M000308284

MAPPING
NEW YORK

MAPPING

NEW YORK

black dog publishing

london uk

CONTENTS

INTRODUCTION
SETH ROBBINS AND ROBERT NEUWIRTH

Uptown, Downtown; East Side, West Side; avenue and street: New York City was invented by a map.

At the dawn of the nineteenth century, the island of Manhattan was a largely bucolic spread of farms, woods, fields, country homes, and villages sprinkled amid the dells. At its southern end there was a small but vigorous harborside settlement: the City of New York.

But in 1807, a state commission drew up a contract with New York's future. It was a map that showed a city sprinting north across an area 20 times larger than the town that huddled at the island's southern tip. A pastoral reality was erased. In its place was a relentless grid of streets and avenues. The map married pragmatism and fancy in stern disregard for any natural form except the island's outline.

That map—known as *The Commissioners Map* and adopted as the city's expansion plan in 1811—was an act of precognition. The conceit of a map that imagined a city of boundless growth at a time when New York had fewer than 90,000 residents was early evidence of an essential characteristic of New York: a place of charge-ahead speculation, ready to rip itself apart and remap itself over and over again.

The complete commoditization of Manhattan's landscape into little marketable boxes followed the example set by the new federal Congress, which had decreed that wilderness territory in the distant west would be mapped in precise 36 square-mile parcels, ready for subdivision and sale. The early American republic was, in a sense, an enormous speculative dream.

The same year the grid plan was adopted, stonemasons finished construction of New York's current City Hall, a French Renaissance-style confection that in its own way confirmed the city's rip-down, build-up spirit. The old city hall, built in 1699 on Wall Street, had played a major role in the development of American society. A jury sitting in one of its chambers rendered the landmark Zenger free press decision in 1735, charting the route to the Bill of Rights' First Amendment that was ratified in that same building in 1791 when it served as the seat of the new federal government. And it was

here, in 1789, that George Washington was sworn in as the new nation's first president. The venerable old structure was razed almost as soon as the new one was up.

Still, the new City Hall turned out to be a strangely backward-looking building. A charming veranda faces the city's past with a vista of the old streets that amble down to the Battery, while it turns its back on the future—the urban expanse stretching away to 'midtown' and 'uptown'.

The maps of the world and the American republic were changing as transportation improvements and the rising market economy announced a new capitalist age, and New York wanted a piece of the action. As America began to fill in the map of the western frontier, New York State planned a new canal cutting from the Hudson River to the Great Lakes. The Erie Canal opened in 1825, anchoring New York's place at the center of a new map of transcontinental trade. When famine and revolution sent the first of successive waves of emigrants to the United States in the mid-1800s, New York was their main arrival point, with the city as the focus of a new global map of human migration.

As New York's exploding population burst beyond its old warrens, construction raced north along the avenues laid out in *The Commissioners Map*. Surveyors traced the lines of streets across farmers' fields or straight through shantytowns and builders filled in estuary marshlands with the detritus of development.

New York's rapid growth redrew the map of rural areas many miles to the north, as the city acquired land to build dams that would impound the Croton River, creating a series of lakes with clean, clear water flowing through a grand new aqueduct system that opened in 1842—a system that is today still spawning maps as the city constructs a new water tunnel to prepare for future needs.

As the city's development cascaded north along the planned avenues and streets, prominent citizens and politicians pushed for another act of visionary cartography: an enormous park in the center of the Island. Central Park, which opened in 1855, was a new kind of park, a carefully planned series of views and experiences with re-imposed pseudo-wilderness and a reconceived topography. This 51 block interruption of the Manhattan grid helps define the modern city's map, and provides a clear visual key for Fifth Avenue's role as the meridian separating the east and west sides. Later, the same landscape architects designed Prospect Park and coined the word "parkways" to describe their plan for a network of broad tree-lined avenues crisscrossing Brooklyn.

This nineteenth century take on green development served the city's speculative ambitions. When a large apartment building rose at West 72nd Street and Central Park West in the early 1880s it was surrounded by shanties and vacant fields, and was far enough from the built-up area of the city to be humorously named "The Dakota". Within a few years buildings filled the surrounding urban prairie.

In the last two decades of the nineteenth century New York City grew more gigantic. In 1883, the Brooklyn Bridge physically linked America's two largest cities— New York and Brooklyn. And in 1898 these two, joined by Queens, the Bronx, and Staten Island, consolidated into the modern 'Five Borough' metropolis.

In 1890, as a new urban age took shape, Joseph Pulitzer invited the public to the top of his downtown New York World Building at a nickel a pop to see for themselves the new metropolis coalescing at their feet. Since then, a host of the city's tallest buildings have accommodated public observation decks. By the early 1930s, New York had a selection of nearly a dozen skyscraper overlooks to choose from, with views offered from high above Brooklyn, from multiple points in the city's downtown, midtown, and in between, from the east side and the west side, and even from a skyscraper church uptown near Harlem. Seen from multiple vantages, the city served as its own life-size map. Sadly, this experience is no longer possible. Just two of these outposts remain open to the public, and they are less than 20 blocks apart.

As the dense urban mass grew above the streets, an infrastructure to feed it tunneled beneath: subway lines, electric cables, telephone wires, steam pipes, and even pneumatic tubes.

Integrating the daylight city and its utilitarian nether reaches in a single map has been a challenge. The first subways were private businesses whose maps ignored rivals' routes, giving no indication of transit connections. The bright, post-groovy 1972 subway map by Massimo Vignelli is an expressive time capsule that tips its hat to emergent solid-state circuitry design. It was a graphic triumph but geographically confusing, providing little sense of where a person might finally re-emerge back onto the streets. The current map, though less graphically appealing, seeks to more literally relate the subterranean routes and the urban landscape above. But New Yorkers continue to navigate without a map showing both worlds on a single surface. A twenty-first century system—including subways and suburban trains, buses, cars, bikes, ferries, foot traffic, and more—cries out for a more comprehensive intermodal map.

One map that provides this kind of overview of the surface of the city is found in the Queens Museum of Art. *The Panorama of the City of New York*—a 9,335 square foot scale model, was commissioned by Robert Moses, the domineering planning czar of the mid-twentieth century city. It shows all five boroughs, down to the smallest building or alley. Updated in 2006, it remains a unique and instructive approach to mapping the city.

Any comprehensive view of the city—the panorama, the high observation decks, or even from an airplane window—conveys a central fact about New York: that it is a maritime metropolis. The waterfront, which for most of its history has been used as a transportation and trading link to the outside world, first studded with piers and later entombed by highways, is now being remapped all around the city. New parks are drawing people back to New York's origin as a spectacular confluence of waters. A city that had, with remarkable success, banished the natural world now seeks to reach new compromises with the reality of its jilted native ecosystems.

The city's bulldozed and buried landscape has inspired a recent adventure in mapmaking. Ecologist Eric Sanderson and the Wildlife Conservation Society (which runs the Bronx Zoo) have created what might be called a memory map of *Mannahatta*, as the island was known before European exploration and colonization reset its history. The *Mannahatta* Project explores the astonishingly diverse interlocking ecosystems that once existed in this spot, providing critical data to plan new, more ecologically

sensitive forms of development. The *Mannahatta* map is in turn indebted to the *British Headquarters Map* of 1782 which showed the natural features of the island in exquisite detail.

Today, just a few years on from the shocking destruction of September 11th, 2001, the city is again remapping itself. New zoning schemes have introduced larger densities for buildings and new residential neighborhoods to displace industrial districts.

Contemporary mapping technologies are offering new ways to look at city planning. New York City's Police Department *CompStat* maps show the location of every crime in every precinct. Site-specific traffic and pedestrian volumes have been charted to plot new bicycle routes. Maps are being rolled out showing the greenest communities in the city, the distribution of bloggers, the neighborhoods with the worst asthma rates, ambulance and police response times, communities with the most overcrowded schools or the highest college application rates, even the streets with the fewest security cameras. These new maps change the way we see, use, relate to, and make plans for the city.

If an early nineteenth century land surveyor returned to the modern city, he would find little to recall in the city's buildings. There is no physical memory of the original Dutch colonial settlement and precious little of the English town that replaced it, or of the city that hosted George Washington and the original framers of the Constitution. But maps survive, tracing the pattern of the Dutch streets that were themselves laid down on ancient Indian trails that wound through woods and bogs that are now nearly impossible to conjure. And Broadway—a native trail, a Dutch path, an English road, and an American icon—still defiantly angles across the rigid grid of *The Commissioners Map*, helping us see historic relationships in a city with an otherwise short memory.

Four hundred years ago, Henry Hudson sailed past the spot that would become New York City looking for the fabled Northwest Passage to Asia. Financed by the largest multi-national corporation of its day, the Dutch East India Company, Hudson's journey was an exploration for speculative profit.

Over the next four centuries, New York developed into a fast-changing speculative enterprise. The maps in this book are charts of its unceasing mutations. Facing challenges to accommodate social inclusion, lifestyle shifts, rising population, the distribution of services, the ongoing communication revolution, and long-term sustainability, these maps provide clues to whether New York will remain the world's urban exclamation point.

———

THE HISTORY OF THE CITY

Founded by the Dutch in 1624, New York is the United States' oldest city. Its history, however, remains shrouded in mystery and intrigue, as the twenty-first century landscape—boasting some of the world's tallest buildings and breathtaking architecture—leaves much of its narrative buried beneath. Maps, and their temporal relationship with reality, provide historians with a way of piecing together this narrative—helping to unearth the diverse history of the city.

The grand early maps of the city of New York show the burgeoning new port at the tip of Manhattan Island after the 1624 discovery by Dutch explorers. Nieuw Amsterdam's proud new inhabitants depicted this rich

———

and fertile land—relatively untouched by human beings—through elaborately decorated cartography as a display to the rest of the world. This all changed, however, with the British arrival in 1664 and their renaming of the island as New York. *A Description of the Towne Of Mannados: Or New Amsterdam* is a patriotic visual celebration of the British acquisition of the port from the Dutch.

The proceeding years saw the rapid development of the city, as the port became an international trading post. The island's settlements extended northwards and commerce and industry began to thrive—as seen in the breweries, markets and tanneries in David Grim's *A Plan of the City of New York as they were in the years 1742 1743 & 1744*. Amongst these settlements, streets began to weave their way northwards, forming the beginnings of a recognizable pattern—the New York City gridiron plan. In 1807 Mayor DeWitt Clinton, proposed the division of the city into a precise grid formation—12 avenues wide and 155 streets long—presented to the city in 1811 in *The Commissioners Plan*.

As the century drew to a close, New York's landscape was to change forever. The building of the world's longest bridge in 1883 saw the city connected to its neighboring city of Brooklyn. This paved the way for the consolidation of the Five Boroughs in 1898—Manhattan, Brooklyn, Queens, Staten Island and the Bronx. Modern day New York City had arrived.

Alongside the extensive urban history of New York, mapping of the city's rich cultural history has also been documented. Ephemera Press' illustrated tours of some of the city's most famous neighborhoods—most notably their *Harlem Renaissance* map—takes the reader on a literary tour of the city's historic neighborhood; whilst Howard Horowitz's cartographically informed word-map takes the reader on an imagined journey of New York City's colorful history: "The riverfront was filled for barnacle-crusted piers, and Minetta Brook wetlands became lots in Greenwich Village."

Finally, a true complexion of New York City's history is not complete without mentioning the events of September 11 2001 and their lasting affects upon New York's physical and emotional landscape—visualized by the technological advancements available to institutions such as NASA, who continue to capture immediate depictions of our landscape through vivid satellite imagery. A new World Trade Center has been scheduled for completion in 2013, which will once again change the face of New York City's famous skyline.

LIST OF WORKS

MAP OF THE ORIGINAL GRANTS OF VILLAGE LOTS FROM THE DUTCH WEST INDIA COMPANY TO THE INHABITANTS OF NEW-AMSTERDAM

HENRY D. TYLER, 1897

This cadastral map—the term pertaining to cartography showing structure and land ownership—depicts an early period study of what would now be South Central Manhattan. New Amsterdam, as it was known at the time, was a colonial trade post founded by the Dutch West India Trading Company, consisting of parts of present day New York State, New Jersey, Delaware, and Connecticut, and which would later become New York City. The image shows the original village lots granted to the town's residents by the company in 1642. One can note the basic perfunctory street and area names from the era; "The Great Highway", "The Shore of the East River", and "The Sheep Pasture" are particularly indicative of their purpose and location.

The Lionel Pincus and Princess Firyal Map Division, The New York Public Library, Astor, Lenox and Tilden Foundations

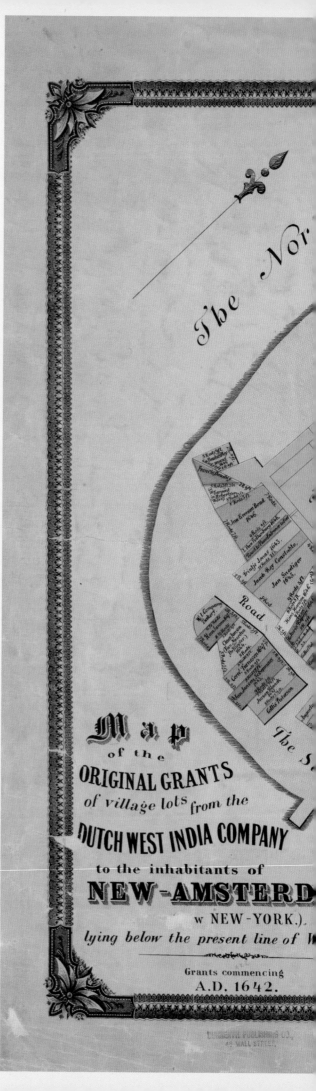

River

West India Company's Garden.

Balthazar Stuyvesant. 1679

20 Rods.

7½ Rods. 7½ Rods.

Formerly West India Company's 1649. *Nich.ᵗ Wᵐ Stuyvesant.* 20 Rods. 20 Rods to Nᵗ River. 16 Rods.

A Rods. Thomas Brown. 1644. 8 Rods 4ft. 4 R. 7½ft.

Hendrick Van Dyck. 167 feet.

7½ Rods. 7½ Rods.

Paulus Leendersen Vandiegrist. 1649 1657.

Old Church Yard.

6 Rods 3 ft.

9 Rods 3 ft.

Dom.ᵉ S. Drissius. 1654.

12 Rods 2 ft.

Jan Stevenson Schoolmaster. 1643.

12 Rods 8 ft.

10 Rods 9 ft. 9½ Rods. 9½ Rods.

8 Rods 8 ft.

11 Rods 8ft.

Arien Pieterson Van Alkmaer. 1645.

6 Rods 9ft. 7 Rods 9ft.

9 Rods.

Martin Cregier. 1643. 11 Rods 6 ft.

Pieter Cocks.

9 Rods 9ft.

The Great Highway

7½ Rods. 7½ Rods. 5 Rods. 4 Rods 5ft. 4 Rods 8ft.

8 Rods 6 ft.

17 Rods. 18 Rods 7ft.

18 Rods 2 feet.

Leendert Jersten.

Thomas Sanderson. 1643.

Andries Wadde. 1643. 17 Rods.

Philip Geraerdy. 1643.

Com.ᵗ Volckertsen.

Cosin Gerritsen 1646. 18 Rods 2 feet.

Rutgers Arentsson. 1643. 18 Rods 2 feet.

Tunis Nyssens. 18 Rods 2 feet.

Isaac Allerton and Govert Loockermans. 1643.

G. Douwman. 10 Rods 2 ft.

Boye Jansen.

8 R. 8ft.

5 Rods 6ft. 4 Rods 9 ft. 9 Rods 8 feet.

8 Rods 9 ft.

Hendrick Jansen Smith.

Jan Snediger. 5 Rods 4ft.

6 Rods 4 ft. 5 R. 8ft.

Coenraet Ten Eyck.

4 Rods 5 feet. 9 Rods 8 ft.

Marsh

The Sheep's Pasture

Wᵐ Bredenbent. 14 Rods 4 feet.

Paulus Vanderbeeck. 1646.

6 Rods 4 ft.

Deacons House. *Poor House.*

11 Rods 8 feet.

Thomas Wandell. 14 Rods.

Tonsiant Briel. 10½ Rods.

Trench

Roelof Jansen Hayes. 1646.

8 Rods 8 feet. 4 Rods 8 feet.

Claes Van Elsland. 1646.

7 Rods 6 feet.

Brarkelfield.

Claes Jansen Van Naarden. 1643. 9 Rods 6 ft.

Isaac De Forrest.

Harman Meyndersen.

Wᵐ Morris.

3 Rods 3 feet.

Brert Jansen. 1646.

3 Rods 4 feet.

Wᵐ Cornelisen. 1647.

5 Rods 8 feet.

Fred Philips. 1653.

The Chique Road, or Walkway to the Ditch and Kerk.

Olof Stevenson Van Cortland.

Jan Cornelisen.

Gysbert Opdyck.

Albert Peterson Trumpeter.

10½ Rods.

Albert Pieterson Drummer.

C. Van Ruyven.

Jacob Steendam.

La Montagnie.

Nicasius De Sille.

26 Rods.

Corn.ᵗ Van Tienhoven. 24 Rods.

Carel Van Brugh. 24 Rods.

Dom.ᵉ Samuel Drissius. 24 Rods.

Pieter Monfort. 1646.

Jan Monfort. 1646.

Swamp.

Bryan Newton.

11 Rods 8 feet.

10 Rods 8 ft.

The Old Ditch

The Common Highway.

Pieter Cornelisen.

Abr.ᵐ Jacobsen Van Steenwidt. 1643.

Michael Paulsen.

Barent Jansen.

Michel Rickel.

The Common Ditch

Road

Wᵐ Rycken. 1643.

Adrian Vincent.

Jochem Calder.

Adrian Dirckson.

Willem Andriesen.

Jacob Wolfertsen Van Couwenhoven.

Evert Duycking. 1643.

Keving.

Kiersted.

Hendrick Jansen.

12 Rods 1 foot 6 in.

15 Rods 5 feet.

Albert Corinch.

Corn.ᵗ Melyn. 1645.

5 Rods.

Abel Riddenhaus.

The Road to the Ferry

Wessel Evertsen. 1646.

17 Rods 5 feet.

Borger Jorisen. 1643. 11 Rods.

The Shore of the East River.

City Hall.

Wᵐ Hall lane. 7 Rods 6in.

Thomas Willet. 1645. 14 Rods 3 feet.

9 Rods 8 feet 6 in.

12 Rods 2 feet.

Richard Smith. 1645. 11 Rods 1 foot.

4 Rods.

Abr.ᵐ Clock. 1655. 3 R.

4 Rods.

Augustyn Heermans. 20 Rods.

Jacob Hendricks Varravanger.

46 Rods 4 feet.

Jan Jansen Damens Farm.

The East River.

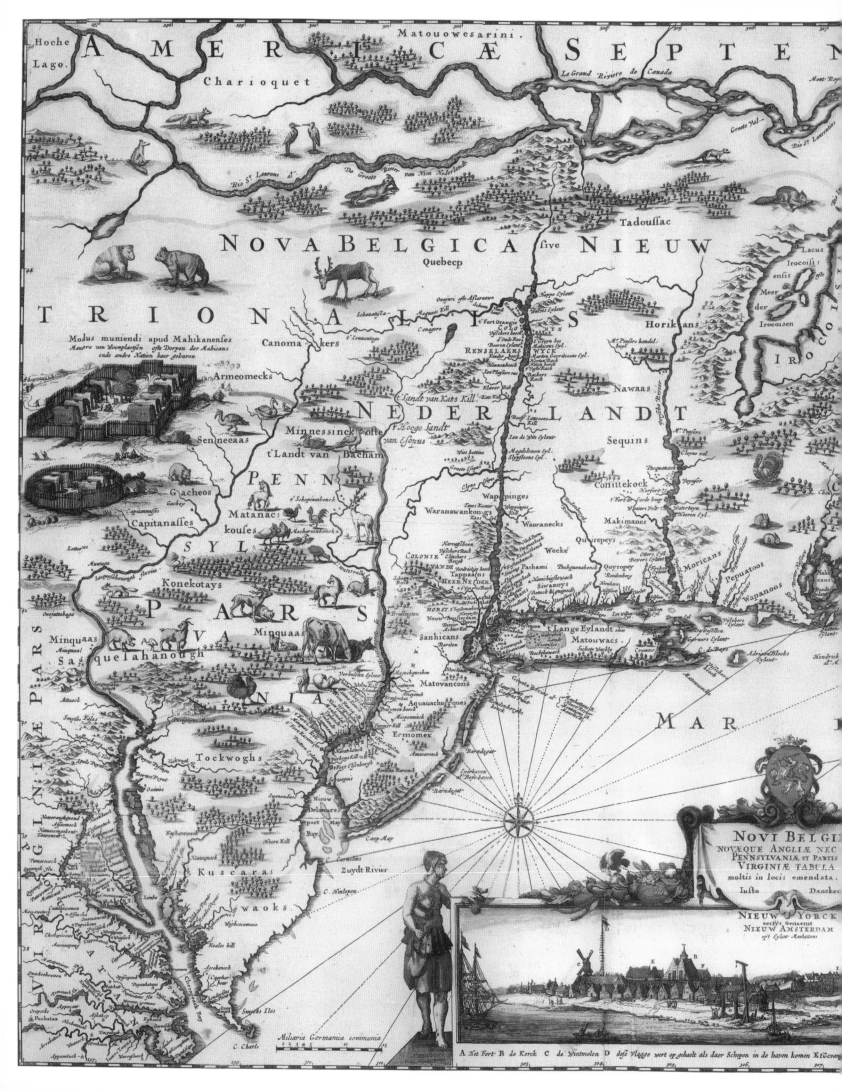

AMERICÆ SEPTEN

Hoche Lago.

Matouowesarini.

Charioquet

La Grand Riviere de Canada

Mont Roy

Croote Val.

Rio St. Laurens d'

De Groote Rivier van Niew Nederlandt

Rio St. Laurentius

Tadoussac

NOVA BELGICA sive NIEUW

Quebecp

Lacus Irocoisi ensis ofte Meer der Irocoisen

TRIONALIS

Modus muniendi apud Mahikanenses
Manero van Woonplaetsen ofte Dorpen der Mahicans
ende andre Natien haer geburen

Canoma-kers

Canomakers

Schanestisa

Aquasi Kill

Ouguri ofte Assareewe
Schoen

Noppe Eylandt

't Fort Orangie COLO

Wischers boeck

Byssi Eylandt

Horikans

IRO

NEDER LANDT

Armeomecks

Sennecaas

Minnessinck ofte
t'Landt van Bacham

'T Hooge Landt van Esopus

't Landt van Kats Kill

RENSELAERS
WYCK

Mr. Pinsers hendel-
huys

Nawaas

Sequins

Mr. Pinsers

Coniittekock

PENN

Gacheos

Matanac-
kouses

Capitanasses

Wappinges

Waranawankongs

Waoranecks

Makimanes

Querepeys

SYL

Konekotays

COLONIE
VANDE
TAPPAEN
HEER NE DER

Wecke

Pachami

Siwanoys

Quyropey

Moricans

Pepuatoos

Wapanoos

PARS VA

Minquaas

Minquaas
Sasquetahanough

Minquaas

Sanhicans

Raritan

't Lange Eylandt alias
Matouwacs.

MAR

NIA

Tockwoghs

Aquaachuques

Matovancons

Ermomex

Nieuw
Delaware
port May
Bay

C. de May

Zuydt Rivier

C. Hinlopen

Kuscaras

waoks.

Miliaria Germanica communia

NOVI BELGI
NOVÆQUE ANGLIÆ NEC
PENNSYLVANIÆ, ET PARTIS
VIRGINIÆ TABULA
multis in locis emendata.
Justo   Dancker

NIEUW YORCK
eertijs Genaemt
NIEUW AMSTERDAM
op 't Eylant Manhattans

A Het Fort B de Kerck C de Wintmolen D dese Vlagge wert op gehaelt als daer Schepen in de haven komen Et Getc.

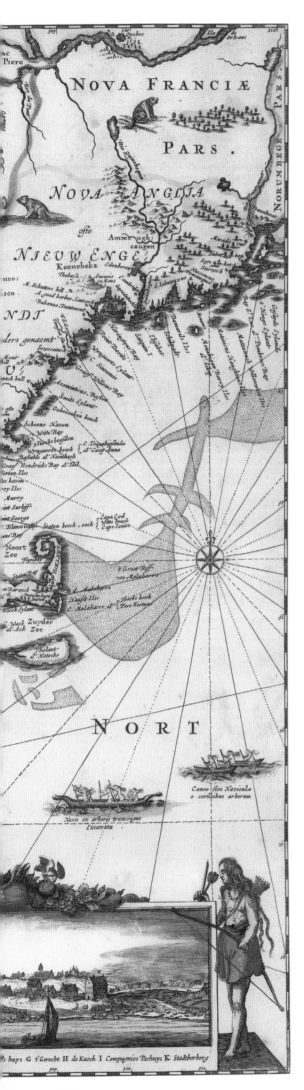

NOVI BELGII NOVAEQUE ANGLIAE NEC NON PARTIS VIRGINIAE TABULA

AUGUSTINE HERMANN, 1651–1653

NOVI BELGII is one of the earliest and most impressive maps depicting the state and city of New York. Alongside the topographical features of the area, intricately drawn animals populate the map in an array of colors. The place names marked out on NOVI BELGII reflect the Dutch colonization of the area—including "Mar Del Nort" and "Neder Landt"—with a grand panoramic view of the city depicted in the lower right hand corner, subtitled as Nieuw Amsterdam.

Historic Urban Plans, Inc., Ithaca, New York, USA

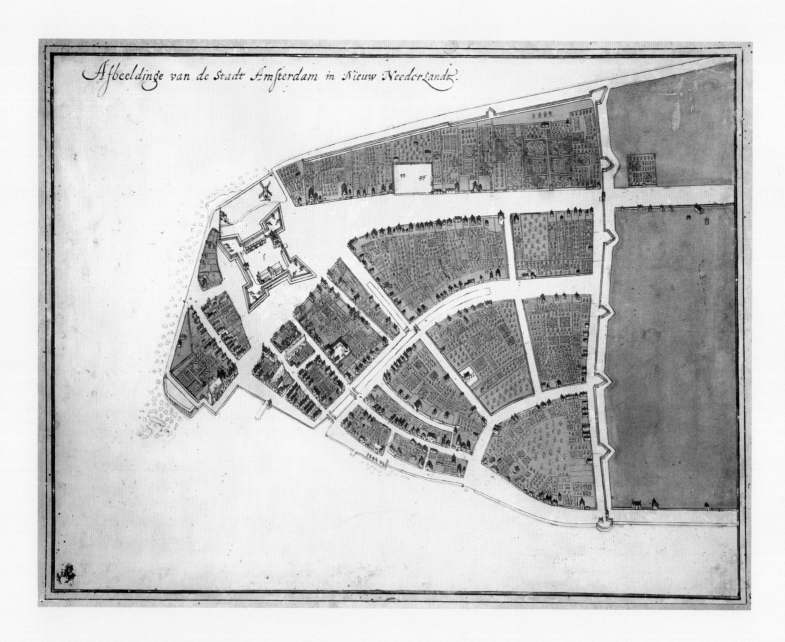

Afbeeldinge van de Stadt Amsterdam in Nieuw Neederlandt.

AFBEELDINGE VAN DE STADT AMSTERDAM IN NIEUW NEEDERLANDT

JACQUES CORTELYOU, 1665–1670

Jacques Cortelyou's plan of the port of Nieuw Amsterdam is the earliest example of a concise street plan of the City of New York. Obsessively precise, each dwelling on the island at the time has been accounted for. Orchards and farmland dominate much of the map—something that Cortelyou was later criticized for, as the city planners interests lay in the growth and development of the settlement into a major trading port. The Castello Plan, as the map is more commonly known, is considered one of the most important early cartographic depictions of Nieuw Amsterdam, due to Cortelyou's meticulous attention to geographical detail.

I.N. Phelps Stokes Collection. Miriam and Ira D. Wallach Division of Art, Prints and Photographs, The New York Public Library, Astor, Lenox and Tilden Foundations

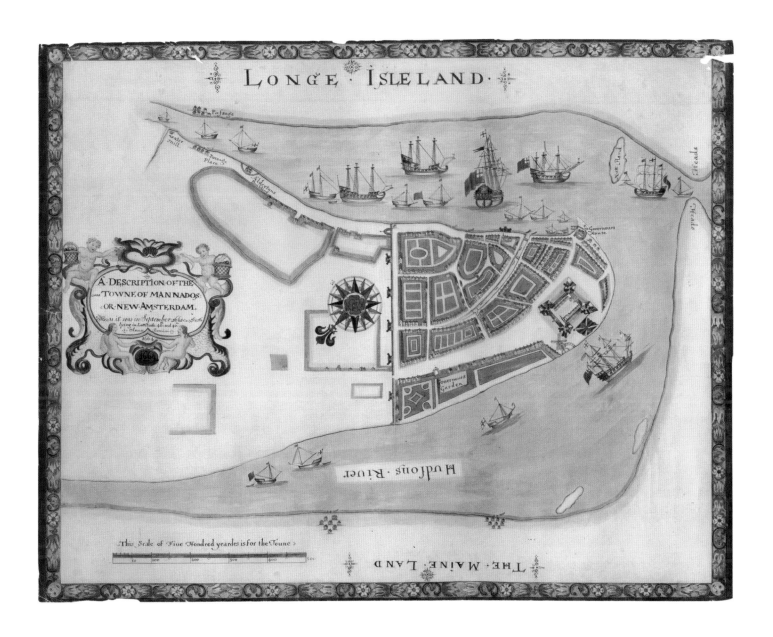

A DESCRIPTION OF THE TOWNE OF MANNADOS: OR NEW AMSTERDAM

JACQUES CORTELYOU, 1664

A Description Of the Towne Of Mannados: Or New Amsterdam is an elegant map of early New York in 1661. The colorful manuscript, found in the collections of the British Library and the New York Historical Society, depicts the original Dutch settlement with Fort Amsterdam standing at the tip of Manhattan Island. Discrepancy over the date arose from the presence of British naval ships moored along the Hudson River, the national flag flying at full mast—the British did not gain control over the island until 1664. It has been suggested that the map is in fact a copy of the earlier Castello Plan (1660), explaining the overlap between Dutch and English details on the manuscript—most notably the title A Description of the Towne of Mannados or New Amsterdam that dates the map as 1661.

Collection of the New Historical Society

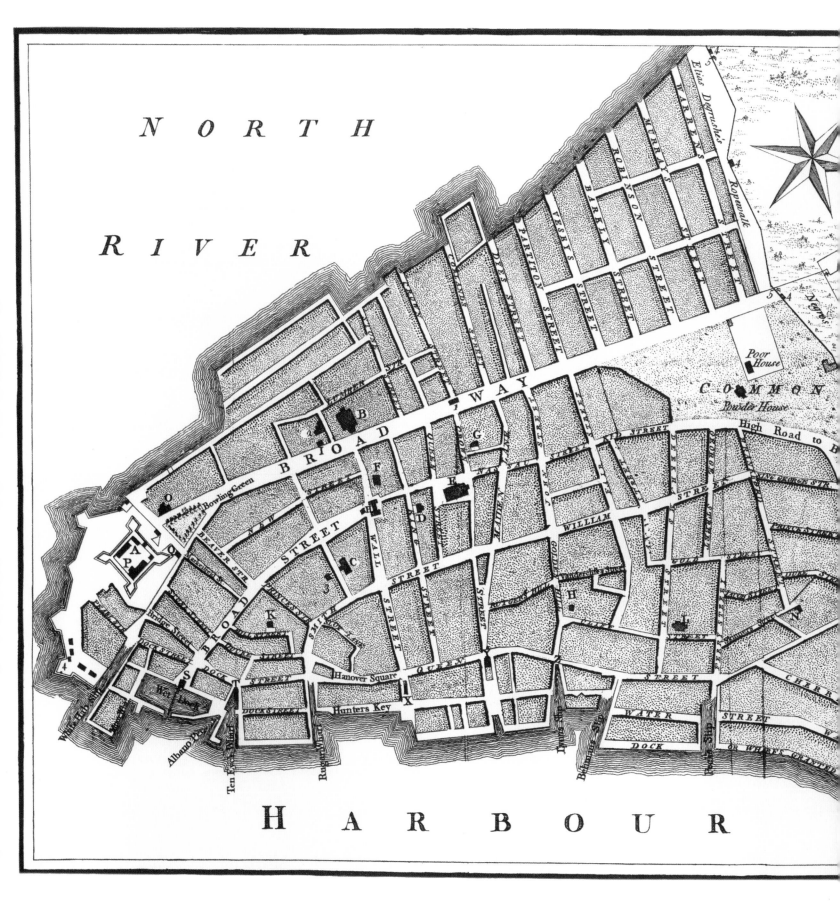

NORTH

RIVER

HARBOUR

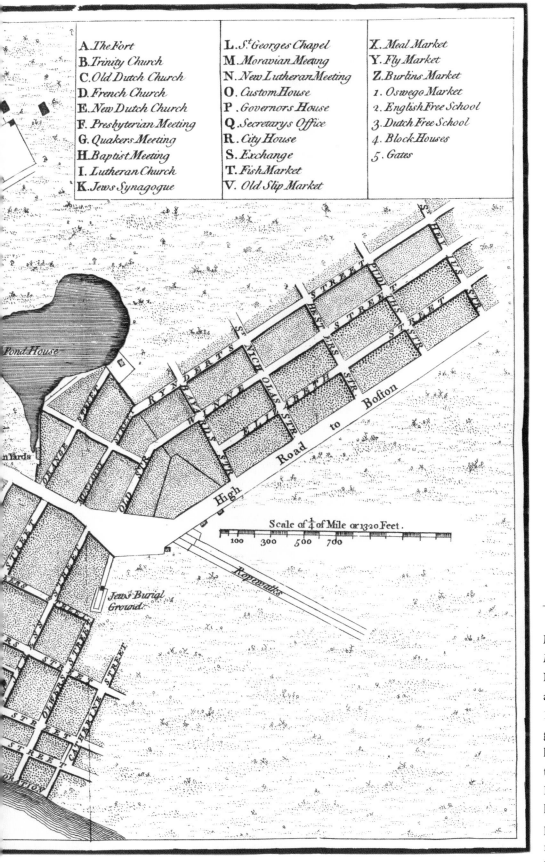

A. *The Fort*	L. *St Georges Chapel*	X. *Meal Market*
B. *Trinity Church*	M. *Moravian Meeting*	Y. *Fly Market*
C. *Old Dutch Church*	N. *New Lutheran Meeting*	Z. *Burlins Market*
D. *French Church*	O. *Custom House*	1. *Oswego Market*
E. *New Dutch Church*	P. *Governors House*	2. *English Free School*
F. *Presbyterian Meeting*	Q. *Secretarys Office*	3. *Dutch Free School*
G. *Quakers Meeting*	R. *City House*	4. *Block Houses*
H. *Baptist Meeting*	S. *Exchange*	5. *Gates*
I. *Lutheran Church*	T. *Fish Market*	
K. *Jews Synagogue*	V. *Old Slip Market*	

Scale of ¼ of Mile or 1320 Feet.

A PLAN OF THE CITY OF NEW-YORK
REDUCED FROM AN ACTUAL SURVEY
T. MAERFCHALCKM, 1763

Maerfchalckm's *A Plan of the City of
New York* is a carefully rendered map of
New York City depicting its development
around the harbour and North River in
1763. Numerous streets run from the port,
gradually extending northwards—with
legendary Broadway running central to
the map towards the Common and Poor
House. A key is shown in the upper right
hand corner with letters corresponding to
points on the map, indicating the different
religious institutions—including both
The Old Dutch Church and The New
Dutch Church, markets and schools
around the island.

Historic Urban Plans, Inc., Ithaca, New York, USA

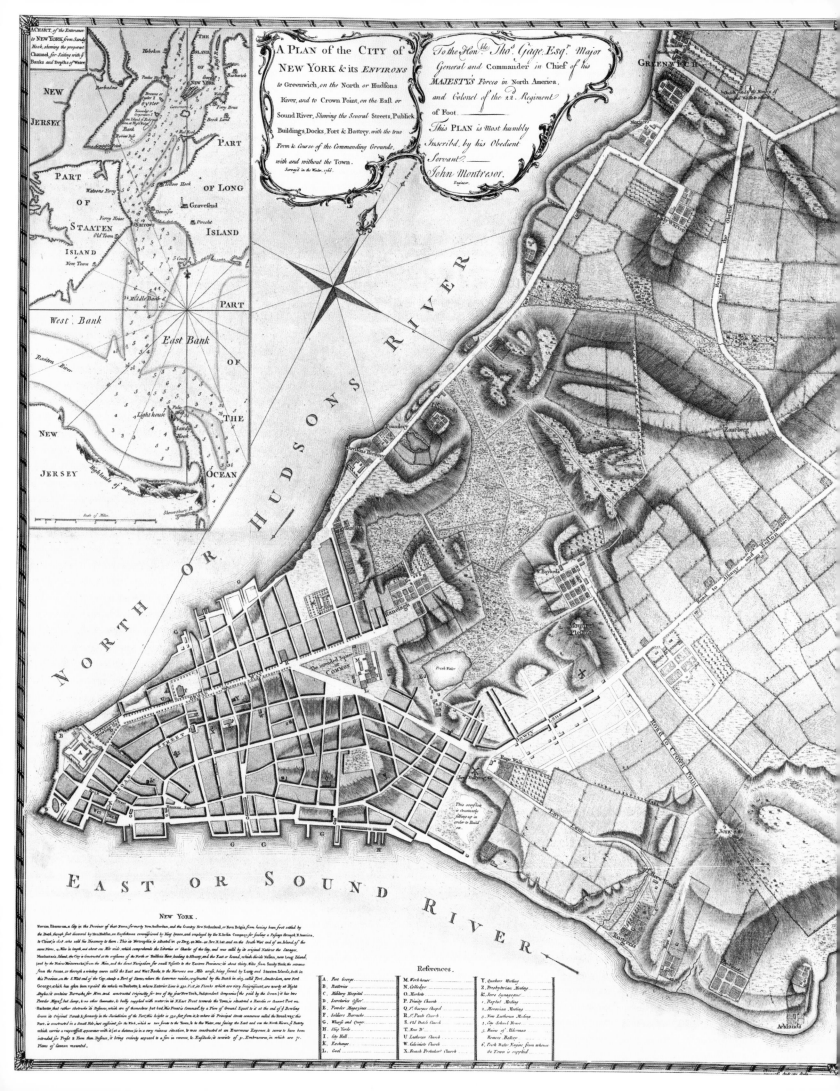

A PLAN of the CITY of NEW YORK & its ENVIRONS to Greenwich, on the North or Hudsons River, and to Crown Point, on the East or Sound River, Shewing the Several Streets, Publick Buildings, Docks, Fort & Battery, with the true Form & Course of the Commanding Grounds, with and without the Town.

Surveyd in the Winter 1766.

To the Honble Thos. Gage, Esqr. Major General and Commander in Chief of his MAJESTY'S Forces in North America, and Colonel of the 22. Regiment of Foot. This PLAN is Most humbly Inscribd, by his Obedient Servant

John Montresor.
Engineer.

A PLAN OF THE CITY OF NEW YORK & ITS ENVIRONS

JOHN MONTRESOR, 1766

A Plan of the City of New York and its Environs to Greenwich, on the north or Hudsons River, and to Crown Point, on the east or Sound River, shewing the several streets, publick buildings, docks, fort & battery, with the true form & course of the commanding grounds, with and without the town.

A Plan of the City of New York and its Environs depicts the settlements of Lower Manhattan and the farmland found further north of the harbour with intricate shading used to represent the steady relief of the area. A sailing chart is shown in the upper-left hand corner of the map depicting the sailing routes from The Ocean past Part of Long Island and Part of Staaten Island towards The Island of New York.

Historic Urban Plans, Inc., Ithaca, New York, USA

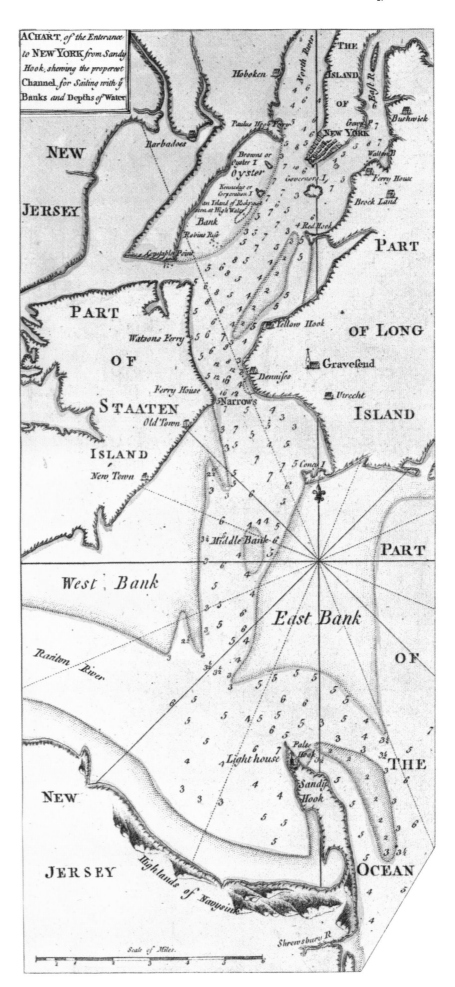

A PLAN OF NEW YORK ISLAND, WITH PART OF LONG ISLAND, STATEN ISLAND & EAST NEW JERSEY

WILLIAM FADEN, 1776

Faden's geographically extensive map, which covers an area as far north and south as what would now be the Bronx, and Staten Island, respectively, and a great deal of New Jersey, is concerned largely with a description of the September 15 1776 taking of New York City by English forces. Published only weeks after the attack it depicts, the image was created from a military point of view for the observing public's consumption; copies of the map were even sold as individual broadside pages on the streets of London. The text pertaining to the campaign is dense and detailed, and the map contains a key specific to the particular movements of the 'Battle on Long Island'.

The Lionel Pincus and Princess Firyal Map Division, The New York Public Library, Astor, Lenox and Tilden Foundations

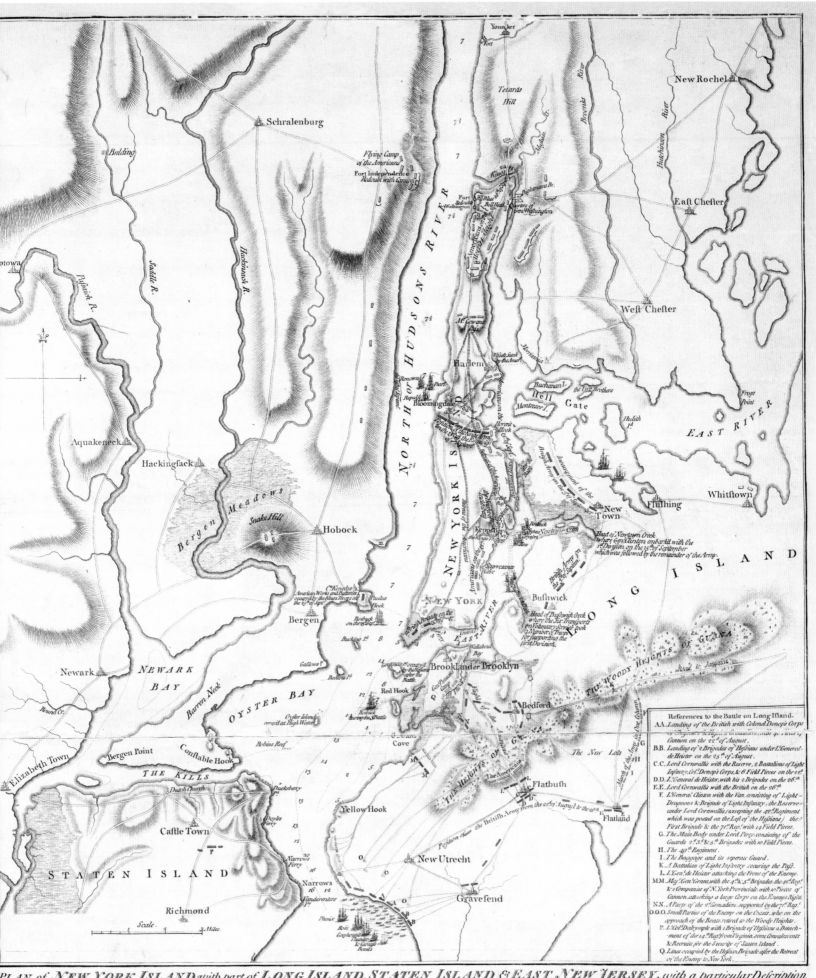

References to the Battle on Long Island.

AA. Landing of the British with Colonel Donop's Corps ...... & ... 6 ... 4 ... first of Cannon on the 22.d of August.

B.B. Landing of 2 Brigades of Hessians under Lt. General de Heister on the 25.th of August.

C.C. Lord Cornwallis with the Reserve, 2 Battalions of Light Infantry, Col.l Donop's Corps, & 6 Field Pieces on the 1.st

D.D. Lt. General de Heister, with his 2 Brigades on the 26.th

E.E. Lord Cornwallis with the British on the 26.th

F. Lt. General Clinton with the Van, consisting of Light Dragoons & Brigade of Light Infantry, the Reserve under Lord Cornwallis ; excepting the 42.d Regiment which was posted on the Left of the Hessians ; the First Brigade & the 71.st Reg.t with 14 Field Pieces.

G. The Main Body under Lord Percy, consisting of the Guards 2.d 3.d & 5.th Brigades with 10 Field Pieces.

H. The 49.th Regiment.

I. The Baggage and its separate Guard.

K. A Battalion of Light Infantry securing the Pass.

L. Lt. Gen.l de Heister attacking the Front of the Enemy.

MM. Maj. Gen. Grant with the 4.th & 5.th Brigades, the 91.st Reg.t & 2 Companies of N. York Provincials, with 10 Pieces of Cannon attacking a large Corps on the Enemy's Right.

NN. A Party of the 2.d Grenadiers supported by the 71.st Reg.t

OOO. Small Parties of the Enemy on the Coasts, who on the approach of the Boats, retired to the Woody Heights.

P. Lt. Col.l Dalrymple with 1 Brigade of Hessians, a Detachment of the 14.th Reg.t on Virginia, some Convalescents & Recruits for the Security of Staten Island .

Q. Lines occupied by the Hessian Brigade after the Retreat of the Enemy to New-York.

PLAN of NEW YORK ISLAND, with part of LONG ISLAND, STATEN ISLAND & EAST NEW JERSEY, with a particular Description of the ENGAGEMENT on the Woody Heights of Long Island, between FLATBUSH and BROOKLYN, on the 27.th of August 1776. between HIS MAJESTY'S FORCES Commanded by General HOWE, and the AMERICANS under Major General PUTNAM. Shewing also the Landing of the BRITISH ARMY on New-York Island, and the Taking of the CITY of NEW-YORK &c. on the 15.th of September following, with the Subsequent Disposition of Both the Armies.

Engraved & Publish'd according to Act of Parliament Oct.r 19.th 1776, by W.m Faden, successor to the late M.r T. Jefferys, Geographer to the King, Charing Cross, LONDON.

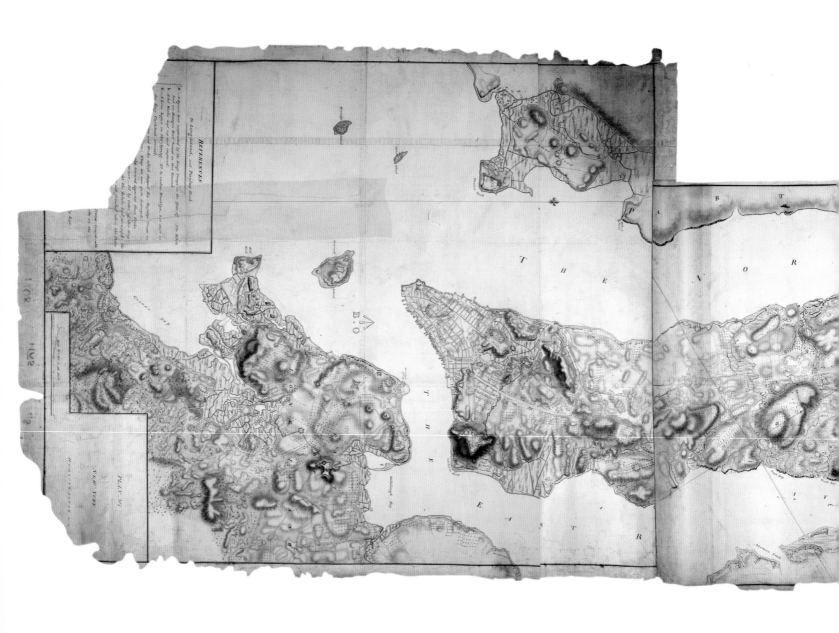

THE BRITISH HEADQUARTERS MAP

1782

Technically untitled, the image popularly
known as *The British Headquarters Map*
is an extensive catalogue of the British
military defences in New York at the time.
Significantly, the map is the only existing
complete record of the island's topography at
a time of early colonization—inevitably it is
unrecognizable given how it appears today.
The primitive appearance of the geography is
startling; conurbations can primarily be seen
around the shorelines and rivers, as well as
in greater density in what would now be the
area around Battery Park. A well-established
network of roads and byways can also be seen,
as well as irrigation ditches and channels.

The National Archives, ref. MR1/463

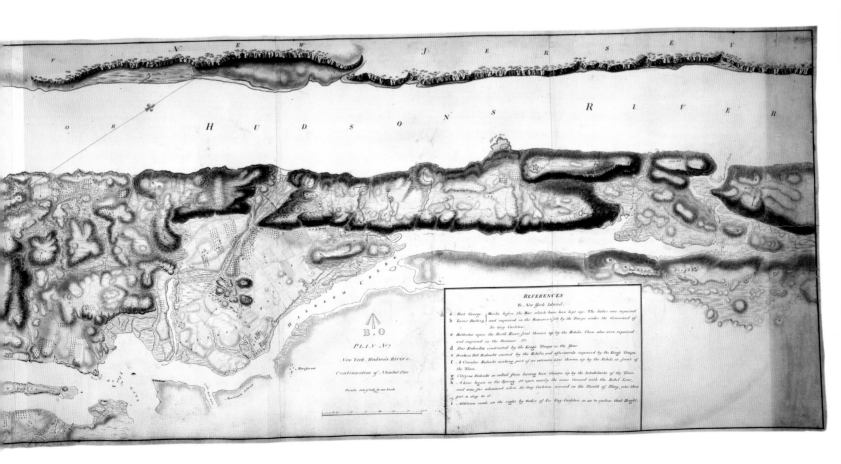

-RIGHT-

A MAP OF THE CITY OF NEW YORK

BY THE COMMISSIONERS APPOINTED BY AN ACT OF THE
LEGISLATURE PASSED APRIL 3RD 1807
JOHN RANDEL, JR., 1811

The study more commonly known as *The Commissioners Plan* is overwhelmingly recognized as being the single most significant document in the history of New York. Proposing an outward expansion of the city by an amount of 11,400 acres, John Randel Jr.'s design envisioned the inception of a modern New York, far removed from the small, clustered urban center it was previously. Interestingly, Randel's manuscript was created by superimposing the new street system and cartographic details over topographic drawings of the existing land, a seemingly unnecessary exercise given that the dense rigidity of the urban plan left no room for difficult geo-physical discrepancies.

-OPPOSITE-

THE NEW COMMISSIONER'S PLAN

JOHN RANDEL, JR., 1814

The New Commissioner's Plan of 1814 is John Randel Jr.'s revision of his earlier, groundbreaking *Commissioners Plan* of 1811, that proposed the ordering of New York by the grid system still in use today. Measuring 26 by 38 inches this colored copperplate engraving is far more precise than its 1811 predecessor. The map depicts the grid plan in greater detail and covers a much larger area—mapping out the streets, piers, and surrounding landscape of Manhattan, "Town of Brooklyn", "County of Queens" and "State of New Jersey". Though stating 1814 as the date, Randel did not publish the map until 1821 due to fears that the accuracy of its details might pose a security threat to the city during The Anglo-American War of 1812.

Collection of the New York Historical Society

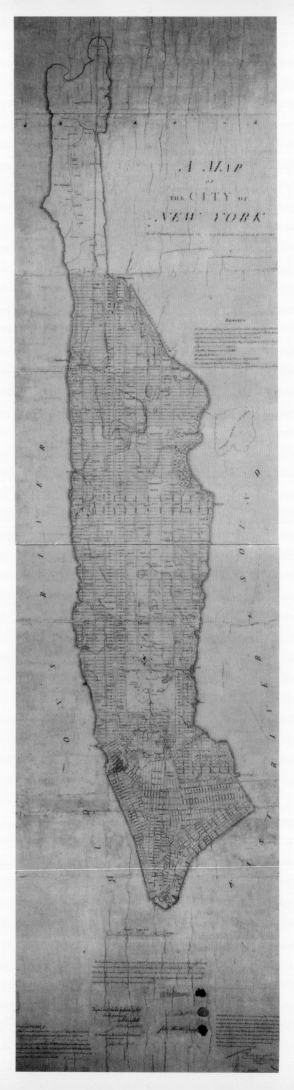

The City of NEW YORK

AS LAID OUT BY THE COMMISSIONERS

with the

SURROUNDING COUNTRY

By their Secretary and Surveyor

John Randel Jun.

1814

Scale of Feet 6165 to a Minute

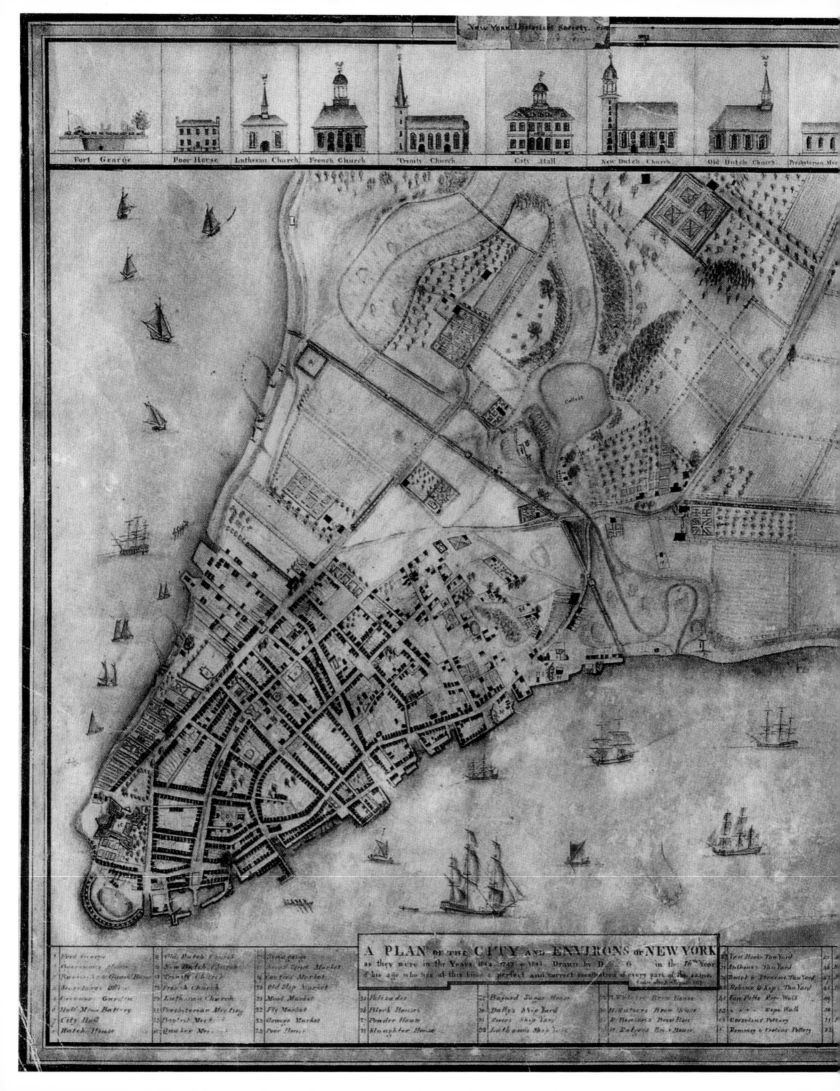

Fort George | Poor House | Lutheran Church | French Church | Trinity Church | City Hall | New Dutch Church | Old Dutch Church | Presbyterian Mee.

A PLAN OF THE CITY AND ENVIRONS OF NEW YORK

as they were in the Years 1742, 1743 & 1744. Drawn by D. G. in the 76th Year

This age who has at this time a perfect and correct recollection of every part of the same.

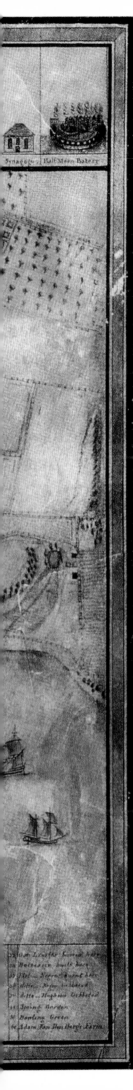

A PLAN OF THE CITY OF AND ENVIRONS OF NEW YORK AS THEY WERE IN THE YEARS 1742, 1743 & 1744

DAVID GRIM, 1813

David Grim's *A Plan of the City of and Environs of New York as they were in the years 1742, 1743 & 1744* is a beautifully illustrated map depicting the early settlement of New York. Grim drew the map in 1813, recalling from memory the city as he knew it as a boy. The map's intricate detailing shows the original settlement built up around the harbor, gradually moving into farmland further north.

Amongst the places referenced on the map are the Bayard Sugar House, Adam Van Den Berg's Farm and Bowling Green. An ornate border lines the top of the map depicting important buildings in Manhattan at the time, including Fort George, City Hall and The New Dutch Church. The plan was donated to the New York Historical Society in 1813.

THIS ACTUAL MAP AND COMPARATIVE PLANS SHOWING 88 YEARS GROWTH OF THE CITY OF NEW YORK

DAVID LONGWORTH, 1817

This engraved study, highly detailed and including intricate drawings of municipal structures such as City Hall and the local asylum, also includes an archaic inset 1729 plan of New York by James Lyne. The juxtaposition is effective; Lyne's sparse design stands in stark contrast to the regimented, dense image presented by the illustrator. Various details are supplied, such as wards, ferry piers, places of interest, and hachure marks to indicate relief.

THE CITY OF NEW YORK AS LAID OUT BY THE COMMISSIONERS WITH THE SURROUNDING COUNTRY

JOHN RANDEL JR., 1821

This gorgeously illustrated *Final Commissioners Plan*—particularly eye-catching due to the collage effect afforded by the rolled paper design of the edge of 'different' constituent documents—was, despite its decorative nature, designed as a street-planning tool. Covering all of Manhattan and its surroundings counties, as well as including two ancillary images of Rhode Island and Connecticut, the map shows both existing and proposed roads, natural geographic features, topographical relief, and political boundary lines. The cartographic tools used by John Randel are sketched in some detail around the title of the image, in the top right hand corner.

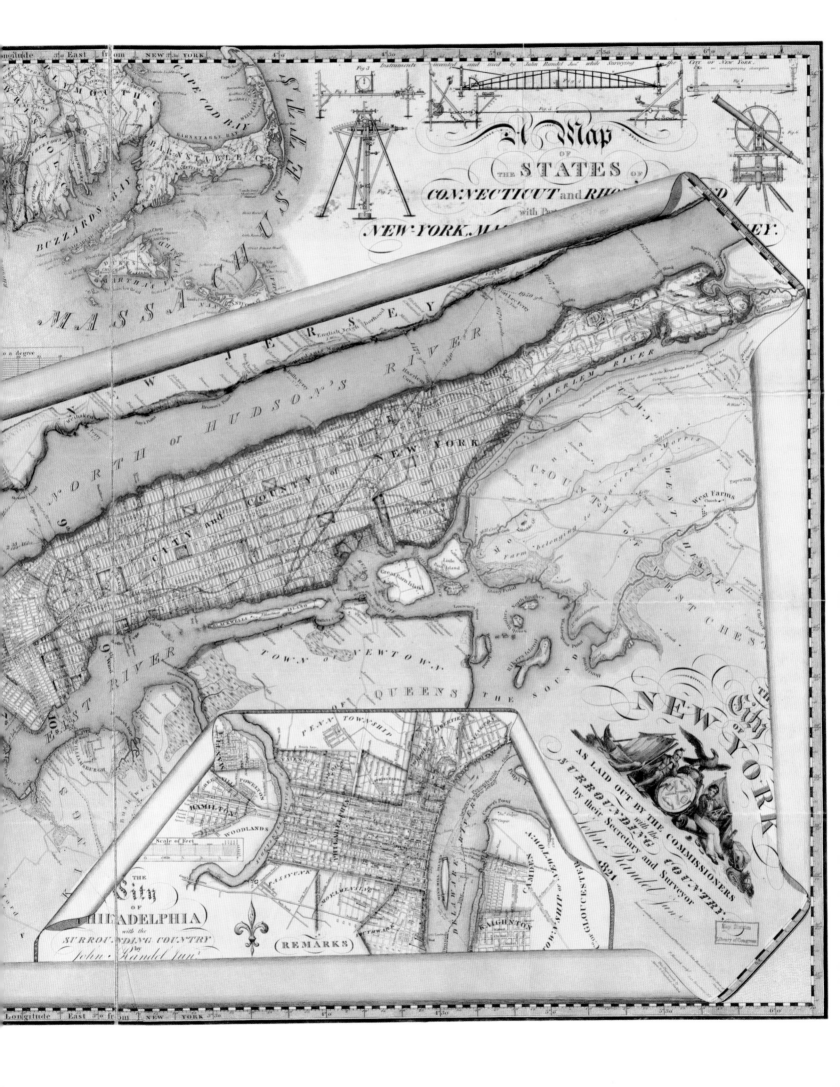

RIOTS TARGET BLACK NEW YORKERS & ABOLITIONISTS JULY 1834

ATTACKS ON WEDNESDAY, JULY 9, 1834

1 THE CHATHAM STREET CHAPEL. Formerly a theater, it was leased by the Tappan brothers for the revival preaching of Rev. Charles G. Finney and called the Second Free Presbyterian Church. It was close to the Five Points and black organizations frequently gathered there. On July 4, 1834, a mob disrupted an abolitionist lecture at the chapel. On the 7th, a melee erupted between black and white groups contending for the use of the room. A false announcement of an abolitionist meeting for the 9th set off three days of rioting.

2 LEWIS TAPPAN'S HOUSE, 40 Rose Street. Silk merchant Tappan and his brother Arthur were the leading advocates of immediate emancipation among white New Yorkers. Tappan's family had taken refuge in Harlem before the attack.

3 Bowery Theater. The English-born manager made ill-advised anti-American comments and saw his theater attacked.

ATTACKS ON THURSDAY, JULY 10, 1834

4 LEWIS TAPPAN HOUSE, 40 Rose Street.

5 Residence of REV. SAMUEL COX, 3 Charlton Street.

6 The BRICK PRESBYTERIAN CHURCH, on Laight Street. Dr. Samuel Cox, an ardent abolitionist, was its pastor.

ATTACKS ON FRIDAY, JULY 11, 1834

6 ARTHUR TAPPAN'S STORE on 122 Pearl Street, near Hanover Square. Arthur, the elder of the Tappan brothers, was president of the American Anti-Slavery Society. His clerks defended the store with firearms.

7 REV. HENRY G. LUDLOW's church, the 8th Presbyterian or Spring Street Church. Ludlow was reputed to have recently presided at the marriage of an interracial couple.

7 Residence of REV. LUDLOW, 148 Thompson Street.

9 AFRICAN AMERICAN MUTUAL RELIEF HALL, 42 Orange Street. This was the headquarters of the most important social organization in black New York, founded in 1808. (Orange is now Baxter Street.)

10 HOUSES AND BUSINESSES OF BLACKS ALONG LEONARD, CENTRE, AND ORANGE STREETS. This was the heart of the Five Points district, center of the black community in 1834.

11 ST. PHILIP'S CHURCH, 31 Centre Street. The leading black Episcopal congregation in the city. A letter to the Mayor from Bishop Benjamin Onderdonk alerted the authorities to the threats against the church. Mr. William Hutson, senior warden of St. Philip's, carried the letter to the mayor. Onderdonk cites his "knowledge of the respectable and uniformly decent and orderly character of the congregation of that Church…."

12 AFRICAN BAPTIST CHURCH, Anthony Street. (Anthony is now Worth Street.)

A LIST OF "CONTEMPLATED ATTACKS" OF SATURDAY, JULY 12, 1834, COMPILED B[Y]

11 ST. PHILIP'S CHURCH, 31 Centre Street.

13 Oliver Street Baptist Church. Rev. Spencer Cone, an ardent evangelical, was the minister of the church at 6 Oliver Street.

14 Bridewell Prison, behind City Hall, the symbol of the police.

15 "Geer's buildings," the landmark Colonnade Row on Lafayette Place, originally twice as long as it is today. Seth Geer's new buildings were targeted "on the ground that the stone is from the State Prison."

16 THIRD FREE CHURCH, Thompson Street. Rev. Dirck Cornelius Lansing, a vice president of the American Anti-Slavery Society, was its pastor.

17 Nassau Street Tract Society, 136 Nassau Street. Rev. John R. McDowall was head of the American Society for Promoting the Observance of the Seventh Commandment and the Magdalen Society, both intended to fight prostitution while assisting prostitutes to reform. A nearby cellar on Nassau Street was targeted because it is "occupied by a colored man who is said to keep a white girl."

18 State Arsenal at Elm Street. Presumably the rioters would want the guns from the armory. Elm is now Lafayette Street.

19 Residence of Rev. Jacob Brouner, Barrow Street, near Bleecker. Perhaps his North Baptist Church, on Bedford near Christopher, was rigidly evangelical or anti-slavery.

20 Residence of Charles King, 455 Hous[e] Street, corner Mercer (where the An[ge] Theatre is now). King, a son of Feder[al] statesman Rufus King, edited the Ne[w] American and later was president of Columbia College.

21 Residence of ABRAHAM L. COX, MD, 434 Broome Street. Dr. Cox was recor[ding] secretary of the American Anti-Slave[ry] Society and one of the city's leading [...]

22 108 GREEN STREET, "occupied by a [...] the note to the mayor said, "is expecte[d] attacked this Evening."

23 The Village Presbyterian Church, on [...] Street. The trustees warned the mayo[r] if "no other guard is present those in[...] will feel it to be their duty to defend themselves and property, holding the authorities responsible for any dama[ge] may arise either to life or property."

24 A letter to the mayor notes that the h[ouse] 11 Vandewater Street "was occupied exclusively by colored people" and "th[e] subscriber makes this application for [...] protection of the premises."

25 HESTER LANE, a respectable colored [...] owned her house at 33 Sullivan Street[...] A note says that "many Families of co[lored] are in her neighborhood." Lane was a[...] in purchasing and freeing slave famil[ies] and was falsely accused of slave tradi[ng in] the late 1830s. (See original on the ri[ght])

26 Store of Roe Lockwood, a bookseller a[nd] publisher, at 415 Broadway.

- ▬ Identified with the Anti-slavery movement
- ▬ People of color & their organizations
- ★ Attacks on July 9, 1834
- ☆ Attacks on July 10, 1834
- ✦ Attacks on July 11, 1834
- ✧ Attacks on July 9 & 10, 1834
- ⬖ Attacks on July 10, targeted for a repeat on July 12, 1834
- ✦ Attacks on July 11, targeted for a repeat on July 12, 1834
- ◆ Potential attacks reported to the Mayor's office, July 12, 1834

er bar of **THOMAS DOWNING**, 5 Broad
et. Downing, a noted black entrepreneur,
the "mayor that he has been inform'd
an attack will be made on his house and
ents the authority to interfere if it should
ecessary." (See original on the right.)

dence of **JOSHUA LEAVITT**, editor, at
Thompson Street. He was editor of *The
ngelist* and a manager of the American
-Slavery Society.

BRICK PRESBYTERIAN CHURCH.

ding owned by **EDWARD DAVIS**, a black
s, 121 Broome Street.

ding owned by **EDWARD DAVIS**, a black
n, 123 Forsyth Street. H. & A. Averill,
chants on South Street, employed Davis
porter in their store. He "possesses,"
wrote, "our entire confidence in point of
grity & is civil & unobtrusive in his
ners & deportment." (See original on
right.)

dence of **REV. PETER WILLIAMS**, 68
sby Street. An Episcopal minister and
leading black churchman in New York
, Williams served on the executive
mittee of the American Anti-Slavery
ety until forced by the bishop to resign
political activities.

ns Building, on Essex Street near the
ex Market, contained notorious brothels.

dence of Henry Pickering, editor of
Countryman, 105 Cross Street. This was
wspaper specializing in news of
land, Ireland, Scotland, and Wales.
do not know why Pickering was targeted.
oss Street was later buried beneath
istopher Columbus Park and the County
rthouse.)

② Magdalen Asylum, 10 Carmine Street, a
refuge for ex-prostitutes.

③ **AFRICAN FREE SCHOOL**, on East Broadway
near Clinton Street. By this time, there were
several such schools for black boys and girls.

⑦ The Spring Street Church.

③ Shop of Wells Philips, a shoemaker, 105
Chatham Street. We do not know why he was
threatened.

③ Dr. Gardiner Spring was an ardent supporter
of evangelical revivals and lived at 3 Bond
Street. He was targeted "on account of
[his agitation against the] Sunday mail."

③ **THOMAS L. JENNINGS**, 35 Chatham Street,
a colored clothier at the edges of the
Five Points, became an active member of
the Committee of Vigilance. In 1854, his
daughter Elizabeth, a schoolteacher, sued to
achieve equal access for black New Yorkers
to street railway lines.

③ **A COLORED PERSON** on Laurens Street
between Broome & Grand

④ Residence of **REV. SAMUEL H. COX**,
3 Charlton Street.

⑥ **ARTHUR TAPPAN'S STORE**, 122 Pearl Street.

④ Residence of Rev. Nathan Bangs, 48
Rivington Street, near Eldridge. Bangs was
editor of Methodist journals and the founder
of the Methodist Missionary Society. He
tried to reconcile both sides in the slavery
controversy.

④ Barzille Knorine's boarding house, 562 Pearl,
near Broadway. This may have been an
interracial dwelling-house.

④ **4 PECK SLIP**. A letter to the mayor from
Dr. John Anderton: "It is intimated that an
attack of the Mob will assail my office on
acct. of renting the Cellar and apartment to a
Colored man that is married to a White
woman they are both excellent Characters
which can be testified by the neighborhood."
(See original to the right.)

④ **AFRICAN METHODIST EPISCOPAL ZION
CHURCH**, 156 Church Street, corner Leonard.
One of the leading black churches in the city.

④ **THE FREE PRESBYTERIAN CHURCH**,
74 Dey Street. This was Lewis Tappan's
church.

④ **UNION CHURCH, PRINCE STREET**. Rev.
Herman Norton, an ardent Presbyterian
revivalist from upstate New York, was
its pastor. Also a "free church," surviving
without pew rents.

④ *The Evening Star* office, 47 William Street,
near Wall. The newspaper was edited by
Mordecai Noah, a lay Jewish leader,
Whig politician, and often caustic critic of
black New Yorkers.

④ **AFRICAN PRESBYTERIAN CHURCH**,
Frankfort Street. **REV. THEODORE
SEDGWICK WRIGHT** was minister of this
church, sometimes called Shiloh Church.
Rev. Wright was an important black leader
of the American Anti-Slavery Society.

RIOTS TARGET BLACK NEW YORKERS & ABOLITIONISTS JULY 1834

The Anti-Abolition Riots of July 1834 have
been documented here in this annotated
poster by the New York Historical Society
as part of their New York Divided: Slavery
and the Civil War exhibition. Beginning
on July 9th 1834, the riots are charted from
the Chatham Street Chapel—where a mob
disrupted an abolitionist lecture—across
Lower Manhattan for the next three days.

Collection of the New York Historical Society

SIDNEY'S MAP OF TWELVE MILES AROUND NEW-YORK

N. FRIEND, 1849

Spanning a radial twelve miles around the southern point of Manhattan Island, publisher J.C. Sidney's aesthetically distinct map, engraved on stone, depicts numerous cartographic details, such as county boundaries, street grids, details of railway lines, water depth soundings, hachure relief, and, as noted below the title, notes pertaining to property ownership around the city. The decorative border and corner illustration surrounding the circular image contain notable features of interest; the 'Arms of the state of New-York' are depicted in the bottom left hand corner, with an iconic Bald Eagle seen opposite.

The Lionel Pincus and Princess Firyal Map Division, The New York Public Library, Astor, Lenox and Tilden Foundations

NEW YORK IN 1642.   NEW YORK IN 1755.   NEW YORK IN 1782.

NEW YORK IN 1642–1782 FROM VOLUME 18 OF THE REPORT ON THE SOCIAL STATISTICS OF CITIES

FROM REPORT OF THE SOCIAL STATISTICS OF CITIES, COMPILED BY GEORGE E. WARING JR., 1886

As the population of the United States grew and urban dwellings increased in size, a need for accurate data mapping arose. The 1880 census saw a new law implemented, which handed over supervision of this data—from mortality rates to agriculture information—to a body of presidentially appointed officers. This series of four maps is taken from Volume 18 of the *Report on the Social Statistics of Cities* by

George E. Waring, Jr. They depict the gradual development of Manhattan Island from 1642 through to 1782. The careful renderings show the extension of the city from its origins at the port, along the bay and eventually northwards as houses and businesses began to thrive in the expanding metropolis.

Courtesy of University of Texas Libraries

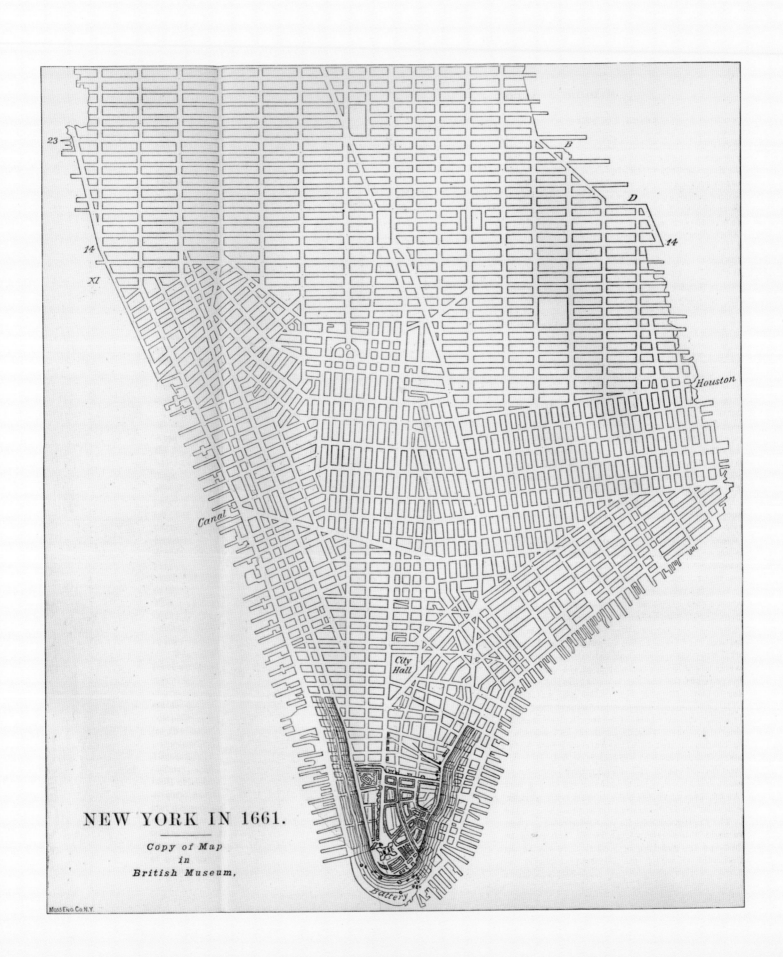

NEW YORK IN 1661.

Copy of Map
in
British Museum,

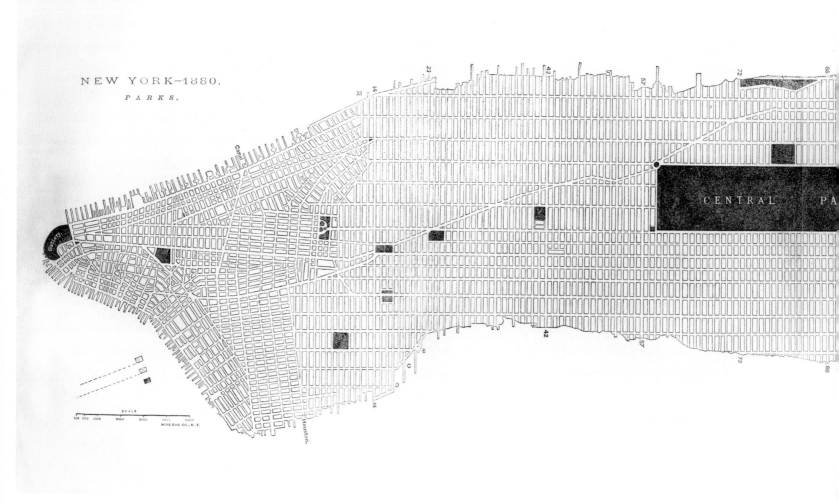

NEW YORK—1880.

PARKS.

CENTRAL PARK

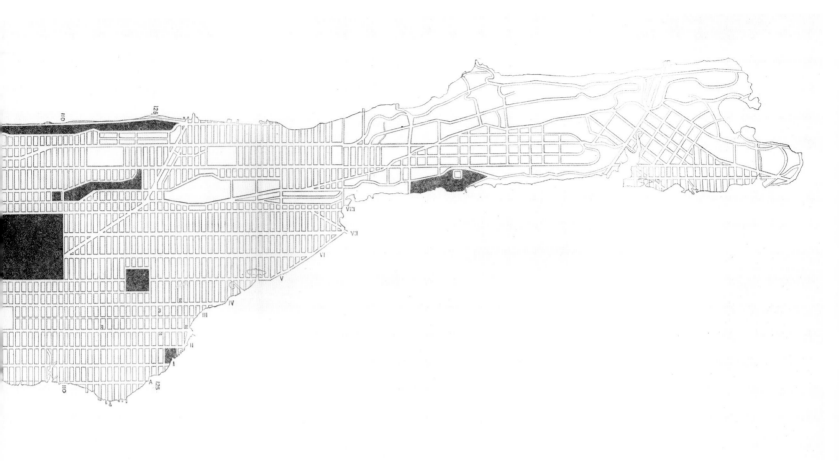

NEW YORK—1880
PARKS
FROM REPORT OF THE SOCIAL STATISTICS OF CITIES,
COMPILED BY GEORGE E. WARING JR., 1886

Waring's aesthetically dense image in reality only conveys very limited information, almost singularly pertaining to the placement of parks around the Manhattan area. With the exception of the Battery and Central Park, the names of these are undisclosed. Other noted features are numbered shoreline points and a canal opening into the Lower West Side.

URBAN DEVELOPMENT OF THE CITY
OF NEW YORK 1625–1988
DEPARTMENT FOR CITY PLANNING, NEW YORK

Here, the New York Department of City
Planning has mapped the city's urban
development from the early Dutch
Settlement through to 1988. The clearly
delineated periods, divided by color
and laid out in the key, collectively illustrate
the rate of development throughout the city's
history. Of particular interest is the city's
development from 1945–1988, of which very
little occurred on Manhattan island itself—
accounted for by the development boom
at the turn of the twentieth century. The urban
sprawl of developed land between1945 and
1988, reinforces New York's position as the
United States' most densely populated city.

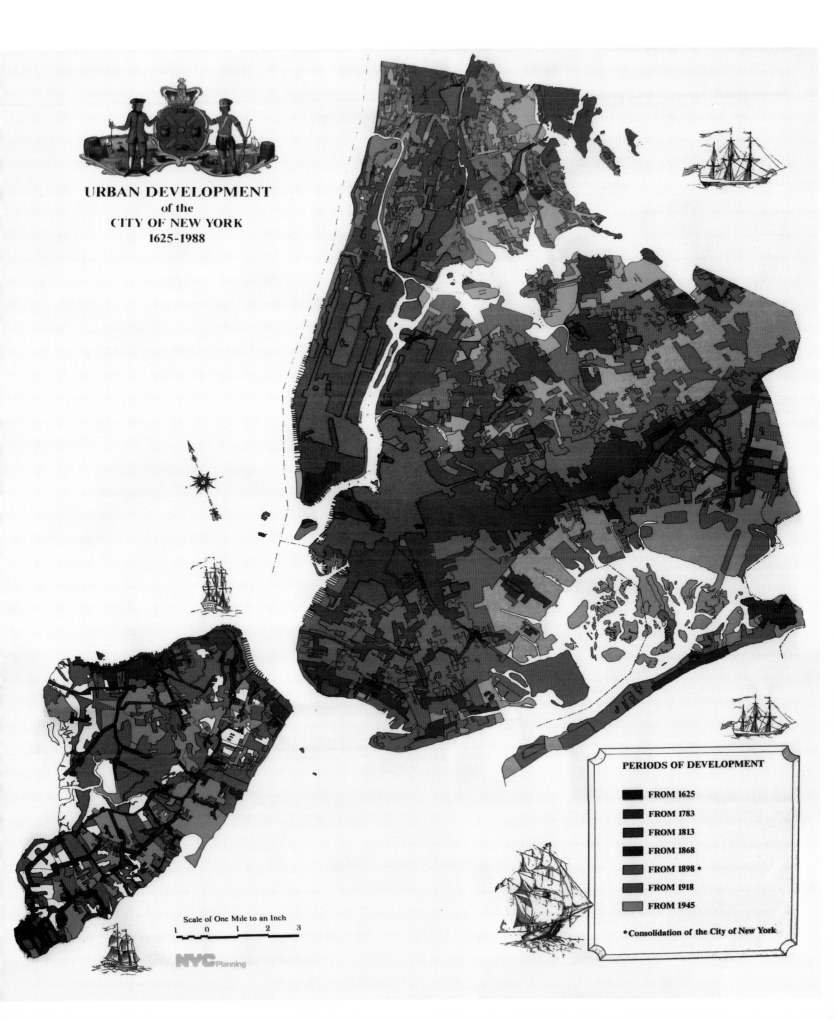

URBAN DEVELOPMENT
of the
CITY OF NEW YORK
1625-1988

PERIODS OF DEVELOPMENT

FROM 1625

FROM 1783

FROM 1813

FROM 1868

FROM 1898 *

FROM 1918

FROM 1945

* Consolidation of the City of New York

Scale of One Mile to an Inch
1   0   1   2   3

NYC Planning

HARLEM RENAISSANCE

ONE HUNDRED YEARS OF HISTORY, ART AND CULTURE

ART BY TONY MILLIONAIRE
© EPHEMERA PRESS 2001

Duke Ellington
935 St. Nicholas Ave.
1939-1961

Paul Robeson
555 Edgecombe Ave.

The Cotton Club
644 Lenox Ave.
Opens 1921; moves to
Broadway 1936

409 Edgecombe Ave.

Rev. Adam Clayton Powell Sr.
435 Convent Ave.

Arctic explorer
Matthew Henson

Justice Thurgood Marshall

THE CRISIS

SUGAR HILL
Overlooking Harlem Plain

Cab Calloway, Ethel Waters and
Bill "Bojangles" Robinson

Ella Fitzgerald

Pianist/composer
Mary Lou Williams
63 Hamilton Terrace

Author Ralph Ellison
749 St. Nicholas Ave.

Jessie Fauset
Literary editor, The Crisis

Savoy Ballroom
596 Lenox Ave.
1926-1958

Composer Billy Strayhorn
315 Convent Ave.

W.E.B. DuBois
Editor, The Crisis

Painter
Charles Alston
306 W. 141st St.

Pianist/composer
James P. Johnson
267 W. 140th St.

Singer Alberta Hunter
133 W. 138th St.

Dancer/choreographer Alvin Ailey
Professor at City College, 1983

STRIVERS ROW
138th & 139th Sts.
between 7th & 8th Avenues

Flecher Henderson

Nobel Sissle Eubie Blake

W.C. Handy

The Abyssinian Baptist Church
136-142 W. 138th St.

Singer Billie Holiday
108 W. 139th St.

Brotherhood of
Sleeping Car Porters
239 W. 136th St.

Howell's Funeral Parlor
137th St. & 7th Ave.
Funeral of Florence Mills, 1927

Universal Negro
Improvement
Association
2305 7th Ave.

108-110 W. 136th St.
Home of Madam C.J. Walker
and The Walker College
of Hair Culture

Tennis champion Althea Gibson
Learns paddleball as child on 143rd St.

City College of New York
Convent Ave. & 138th St.

Wallace Thurman, Zora Neale
Hurston and Aaron Douglas
Publish Fire!, 1926

Boarding House
267 W. 136th St.

Urban League Offices,
202-206 W. 136th St.

Marcus Garvey

St. Philips Apt. Buildings
107-145 W. 135th St.

Arturo Schomburg
Bibliophile and
art collector

187 W. 135th St.
James Weldon
Johnson

Charles S. Johnson
editor of Opportunity

FIRE!

Union leader
A. Philip Randolph
City College
class of 1919

Harlem YMCA
180 W. 135th St.

New York Public Library, 135th St. Branch
Schomburg Center for Research in
Black Culture

Madam C.J. Walker with friend
and daughter A'Lelia Walker, c. 1918

Augusta Savage's
Studio of Arts
and Crafts, c. 1935
239 W. 135th St.

St. Philip's
Episcopal Church
210-216 West 134th St.

Smalls' Paradise,
2294 1/2 7th Ave.

Writer Claude McKay

Barron's Exclusive Club
198 W. 134th St.

JUNGLE ALLEY
Nightclub row on 133rd St.
The Clam House, 146 W. 133rd St.
Pod and Jerry's, 168 W. 133rd St.
The Nest, 169 W. 133rd St.

The Tree of Hope
Destroyed 1934

Connie's Inn,
Lafayette Theater,
Rhythm Club
East side 7th Ave.
131st –132nd Sts.

67 W. 131st St.
James Reese Europe

Singer
Marian Anderson
1200 Fifth Ave.

Rev. Frederick Cullen

Poet Countee Cullen

Salem Methodist
Episcopal Church
2190 7th Ave.

Pianists Willie "The Lion"
Smith "Fats" Waller, & "Jelly Roll" Morton

Malcolm X
Assassinated 1965
Audubon Ballroom
166th St & Broadway

Trumpeter and singer
Louis Armstrong

Artist Romare Bearden
154 W. 131st St.

17 E. 126th St.
Site of "Great Day in Harlem"
photograph, 1958

20 E. 127th St.
Langston Hughes, 1947-1967

Writer James Baldwin
Born 1924
Harlem Hospital
136th & Lenox

Apollo Theater
253 W. 125th Street
Opened 1935; still active.

Marvin & Morgan Smith
Photography Studio
243 W. 125th St.

Adam Clayton Powell, Jr.
Elected to Congress, 1944

THE JAZZ AGE
DOWNTOWN

International House
500 Riverside Dr.
Harmon art exhibits, 1928-30

Boxer
Joe Louis

125th MARTIN LUTHER KING, JR. BLVD.

Carl Van Vechten
Writer photographer,
promoter of Harlem

Blumstein's
Department Store
230 W. 125th St.
Boycott for jobs, 1934

Hotel Teresa
2090 7th Ave.

Eugene O'Neill's
The Emperor Jones
opens in
Greenwich Village, 1920

Painter William H. Johnson
311 W. 120th St.

2040 7th Ave;
Dizzy Gillespie, 1940s

Mt. Morris Fire
Watchtower, 1855
Marcus Garvey Park
122nd St. & Fifth Ave.

George Gershwin's
"Rhapsody in Blue"
debuts Aeolian Hall
34 W. 43rd St., 1924

272 Lenox Ave.
Photography Studio
of James Van Der Zee

Dancer/choreographer
Katherine Dunham

Minton's Playhouse at the
Cecil Hotel, 210 W. 118th St.

Bop pioneer
Dizzy Gillespie

Alain Leroy Locke
Editor, "Harlem" issue of
Survey Graphic, 1925

Hotel Olga, 42 W. 120th St.

Thelonious Monk leads
jam sessions, c. 1941

AFRICAN AMERICAN NEW YORK C. 1900

The Tenderloin, 23rd to 42nd Sts.
along 8th and 9th Aves.

San Juan Hill, 58th to 65th Sts.
between 8th and 11th Aves.

Songwriters Bob Cole,
James Weldon Johnson, and J. Rosamond
Johnson At The Marshall Hotel
260 W. 53rd St., c. 1903

James Reese
Europe Organizes Clef Club,
134 W. 53rd., c. 1905.
Leads Harlem's 369th
Infantry Regimental
Marching Band in
victory parade, 1919

ON BROADWAY

George
Walker

Bert Williams

Will Marion Cook's Clorindy, the Origin of the Cake-Walk
Opens Casino Theatre Roof Garden, 1898

In Dahomey opens
New York Theatre, 1903

Charles Gilpin as Emperor Jones
Princess Theatre, 1921

Eubie Blake, Flournoy Miller
Nobel Sissle & Aubrey Lyles
Shuffle Along opens 63rd Street Theater, 1921

HARLEM RENAISSANCE
EPHEMERA PRESS, 2001

The *Harlem Renaissance* map depicts a colorful literary tour of Manhattan's historical district of Harlem. Created by Ephemera Press, the map celebrates the district's rich cultural history with illustrations of the people and places central to the Renaissance movement that spawned a multitude of African American music, art and literature during the 1920s and 1930s. The tour includes Singer Billie Holiday at 108 West 139th Street and Marcus Garvey's United Negro Improvement Association on Seventh Avenue.

Ephemera Press, Brooklyn, NY; Art by Tony Millionaire

PANORAMA OF THE CITY OF NEW YORK
ROBERT MOSES, 1964

Robert Moses' expansive diorama, built as a city planning tool and displayed at the 1964 World's Fair, is a dense reconstruction of New York City featuring every single building constructed prior to 1992 in all of the Five Boroughs, and totalling 895,000 individual structures.

Built by a team of 100 for the architectural model makers Raymond Lester Associates, the Panorama took three years to complete. Planned from aerial photographs, insurance maps, and other city planning documents, the model was initially stipulated to have less than a one per cent margin of error in physical accuracy.

Moses was a highly controversial figure in the history of New York; his city planning in the early to mid-twentieth century featured a notable focus on the development of city-wide expressways, and despite his lasting legacy, he is seen by his detractors as displacing entire neighborhoods and creating disinvestment in public transport through his work.

Courtesy of Queens Museum of Art

MANHATTAN

HOWARD HOROWITZ, 1997

"The island's tip was sliced by a ship" upon the
Dutch arrival in 1624. The impressive rise of
the City of New York is documented within
Howard Horowitz's *Manhattan*, with each word
and sentence crucially arranged, provoking
the examination of Manhattan's colorful
history in this meta-cartographic word-map.
From the "midtown: skyscrapers at Columbus
Circle, Fifth Avenue, and Park Avenue" to the
"wind-swept docks at Battery Park"—Horowitz
takes the reader on an animated journey of
Manhattan past and present.

Originally appeared in *The New York Times*, August 30
1997, courtesy of the Author

The island's tip
was sliced by a ship
canal that tamed the
Spuyten Duyvil shoals,
but severed Marble Hill
from Inwood. Medieval
tapestry unicorns grace
the Cloisters; a flag-
pole and stockade mark
old Fort Tryon. Lofty
crags overlook the
broad Hudson River
as bedrock & history
anchor the Heights to
the George Washington Bridge. Walk east
toward the Bronx across High Bridge;
gaze to the south
from Sugar Hill,
where trumpeters
and tap dancers
stepped up into
the sun. Ages ago
Iapetus (an older
Atlantic Ocean)
closed; the kiss
with Africa heated
a melting pot. Lava
was injected in veins
of rock and coagulated
to form Palisade cliffs.
The legacy of Algonquian
life is hidden in our place
names and our meals. The new-
comers (first the Dutch, then
English, African, Irish, German,
Italian, Jewish, Chinese, Greek,
Ukrainian, Armenian, Puerto Rican,
Pakistani, Cuban, Dominican, Haitian,
Filipino, and all), have shed blood in a
thousand places, but millions live. Legends
of Gotham: Father Knickerbocker, Boss Tweed,
Emma Lazarus, Fiorello, the roar of the El,
the blizzard of '47, Giants at the Polo Grounds.
Offshore, barges ply swirling brown water near
North River sewage pipes, as striped bass and
shad swim up "the river that flows both ways": a
tidal reach of the sea all the way up to Albany.
Brownstone, bodega, ball court & bus stop: on warm
nights in Harlem, noisy streets and quiet rooftops.
Kids splash around a hydrant as lovers embrace on a
Riverside Park bench and rush-hour traffic is stalled on the Triborough Bridge.
Some uptown options: gospel choir on Sunday, sooty
Grant's Tomb, hiphop the Apollo, ribs at Sylvia's,
law at Columbia, mangos in El Barrio, peace garden
in the Cathedral, rowboat on the Meer, pub-crawl the
West Side, listen to poetry at the 92nd St. Y, nosh at
Zabar's, spiral up the Guggenheim, tour Gracie Mansion.
Songbirds alight in leafy woods as a turtle lays eggs
near a pond in Central Park. Grand museums flank the
green with dinosaur bones and Egyptian tombs. When it
snows, we ramble out to Sheep Meadow & the Great Lawn;
in sunshine, to Strawberry Fields, the Lake, & the Zoo.
Buy hot dogs from pushcarts near Madison boutiques, or
hear grand opera at the Met. Step down to the world of
subways. (Take the A train, ride the Lexington line,
or change at 59th Street for the IRT. Catch the F out to Queens.)
Gneiss but full of schist, the bedrock sparkles with
mica. It bears the weight of midtown: skyscrapers
at Columbus Circle, Fifth Avenue, and Park Avenue.
Attend concerts at Carnegie, ice skating shows at
Rockefeller Center, Mass at St. Patrick's Cathedral.
Our eyes are drawn up to a blue slice of sky as
vertical walls enclose us. 100 gridlocked taxis honk
at police blockades as Fidel speaks at the U.N.
Revelers jam Times Square on New Year's Eve, to
jostle and sing as the ball drops. Buses come in
(the Lincoln Tunnel) to Port Authority, trains to Grand Central. The
lion-flanked public library was once a reservoir;
we love the Art Deco classic Chrysler spire. From
Hell's Kitchen walk to Broadway, buy tickets for
"Showboat" or "Cats"— hey, the Knicks won at the
buzzer in the Garden! See Macy's float parade, then
gape from atop the Empire State, where mighty Kong
took a fall. Diamond jewelers join fur-clad window
shoppers as herds of jaywalkers cross against the
light in the Garment District. Graffiti-scrawled
boards near the Flatiron Building enclose pits
of unconsolidated sediment Consolidated Edison
must dig. Workers repair Gramercy Park cables,
reroute Chelsea steam pipes, plug a burst main
flooding streets by Union Square. (Tap water
flows down from the Catskills in deep tunnels;
garbage is hauled to a landfill at Fresh Kills.)
The riverfront was filled for barnacle-crusted
piers, and Minetta Brook wetlands became lots
in Greenwich Village. A sweatshop horror: 146
locked-in women lost their lives in the Triangle
Shirtwaist fire. Watch skateboard demons cavort
among panhandlers as old men play chess near the
arch in Washington Square. N.Y.U. students, art
film fans, coffee drinkers, & East Village poets
crowd smoky joints on Saturday night; some cross
(the Holland Tunnel) back out to New Jersey. Cheap gallery space
is a memory in SoHo; cast-iron lofts rent high,
as do TriBeCa warehouses. A bag lady seeks warmth
huddled over a sidewalk grate on the Bowery, where
Stuyvesant's farm once spread in old New Amsterdam.
The original steal (this island, traded for $24 in
beads) lies plastered in myth and concrete, obscured
like the African Burial Grounds. A Lower East Side
delicatessen sells good chicken soup; enjoy zuppa di
pesca at the Festival of San Gennaro, or bird's nest
soup in Chinatown. Marchers to City Hall cross the Brooklyn Bridge
to demonstrate, as tourists at South Street Seaport
eat lunch with a view. The Fulton Fish Market is
mobbed before dawn. Precambrian stocks bond the
upper crust with solid foundations below the
Trade Towers, Trinity Church and Wall Street.
Ferryboats to Staten Island, Ellis
Island, the Statue of Liberty,
and Governor's Island
depart from wind-
swept docks
at Battery
Park.

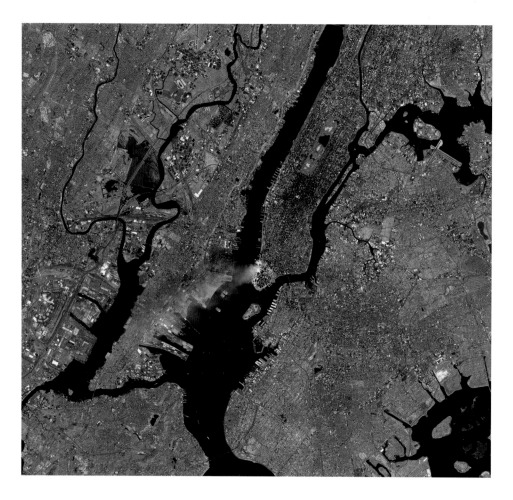

-ABOVE-

AFTERMATH OF WORLD TRADE CENTER ATTACK
NASA EARTH OBSERVATORY, SEPTEMBER 12 2001

NASA's image, taken the day after the 9/11
attacks, is remarkable for a number of reasons.
As well as showing the incredible photographic
detail afforded by modern satellite imagery, the
small-scale focus gives the catastrophic events
documented by the image an almost banal,
disconnected feel. By highlighting the greater
space of New York city and its surrounding
areas, the viewer sees the focus of the map—
a plume of smoke rising from Ground Zero—
in a far less immediate or dramatic context.
The catastrophe itself appears fairly miniscule
and incidental to the area surrounding it. Only
by associating what we are seeing with the date
of its recording do we understand the gravitas
and significance of the image.

Image courtesy NASA: Earth Observatory and USGS

Landsat 7 team

-RIGHT-

AERIAL VIEW OF GROUND ZERO AND
THE FINANCIAL DISTRICT
LIBRARY OF CONGRESS, 2001

A thematic partner to *Aftermath of the World
Trade Center Attack*, this photograph from the
Library of Congress archives—almost surreal
in its large-scale clarity—highlights the sheer
destruction of the September 11 attacks which
NASA's shot can only hint at in its small scale.
The clear image of a working city, and an
abundance of recognizable public and service
vehicles, gives the 'map' a profoundly human
feel, and the reader an almost voyeuristic
perspective into one of the formative events
of the twenty-first century.

Courtesy Library of Congress, Geography and Map Division

SERVICING THE CITY

Cartography is an essential tool in urban management. Whether used in the defining of official district organization, compiling historical land ownership details, providing resources for municipal services, or documenting construction and development, the medium is invaluable in tracking New York's growth as a city. The maps selected for this chapter fundamentally offer a commentary on the basic details that make an urban center; streets, wards, bridges, piers, transport routes, and waterways, as well as radial distances from points in the city and topographic features such as different relief and water depth marks. Information like this, seemingly banal at times, is what provides New York with its basic character and status, and by reading into census details, geographical elements, and municipal city data, we form an understanding of how the conurbation has grown so significantly from its inception as a minor Dutch colonial trading post.

Whilst some of the themes of the maps in this chapter may seem interchangeable with those to do with simply living in the city, such as the examples pertaining to transport or perhaps the more comprehensive street maps, all are chosen with perfunctory services in mind.

Thus, an image such as the 1922 *Third Avenue Railways System Map*, whilst perhaps being useful for the casual commuter, is included due to its recording of disused and disenfranchised railway lines, revealing a glimpse into the historical development of transit systems around the city.

Maps depicting contemporary topographic and cartographic detail also afford an inadvertent chronological overview of the growth of their subject. Egbert L. Viele's hugely influential *Sanitary and Topographical Map of the City and Island of New York*, 1865, records the original shoreline, natural springs, marshland, and meadows of Manhattan before city development and expansion began. It is still used in modern city planning as a preventative guide to flooding dangers and construction suitability.

Other images reveal subsequent private land ownerships of municipal and residential space. In the case of Henry Fulton's *Farm Line Map of the city of Brooklyn (Section 3)*, we see the example of the dominance of Ward 12 by a number of families, as well as a highlighting of the evolution of the separate towns of Bushwick and Brooklyn prior to their 1853 consolidation to become the City of Brooklyn.

As a modern example of the outlay of the city, *New York: The City's Land Use*, developed by the Department of City Planning in 1995, separates and color codes the many different uses of land around the extended city area. Inevitably, and in great contrast with the Viele map, land designated as 'vacant' is notably sparse. Manhattan Island's development is fascinating partly because of its disconnected status; its development as a borough 'guided' by water—the Hudson, East River and underground systems—means that it has only been able to develop vertically in recent years. The city's urban sprawl has thus spread to the boroughs of Queens, the Bronx, and Brooklyn, and it is intriguing to track such development through these maps; both increasing density of construction and the stages of consolidation that created the New York City one knows and recognizes today.

LIST OF WORKS

NEW YORK

FROM AN ILLUSTRATED ATLAS, GEOGRAPHICAL,
STATISTICAL, AND HISTORICAL, OF THE UNITED STATES
AND THE ADJACENT COUNTIES
T.G. BRADFORD, 1838

Thomas G. Bradford's beautifully engraved map covers the majority of Manhattan, as well as portions of Brooklyn and the west New Jersey shore. The latter, despite the relative disparity of topographical detail, contains a number of interesting features; the Hoboken shore north of the peninsula is dotted with woodland, an indication of the lack of dockside development prevalent in this area at the time of publication, and the grid pattern can be seen to have clearly overprinted into the docks above Jersey City.

Manhattan's street names, parks, and a number of dockland slips on the southeast side are provided. City districts are numbered and color-coded, though no key is provided for these on the map. The legend references only six locations of municipal interest, such as City Hall and New York University.

The recording of Forts Greene and Columbus—located in the Bronx and on Governors Island, respectively—are noteworthy. At the time of the map's creation, the former was still largely arable farm land, only in the initial stage of being sold by landowners for the development of city commuter housing. The area is now an established multi-racial neighborhood and the site of the Brooklyn Academy of Music and the Museum of Contemporary African Diasporan Arts, a far cry from its poverty-stricken beginnings. Fort Columbus, a harbor fortification originally designed to protect Upper New York Bay, had by this period begun to diminish in its function with improving weapons technology, though it was still utilized by the military for other purposes. It reverted back to its original name of Fort Jay in 1904.

David Rumsey Map Collection www.davidrumsey.com

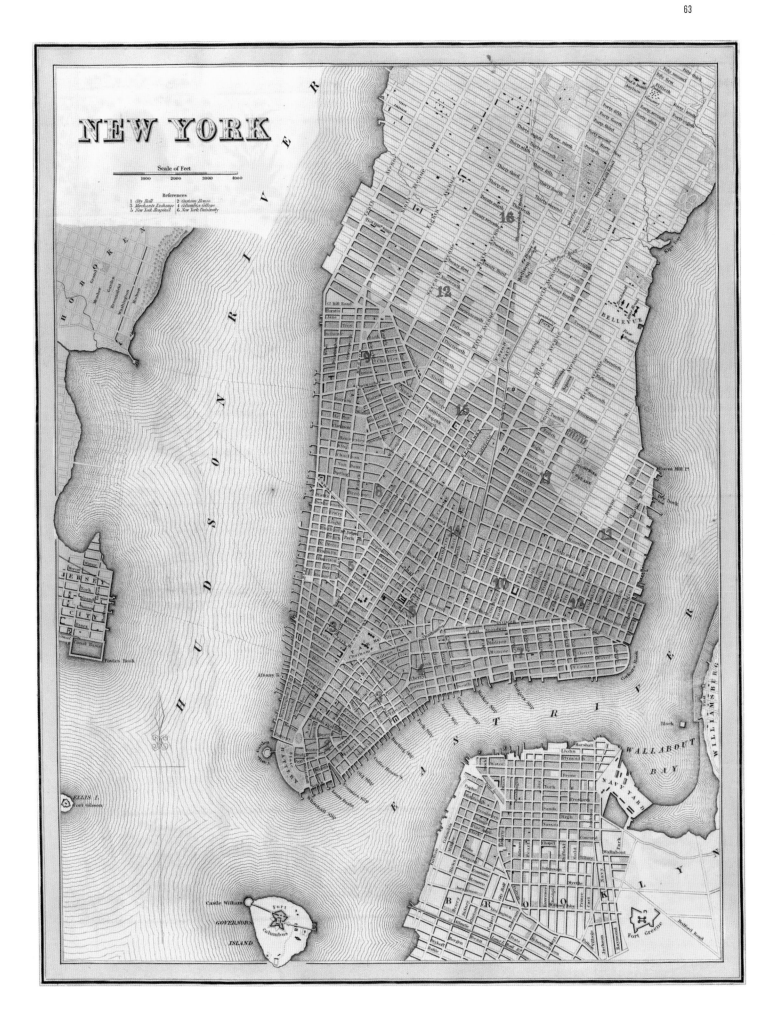

STATIONS OF ENGINES, HOSE & HOOKS & LADDERS.

Buildings having Cisterns.

Indication of Districts.
- 1st — One Stroke of Bell.
- 2d — Two do.
- 3d — Three do.
- 4th — Four do.
- 5th — A continual ringing.

NORTH RIVER

Castle Garden

Battery

THE FIREMEN'S GUIDE

A MAP OF the City of NEW-YORK

Showing the Fire Districts, Fire Limits, Hydrants, Public Cisterns,
Stations of Engines, Hooks & Ladders, Hose Carts, &c.

PUBd. BY P. DESOBRY.
171 Broadway.

Under the Direction of U. Wenman.

Scale of ½ a Mile.

THE FIREMEN'S GUIDE
A MAP OF THE CITY OF NEW-YORK
PROSPER DESOBRY (PUBLISHER), 1843

Keeping in context with its title by showing
city fire districts, fire limits, hydrants, public
cisterns, stations of engines, hooks and
ladders, and contemporary illustrations of
hose carts and equipment, Prosper Desobry's
map accurately records city street grids
and numbers around lower Manhattan. Its
district delineation is particularly fascinating;
emergency response zones are indicated with
specific numbers of fire service bell rings,
growing from the west to east shorelines,
and with the southernmost point around the
Battery signalled with a continuous chiming.

The Lionel Pincus and Princess Firyal Map Division, The New
York Public Library, Astor, Lenox and Tilden Foundations

MAP OF THAT PORTION OF THE CITY AND COUNTY OF NEW-YORK NORTH OF 50TH STREET

MATTHEW DRIPPS. 1851

Matthew Dripps' maps are easily identifiable through the considerable body of information the cartographer includes in each. In his *Map of that Portion of the City and County of New-York North of 50th Street* he depicts the streets and topography of uptown Manhattan in 1851. The map includes the original names for the neighborhoods of the city—including the historic Dutch settlement of Bloomingdale Village, which ran from 23rd to 125th street. Also shown are the neighborhoods of Yorkville, Manhattanville and Harlem—all of which still exist today. An inset image of the streets and topography of the area north of that delineated on the map is also depicted, with three impressive views of the High Bridge, New York State Arsenal and a Blind Asylum pulled out by the cartographer as places of importance.

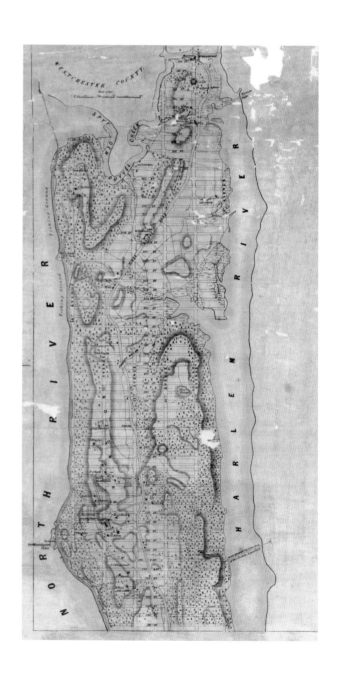

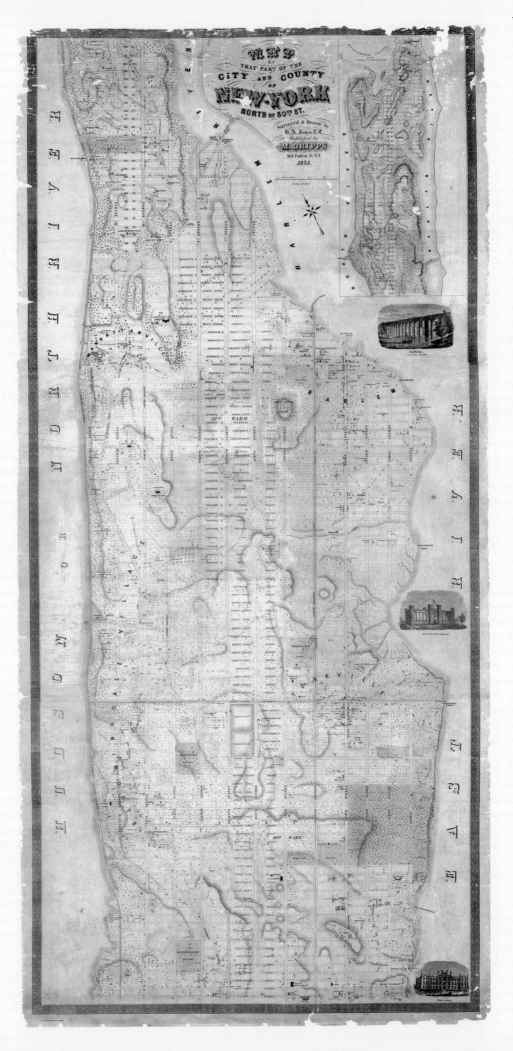

MAP OF THE CITY OF NEW YORK EXTENDING NORTHWARD TO FIFTIETH ST.

MATTHEW DRIPPS, 1852

Dripps *Map of the City of New York*, published in 1852, is the first of its kind to show all the buildings and lots in New York City before the publication of the first Fire Insurance maps by Perris later that year. This highly detailed map of the city provides exact measurements of the avenues and streets below 50th Street—including a Table of Distances between the Avenues, a Table of Distances between streets and a detailed description of all avenues and streets "All the Avenues are 100 feet wide except South of 23rd Street, where Avenues A and C are each 80 feet." Around the edge of the map is an ornate border showing views of the important buildings in the city at the time—including The Grace Church and City Hall.

David Rumsey Map Collection www.davidrumsey.com

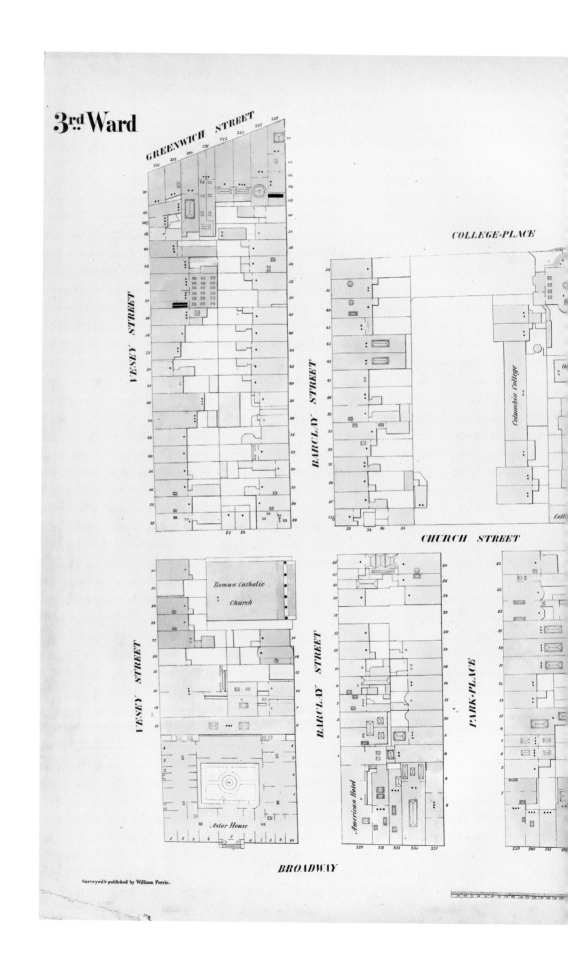

3rd Ward

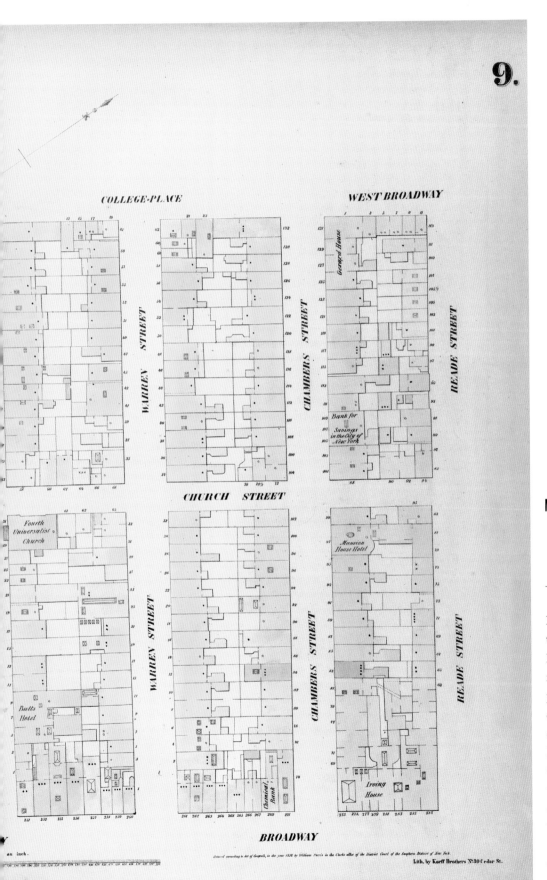

9.

COLLEGE-PLACE

WEST BROADWAY

WARREN STREET

CHAMBERS STREET

READE STREET

CHURCH STREET

Fourth Universalist Church

Butts Hotel

WARREN STREET

CHAMBERS STREET

READE STREET

Mansion House Hotel

Irving House

Chemical Bank

BROADWAY

an inch.

Lith. by Korff Brothers N° 30 Cedar St.

PLATE 9:
MAP BOUNDED BY GREENWICH STREET, BARCLAY STREET, COLLEGE PLACE, WEST BROADWAY, READE STREET, BROADWAY, VESEY STREET
WILLIAM PERRIS, 1852

Perris' comprehensive illustrations were the first of the subsequently numerous Fire Insurance maps of the New York area, replacing the work of Matthew Dripps in providing the definitive detailed cartographic documents of the city at the time. This example, depicting the 3rd Ward area of Manhattan and, as cited, entered according to an Act of Congress in "the Clerks office of the District Court of the Southern District of New York", provides detailed property boundaries and building numbers.

The Lionel Pincus and Princess Firyal Map Division, The New York Public Library, Astor, Lenox and Tilden Foundations

MAP OF NEW YORK AND VICINITY

MATTHEW DRIPPS, 1863

This elegant map of New York, bedecked
with the New York City Arms, is a colorful
depiction of the city's avenues and wards.
Particular attention, however, has been paid to
the city's relationship with the Hudson River
and East River. Each pier has been carefully
drawn, with hundreds of depth measurements
written along the two rivers, interspersed with
positions of buoy's and the various ferry lines
from the harbor to the surrounding boroughs.

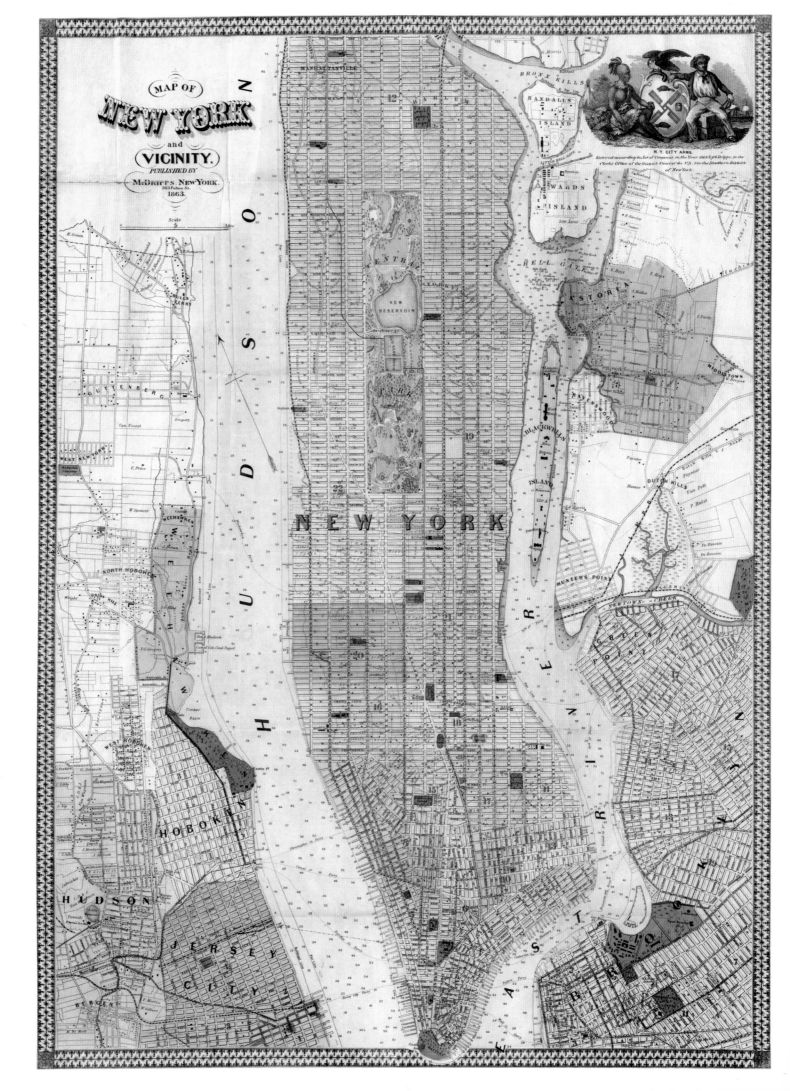

MAP OF
NEW YORK
and VICINITY.
PUBLISHED BY
M. DRIPPS, NEW YORK.
103 Fulton St.
1863.

Scale

N. Y. CITY ARMS.

Entered according to Act of Congress in the Year 1863 by M. Dripps, in the Clerks Office of the District Court of the U.S. for the Southern District of New York.

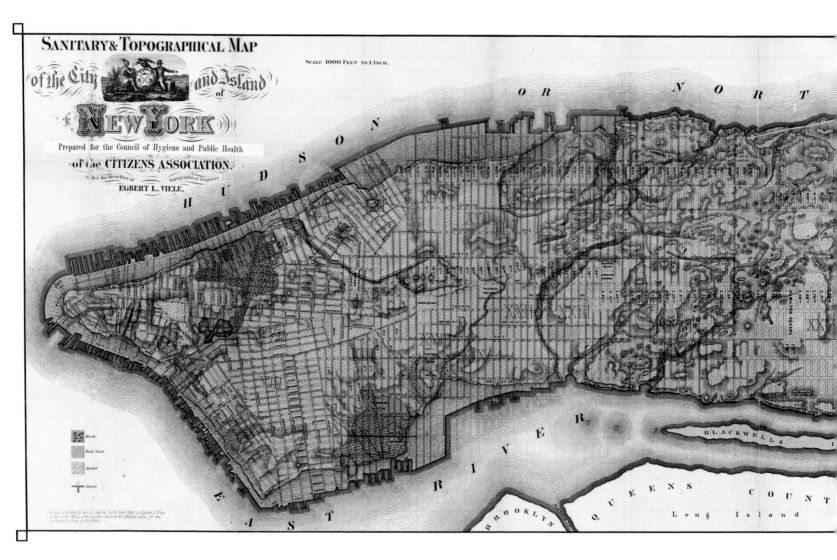

SANITARY AND TOPOGRAPHICAL MAP OF THE CITY AND ISLAND OF NEW YORK

EGBERT L. VIELE, 1865

Egbert Viele's *Sanitary and Topographical Map of the City and Island of New York* can be considered one of the most influential maps in the development of New York City as we know it today—despite its creation date of 1865. The map presents the original shoreline, natural springs, marshes and meadows of Manhattan before the expansion and development of the island due to landfill. The map was originally presented to the U.S. Sanitary Commission, as part of a case by Viele to prevent the spread of disease through the preservation of Manhattan Island's natural waterways. It depicts Manhattan in 1865 as a vast expanse of lush meadow and marshland with "Made Land" running only along the southern tip of the island. This was all to change, however, as developers ignored Viele's argument and the island's natural landscape made way for settlements and streets. Viele's map did not disappear into obscurity, however, but adopted an entirely different role as an indispensable tool for the development of the future city. To this day developers still refer to the *Sanitary and Topographical Map* to ascertain the likelihood of flooding and the suitability of land for building upon.

David Rumsey Map Collection www.davidrumsey.com

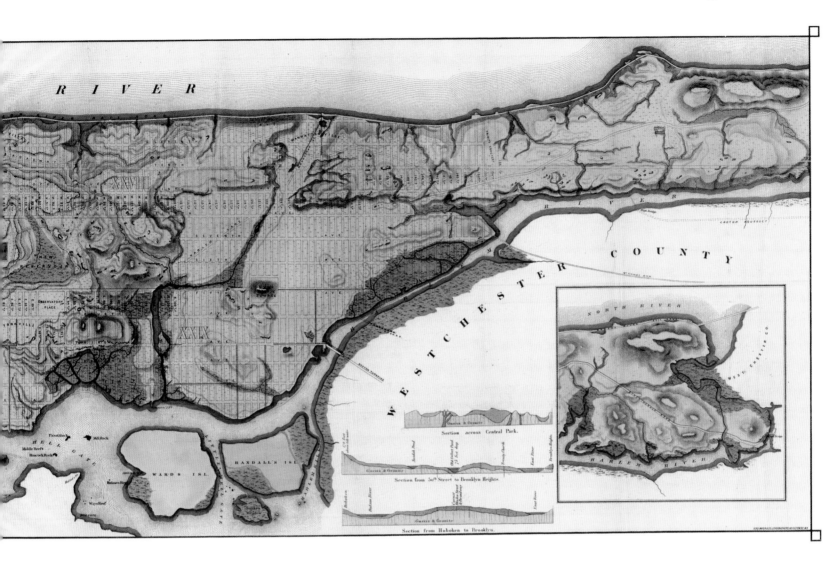

-OVERLEAF-

NEW YORK AND BROOKLYN

SAMUEL AUGUSTUS MITCHELL, 1890

Samuel Augustus Mitchell's map of New York and Brooklyn is taken from his New General Atlas, which detailed 'various' global countries and was published in 1890. Appearing especially dense due to the full referencing of street names and a number of major public buildings, the map also supplies comprehensive portrayal of the walkways and reservoirs of Central Park, railroads, a number of river ferry routes, and contour lines to show under-river depth gradients. Also highlighted are certain benevolent institutions, notably the lunatic asylum and Alms House of Blackwell's Island. City wards are both numbered and, as well as Long Island City, Ward's and Randall's Islands, Ravenswood, and South Astoria, are hand-colored. An inset shows the northern portion of New York City and County as far as the southern Bronx district border.

David Rumsey Map Collection www.davidrumsey.com

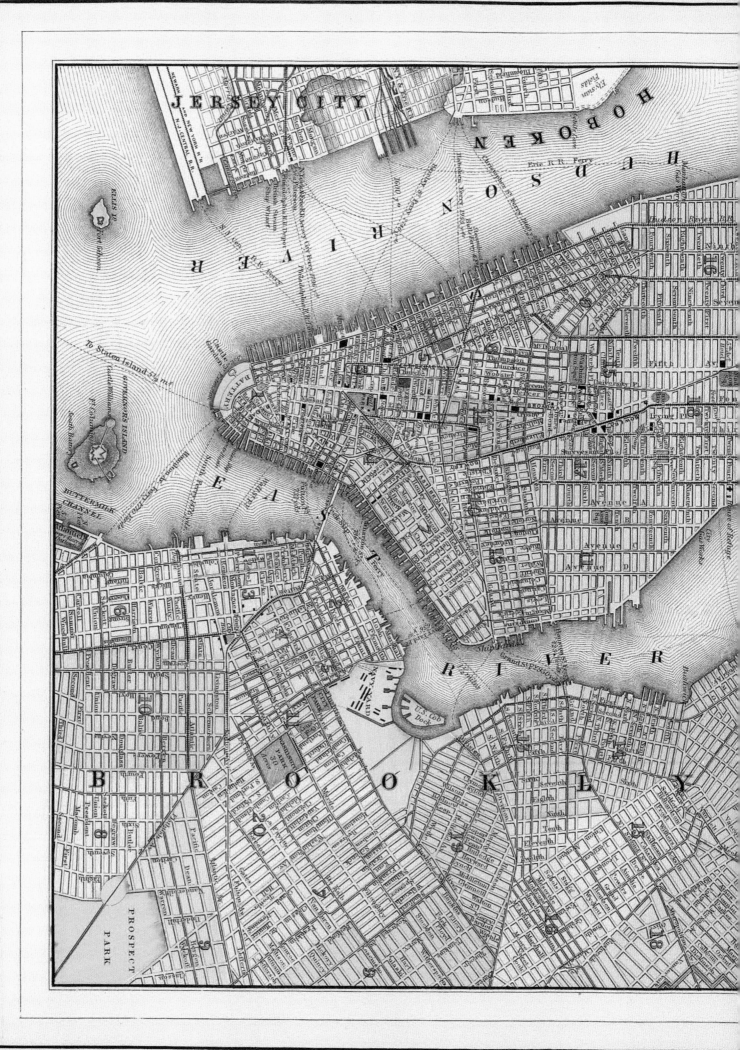

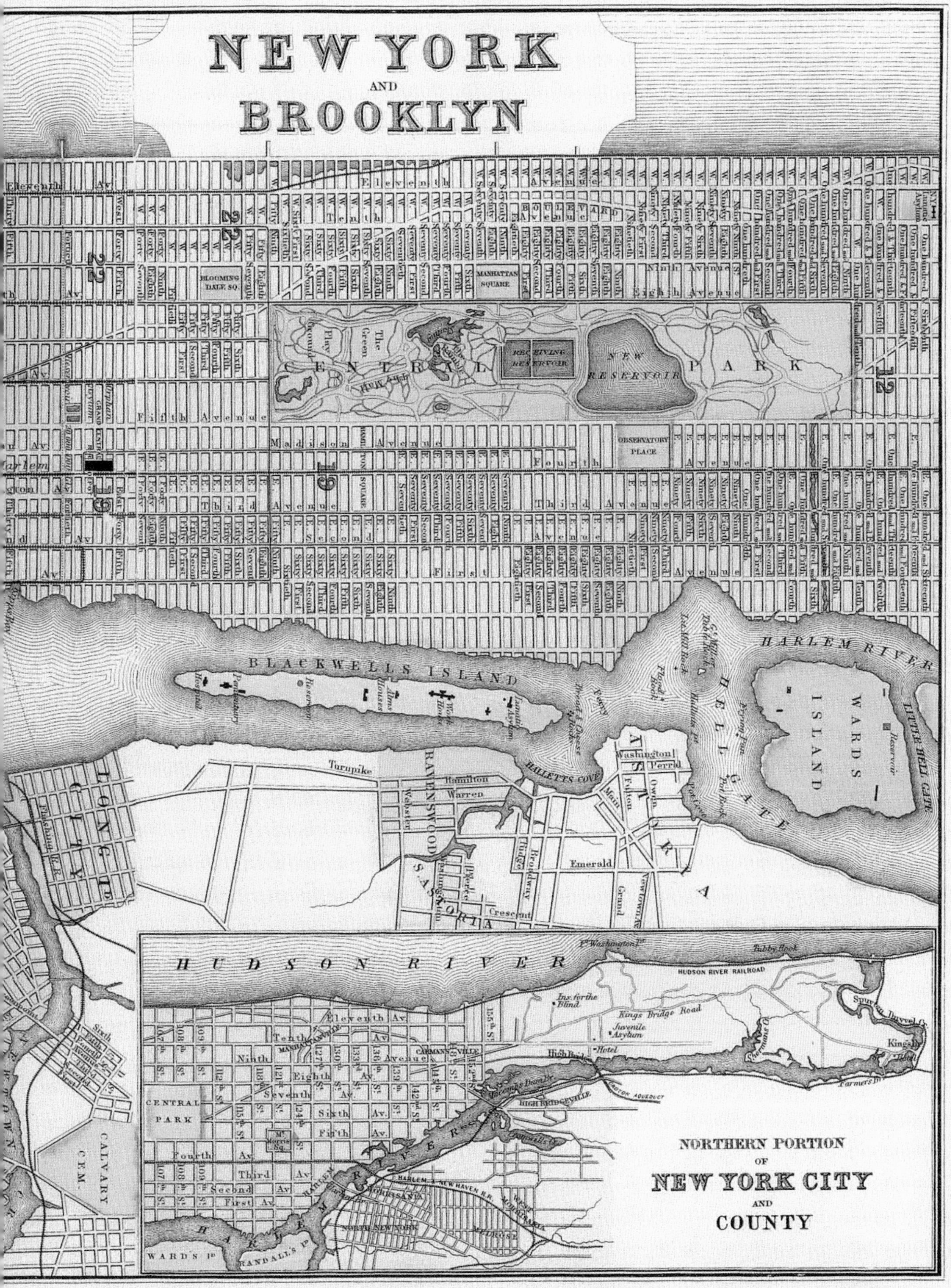
NEW YORK
AND
BROOKLYN
Eleventh Av.
Tenth Av.
Boulevard
Ninth Avenue
Eighth Avenue
Fifth Avenue
Madison Avenue
Fourth Av.
Third Avenue
Second Av.
First Avenue
BLOOMING DALE SQ.
MANHATTAN SQUARE
CENTRAL PARK
Play Ground
The Green
RECEIVING RESERVOIR
NEW RESERVOIR
OBSERVATORY PLACE
HAMILTON SQUARE
BLACKWELLS ISLAND
HARLEM RIVER
WARDS ISLAND
HELL GATE
LITTLE HELL GATE
HALLETTS COVE
ASTORIA
RAVENSWOOD
LONG ISLAND CITY
Turnpike
Hamilton
Warren
Webster
Washington
Main
Fulton
Emerald
Broadway
Grand
Crescent
CALVARY CEM.
HUDSON RIVER
HUDSON RIVER RAILROAD
Kings Bridge Road
Ins. for the Blind
Juvenile Asylum
MANHATTANVILLE
CARMANSVILLE
High Bridge
HIGH BRIDGEVILLE
CROTON AQUEDUCT
HARLEM RIVER
HARLEM & NEW HAVEN R.R.
MORRISANIA
NORTH NEW YORK
MELROSE
CENTRAL PARK
WARD'S I.
RANDALL'S I.
NORTHERN PORTION
OF
NEW YORK CITY
AND
COUNTY

-RIGHT-

SECTION 10 (FARM LINE MAP OF THE CITY OF BROOKLYN)

HENRY FULTON AND J.B. BEERS & CO., 1874

Henry Fulton's *Farm Line Map of the City of Brooklyn*, depicts a lush, green Prospect Park in its foreground. The park's landscape is a labyrinth of paths and concourses, shown traversing the length and breadth of the park and circling the intricately detailed meadows, woods and orchards.

David Rumsey Map Collection www.davidrumsey.com

-OPPOSITE-

SECTION 3 (FARM LINE MAP OF THE CITY OF BROOKLYN)

HENRY FULTON, 1874

Taken from the *Farm Line Map of the City of Brooklyn*, Henry Fulton's comprehensively detailed study of the New York district documents an extensive range of cartographic features; street names, block numbers, and ward boundaries are noted in full, as are closed thoroughfares, harbor depths, and farm lines with corresponding names, signifying traditional property and land ownership. The latter can be seen in the hand colored areas covering the central regions of the lithograph, and highlight the Van Dyke and Luqueer family's domination of the area in the mid-nineteenth century. The inclusion of historical details such as these serve to highlight the then evolving status of the area, from its beginnings in the separate towns of Bushwick and Brooklyn, to the 1853 City of Brooklyn documented by Fulton.

David Rumsey Map Collection www.davidrumsey.com

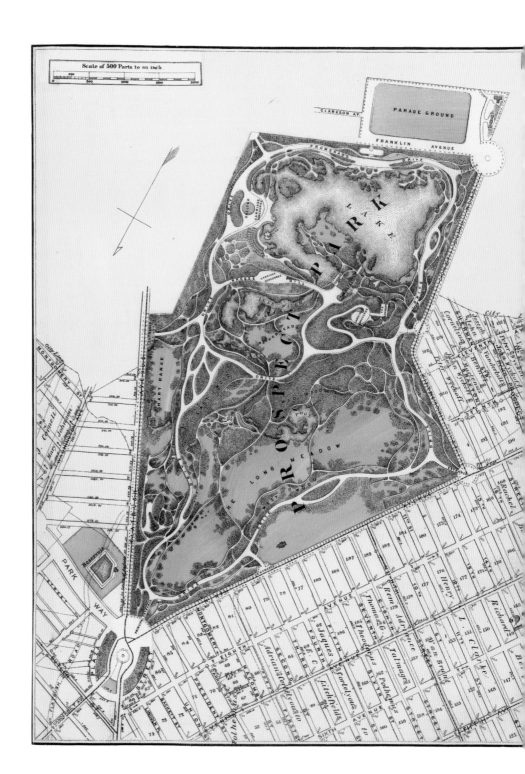

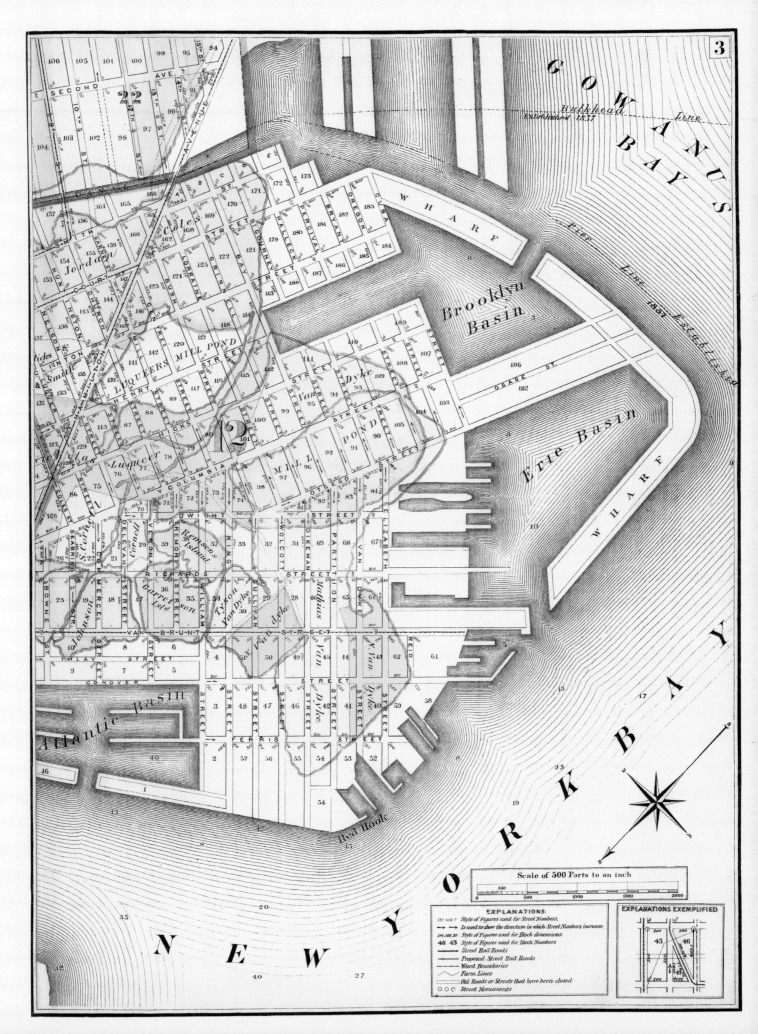

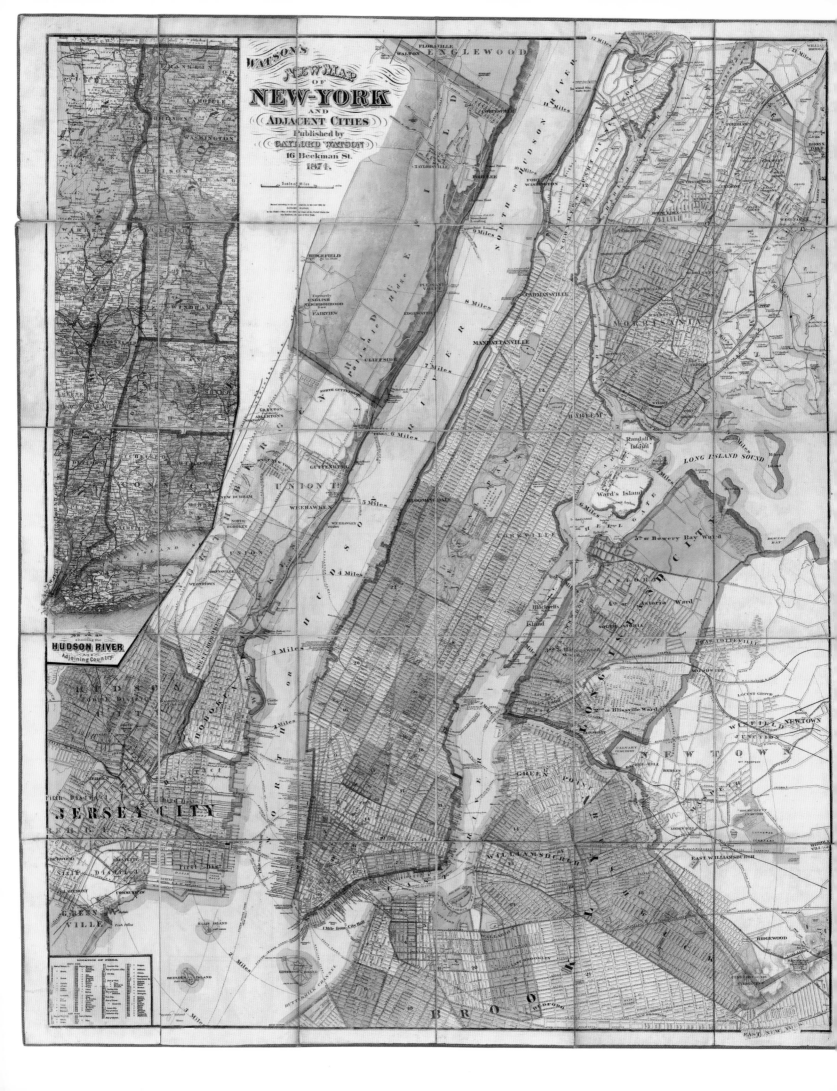

WATSON'S
New Map
OF
NEW-YORK
AND
ADJACENT CITIES
Published by
GAYLORD WATSON
16 Beekman St.
1874.

Scale of Miles

MAP
showing the
HUDSON RIVER
AND
Adjoining Country

-OPPOSITE-

WATSON'S NEW MAP OF NEW-YORK AND ADJACENT CITIES

GAYLORD WATSON, 1874

Gaylord Watson's delightfully colorful *Map of New-York and Adjacent Cities* is a highly detailed view of the streets and lots of New York City, Brooklyn, Jersey City and Long Island City in 1874. The map pays particular attention to the piers running from Manhattan Island into the Hudson and East Rivers, all of which are referenced in a detailed key on the map. An inset map of the *Hudson River and Adjoining County* is also shown, placing the city in perspective, relative to its surrounding area.

-OVERLEAF-

OUTLINE AND INDEX MAP OF NEW YORK CITY, NEW YORK

G.W. BROMLEY AND E. ROBINSON, 1879

From the *Atlas of the Entire City of New York*, G.W. Bromley's and E. Robinson's Outline *and Index Map of New York City* acts as a detailed guide for the rest of the atlas. Streets, wards, neighborhoods and railroads are all shown on the map—describing both Manhattan and the Bronx—alongside a note stating "The red numbers indicate the plates in the atlas and the red lines the boundaries of the same." To find a more detailed plan of a particular area of the city one can turn to the correct plate indicated by the index in red.

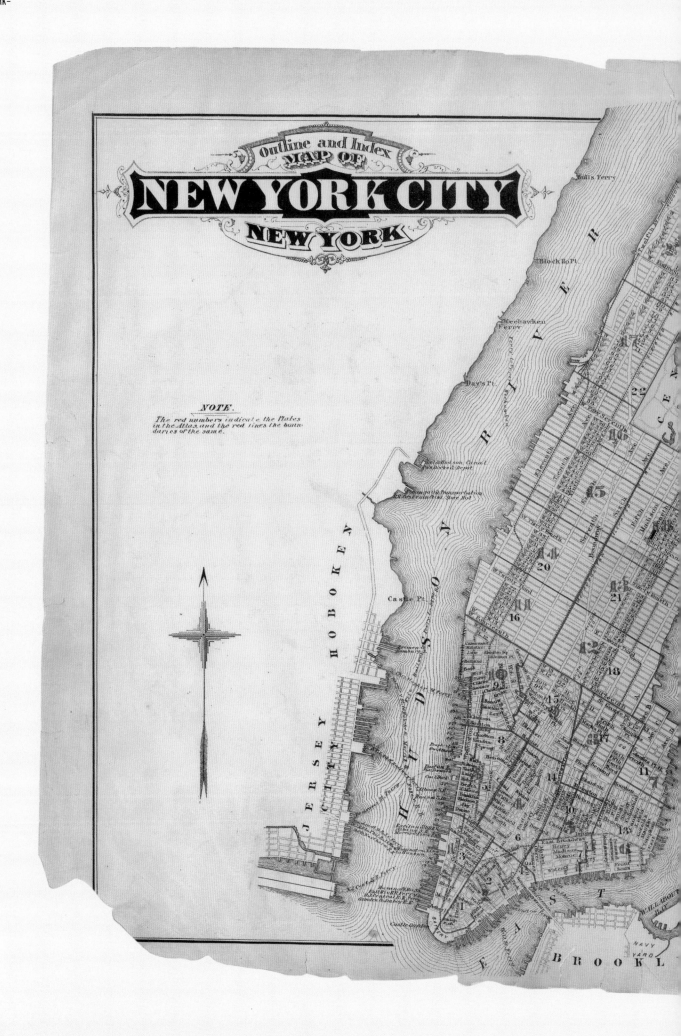

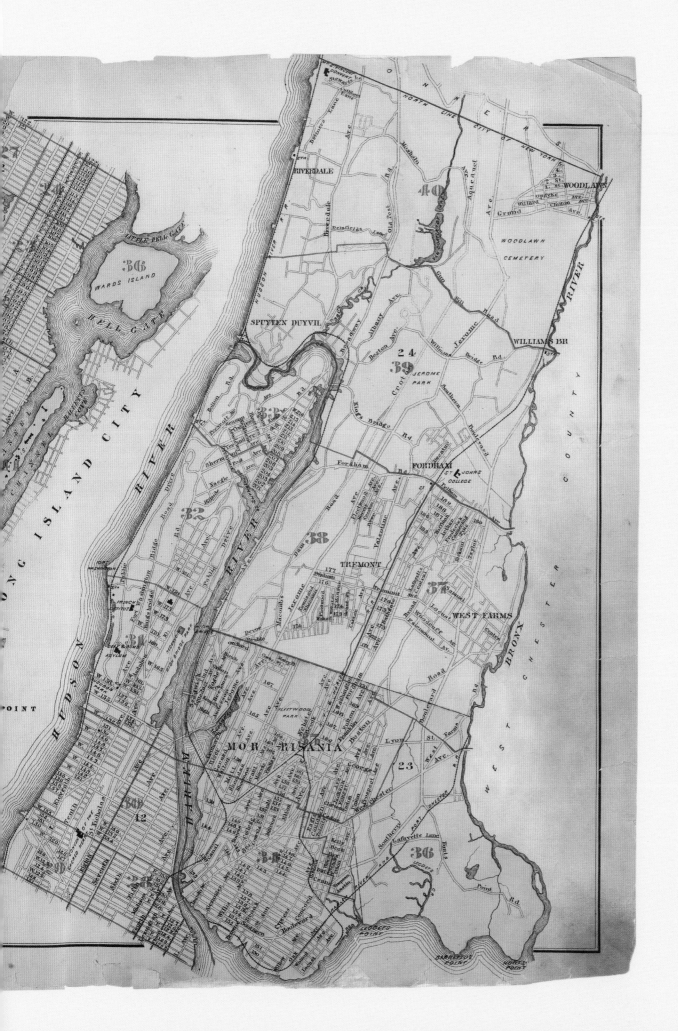

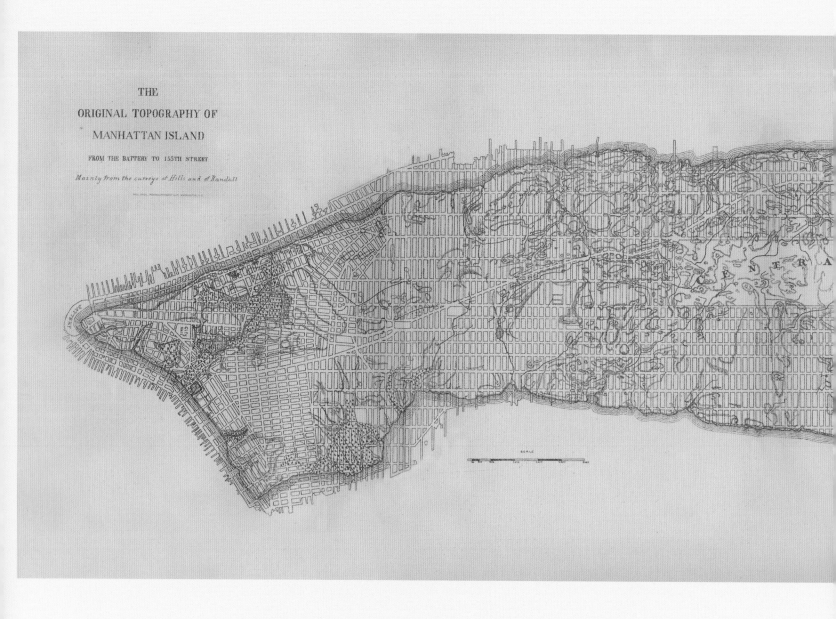

THE
ORIGINAL TOPOGRAPHY OF
MANHATTAN ISLAND
FROM THE BATTERY TO 155TH STREET
Mainly from the surveys of Hills and of Randall

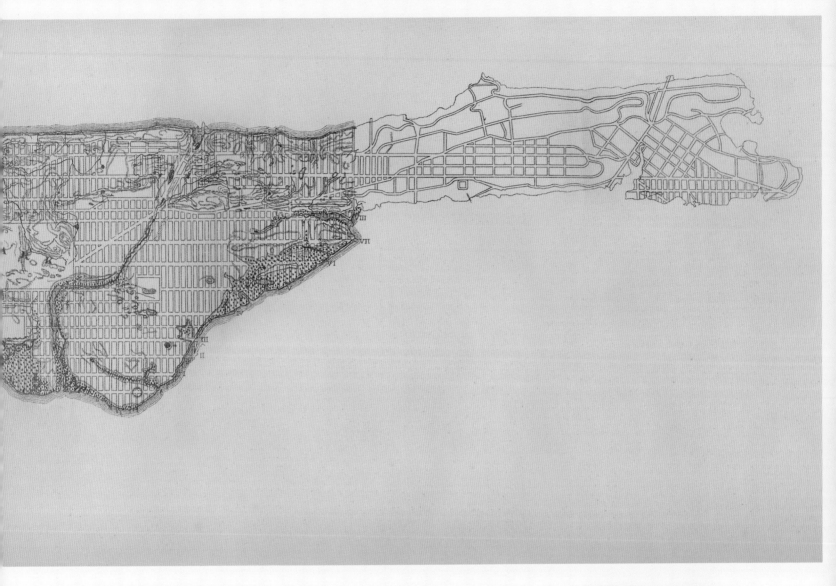

THE ORIGINAL TOPOGRAPHY
OF MANHATTAN ISLAND: FROM BATTERY
TO 155TH STREET

FROM REPORT OF THE SOCIAL STATISTICS OF CITIES,

COMPILED BY GEORGE E. WARING JR., 1886

The Original Topography of Manhattan Island: From Battery to 155th Street is a precise survey depicting the city's streets and relief along the length of Manhattan Island. The city's famous grid system is mapped out to scale, indicating Houston Street, 42nd Street and 125th Street, amongst others. City Hall is shown at the bottom of the map alongside Central Park between 57th and 110th Street.

Courtesy of University of Texas Libraries

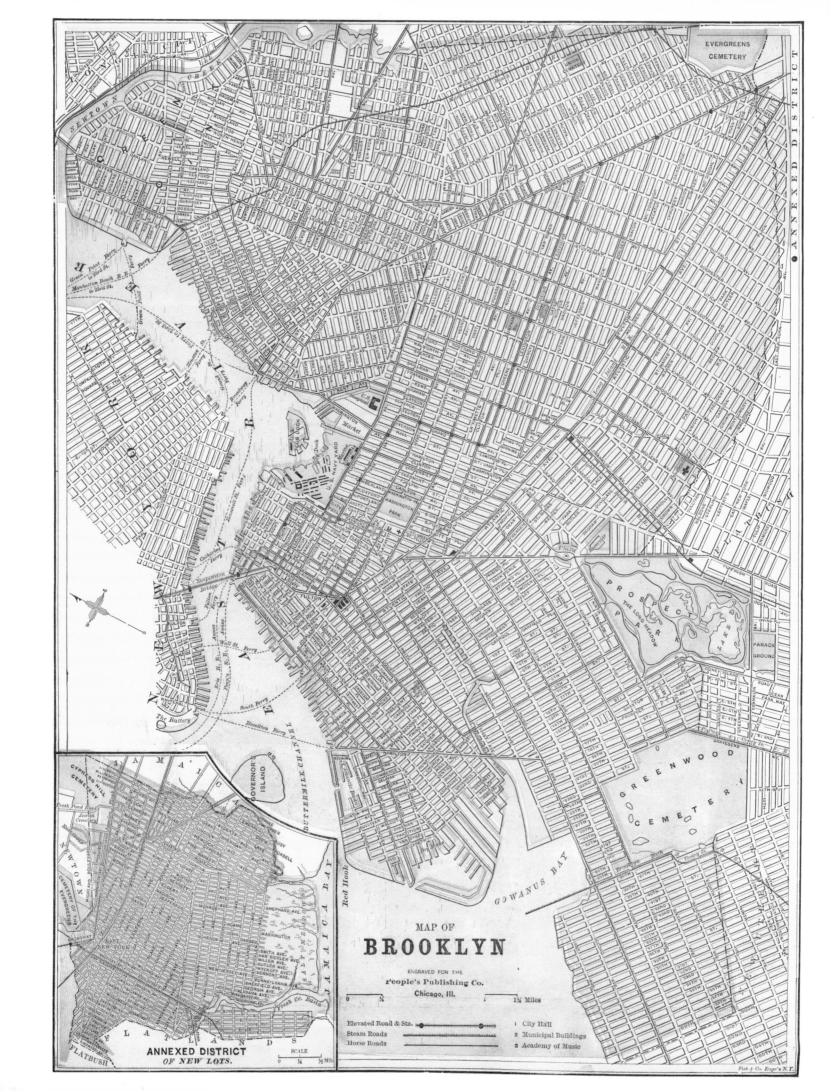

MAP OF
BROOKLYN

ENGRAVED FOR THE

People's Publishing Co.

Chicago, Ill.

SCALE

0   ¾   ½   1   1¼ Miles

Elevated Road & Sta. ●━━━━━━━━━●   1   City Hall
Steam Roads ━━━━━━━━━━━━━   2   Municipal Buildings
Horse Roads ━━━━━━━━━━━━━   3   Academy of Music

ANNEXED DISTRICT
OF NEW LOTS.

SCALE
0   ¼   ½ Mile

EVERGREENS
CEMETERY

GREENWOOD
CEMETERY

PROSPECT PARK

THE LONG MEADOW

PARADE GROUND

GOWANUS BAY

Fisk & Co. Engr's N.Y.

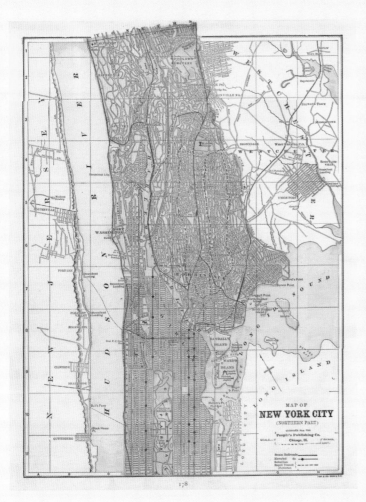

MAP OF NEW YORK CITY (NORTHERN PART) AND NEW YORK CITY (SOUTHERN PART)

PEOPLE'S PUBLISHING CO., 1886

Produced by the publishers of the 1886 *Street Map of Brooklyn*, these illustrations of north and south Manhattan—the former encompassing significant swathes of the Bronx (then Westchester County), New Jersey, and Long Island—follow an identical aesthetic style. Cartographic detail in the northern portion is limited to street labelling and railway lines around Manhattan, as well as the gridding of smaller urban areas within the larger conurbation. In addition to this, the map of Lower Manhattan also includes wharf and pier numbers, ferry routes, bridges, and municipal and business locations of interest.

STREET MAP OF BROOKLYN

PEOPLE'S PUBLISHING CO., 1886

This disorientatingly-angled print of the streets of Brooklyn and the shore of Lower Manhattan provides an intricate gridding of the borough's street system. An inset study of the New Lots area around Jamaica Bay, annexed from the original City of Brooklyn—as set out in 1834—in the year of the map's production can be seen in the bottom left corner.

Map image courtesy of Stuart Brorson

Map image courtesy of Stuart Brorson

WATSON'S NEW MAP OF NEW-YORK AND ADJACENT CITIES

F.W. BEERS, 1891

PUBLISHED IN ATLAS OF THE HUDSON RIVER VALLEY, FROM NEW YORK CITY TO TROY, 1891

Showing the Upper End of Manhattan and its surrounding area—Morrisania, the Hudson River, Long Island Sound, and an inset map of land west of the Westchester County border towards Spuyten Duyvil—this extract from the publisher Gaylord Watson's study of New York shows many comprehensive topographical details. As well as street numbers, railways, and ferry routes, Beers also includes more specialist points of interest such as radial distances from City Hall and hachure marks to indicate relief.

The included illustration of the New Jersey shore, from North Hoboken up to Fort Lee, is notably detailed, more so than many of these maps, which tend to supply only rudimentary cartographic information for areas outside of the Five Boroughs.

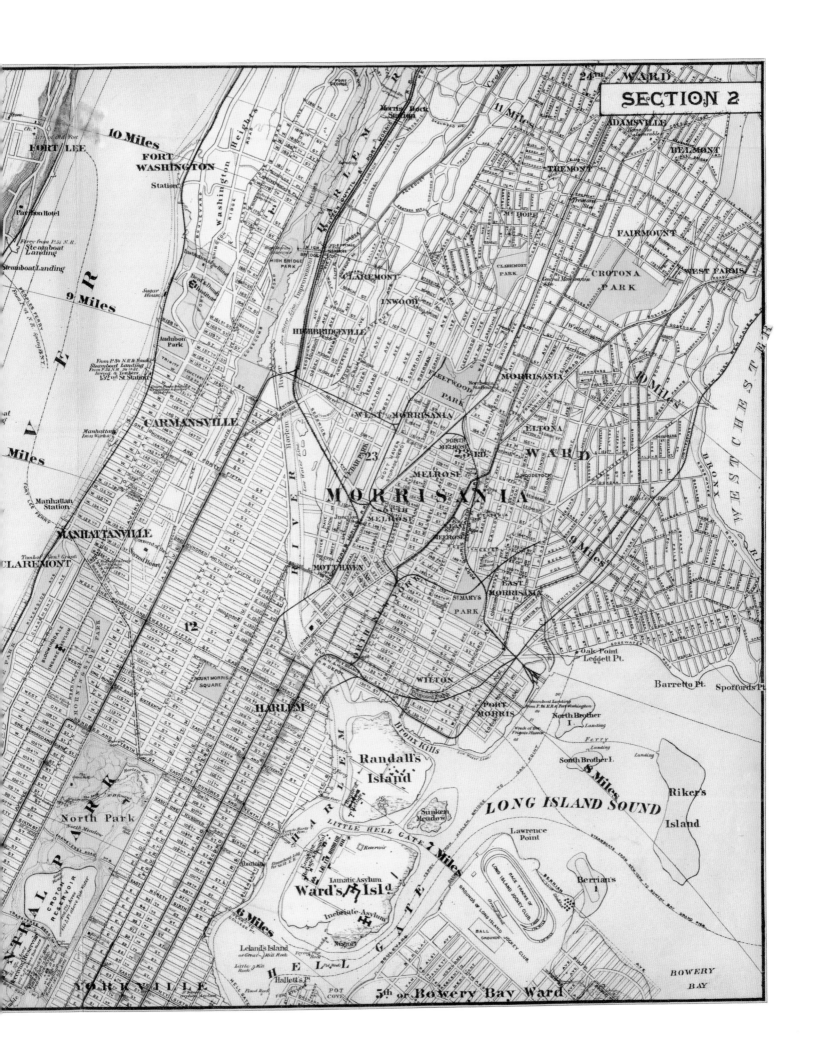

24TH WARD

ADAMSVILLE

BELMONT

TREMONT

FORT LEE

10 Miles

FORT WASHINGTON
Station

MT HOPE

FAIRMOUNT

WEST FARMS

Pavilion Hotel

11 Miles

Steamboat Landing

CLAREMONT
PARK

CROTONA
PARK

Steamboat Landing

9 Miles

CLAREMONT

INWOOD

MORRISANIA

HIGHBRIDGEVILLE

Audubon Park

FLEETWOOD PARK

ELTONA

WEST MORRISANIA

CARMANSVILLE

NORTH MELROSE

23RD   WARD

Miles

23

MELROSE

MORRISANIA

MANHATTANVILLE

MELROSE

CLAREMONT

MOTT HAVEN

EAST MORRISANIA

St MARYS
PARK

MOUNT MORRIS
SQUARE

12

WILTON

Oak Point
Leggett Pt.

Barretto Pt.   Spuffords Pt.

HARLEM

PORT
MORRIS

North Brother
I.

NORTH
PARK

Randall's
Island

Bronx Kills

South Brother I.

8 Miles

Riker's
Island

LONG ISLAND SOUND

North Park

North Meadow

Sunken
Meadow

Lawrence
Point

Berrian's
I.

CROTON
RESERVOIR

LITTLE HELL GATE 7 Miles

Reservoir

Lunatic Asylum

Ward's Isld

Inebriate Asylum

6 Miles

Leland's Island
or Great Mill Rock

Little Mill Rock

Hallett's Pt.

POT
COVE

BOWERY
BAY

YORKVILLE

5th or Bowery Bay Ward

CITY AND COUNTY OF NEW YORK

CITY AND COUNTY
OF NEW YORK

JOSEPH RUDOLF BIEN, 1891

Joseph Rudolf Bien's *City and County of New York* map from the Atlas of Westchester County, New York, is a lithographed map depicted in full color. The area's rich geography is represented by the lush meadows, marshlands and winding rivers of New Jersey, Westchester and Queens and is visibly juxtaposed with Manhattan's developed grid system and the built up area of "Kings"—better known as the borough of Brooklyn. Prominence is given to the striking turquoise of The Hudson and East Rivers flowing into Flushing Bay, with each of the different ferry lines carefully drawn on by Bien.

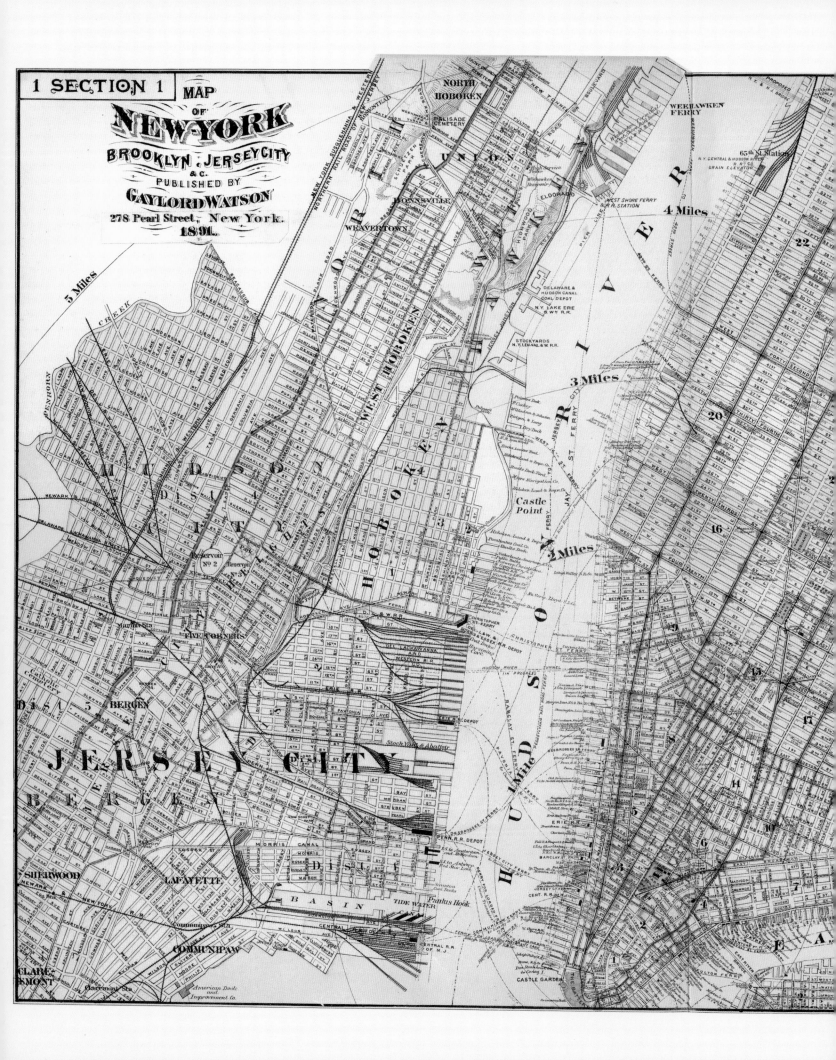

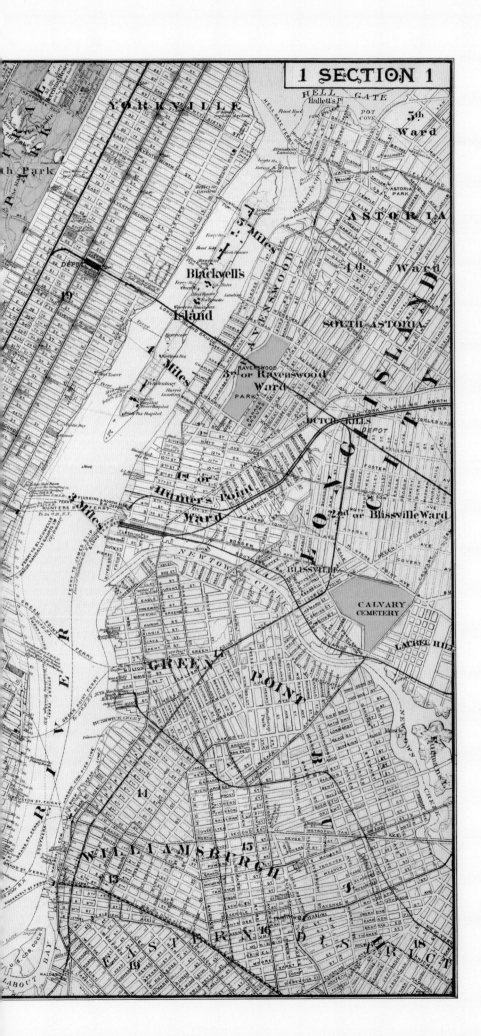

MAP OF NEW-YORK, BROOKLYN, JERSEY CITY & C.

GAYLORD WATSON, 1891

Gaylord Watson's *Map of New-York, Brooklyn, Jersey City & C.* is a thorough geographical overview of New York and its surrounding boroughs crammed with information on the city's streets, railroads, piers and parks. Each of Manhattan's piers has been intricately labelled, alongside the different ferry routes leaving the island, travelling to the surrounding boroughs—with each painstakingly labelled with the ferry's name. Radial distances are also highlighted on the map extending out from City Hall one mile at a time.

David Rumsey Map Collection www.davidrumsey.com

-OVERLEAF-

OUTLINE AND INDEX MAP OF NEW YORK CITY MANHATTAN ISLAND

GEORGE W. BROMLEY & CO., 1891

New York City Fire Insurance maps provide some of the most comprehensive guides to the city. The eye-catching full color maps were published under a variety of different authors throughout the nineteenth century—including William Perris in 1852 with his *Maps of the City of New York*. The fire insurance maps give detailed information on land-use, building type and water mains, whilst also depicting the city's famous grid system to an exact scale. This *Outline and Index Map* by George W. Bromley acts as a colorful guide to the map plates that follow in his *Atlas of the City of New York*. This elegant image reflects the level of development of New York City in 1891, when used in conjunction with its 'Explanations' Key. Whilst Lower Manhattan is depicted as a colorful grid of built land—in contrast, Upper Manhattan and the Bronx remain markedly undeveloped.

David Rumsey Map Collection www.davidrumsey.com

EXPLANATIONS.

Denotes	Brick Building	
"	Stone "	
"	Wood "	
"	Iron "	
"	Brick Building with Stone Front	
"	" " " Iron "	
"	Wood " " Brick "	
"	" " Covered with Iron	
"	Brick Stable or Shed	
"	Wood " "	
"	Water Main with size	

Denotes	Sewers	
"	Old Farm Lines	
"	Old Water Course	
"	Block Dimensions & Street widths	
"	Lot Numbers	
"	Lot Dimensions	
"	House Numbers	
"	Number of Stories & Basement	
"	Number of Stories	
"	Elevations above high tide	
235 "	Block Numbers	
⑦ "	Adjoining Plate	

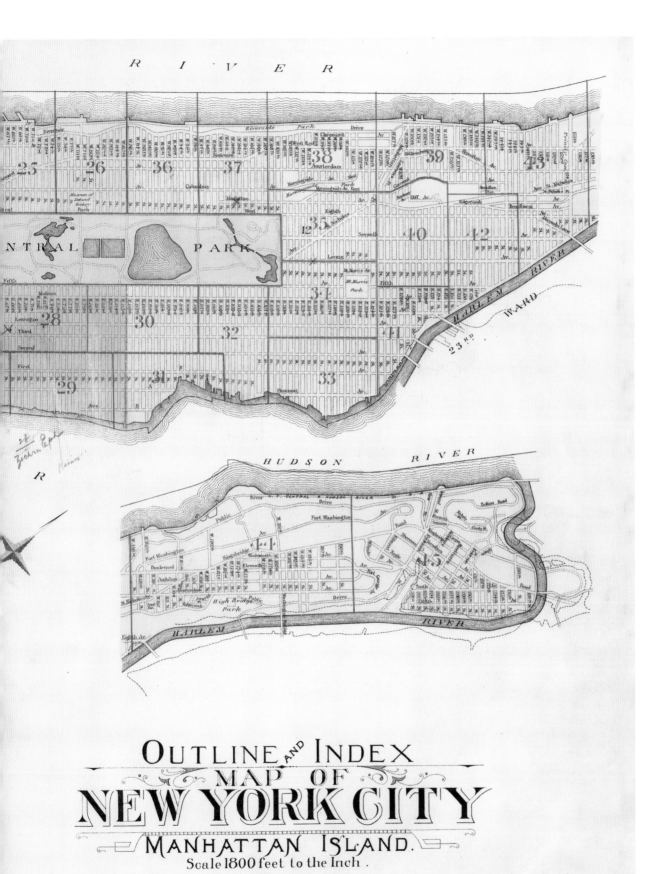

OUTLINE AND INDEX
MAP OF
NEW YORK CITY
MANHATTAN ISLAND.
Scale 1800 feet to the Inch.

Note. Red figures & lines indicate names
& boundaries of plates in the Atlas.

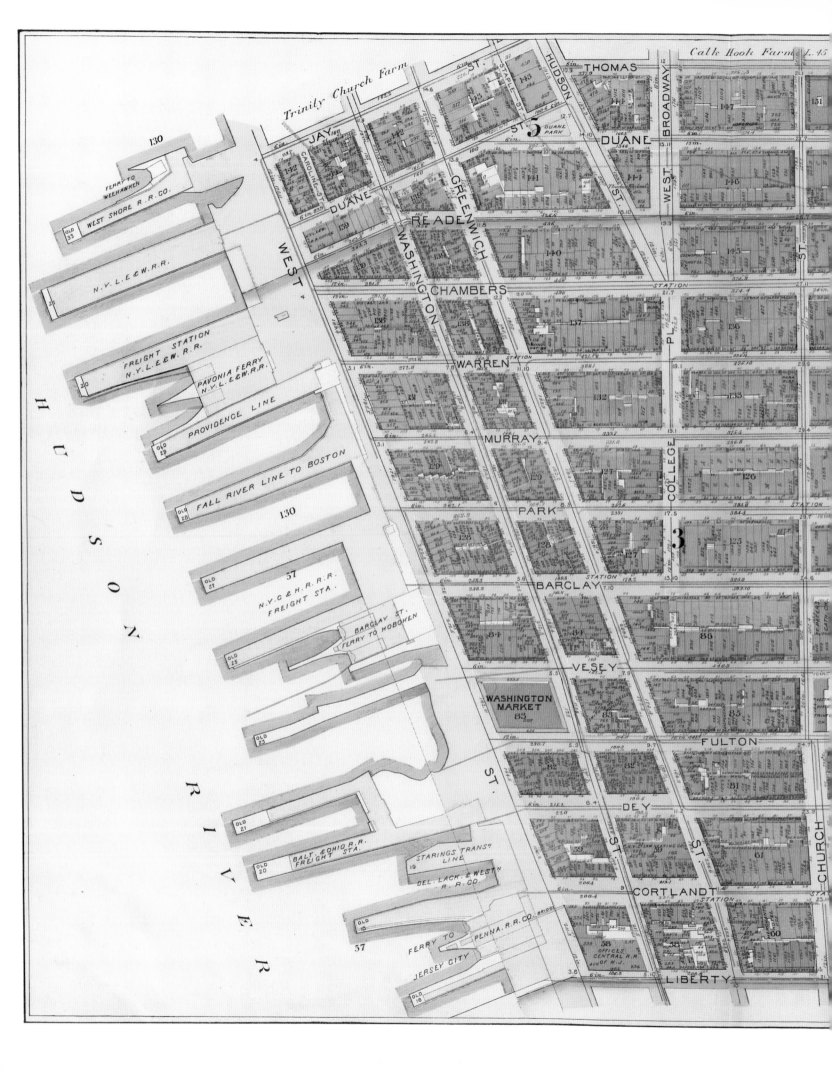

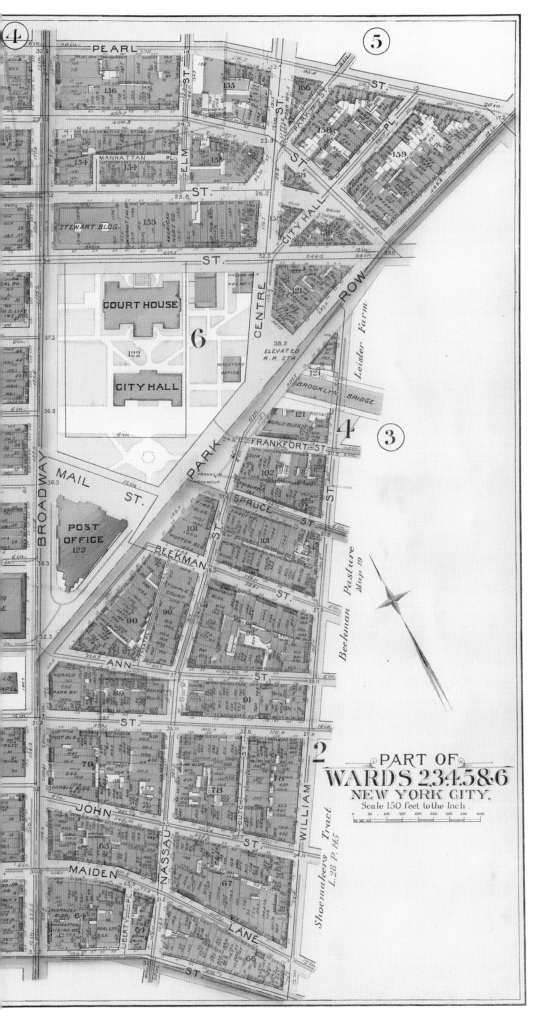

PART OF WARDS 2, 3, 4, 5, & 6, NEW YORK CITY

GEORGE WASHINGTON BROMLEY
& WALTER SCOTT BROMLEY, 1891

Civil engineers Bromley and Bromley's hand-colored study of the area north of Liberty and south of Jay, Thomas, and Pearl Streets, is another detailed example of the city's dense collection of Fire Insurance maps. Even for a map of this type, some of the details noted are particularly obscure; property use or occupant, sewers, antiquated farm line delineation, street widths, and old water courses are all observed, as well as more generic labelling of street and wharf names, and building construction materials. Notable municipal buildings, such as City Hall and the Post Office, are picked out in a subtle brown, a juxtaposition to the vivid, almost neon quality of the rest of the image.

David Rumsey Map Collection www.davidrumsey.com

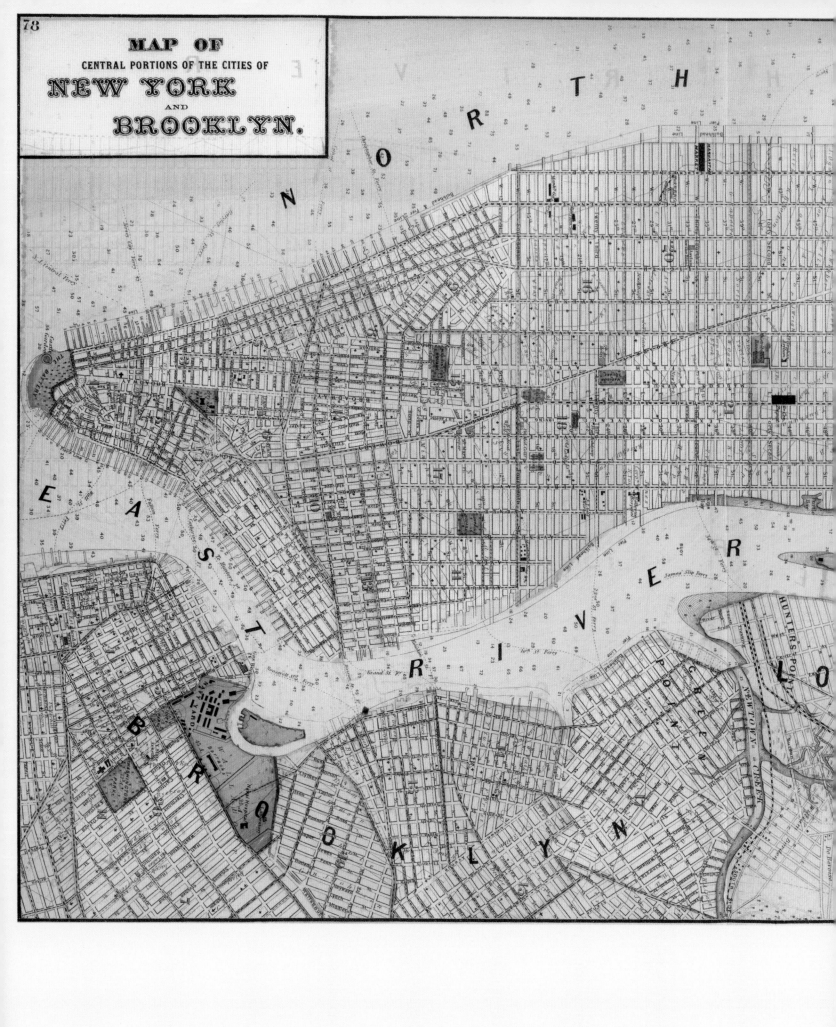

MAP OF
CENTRAL PORTIONS OF THE CITIES OF
NEW YORK
AND
BROOKLYN.

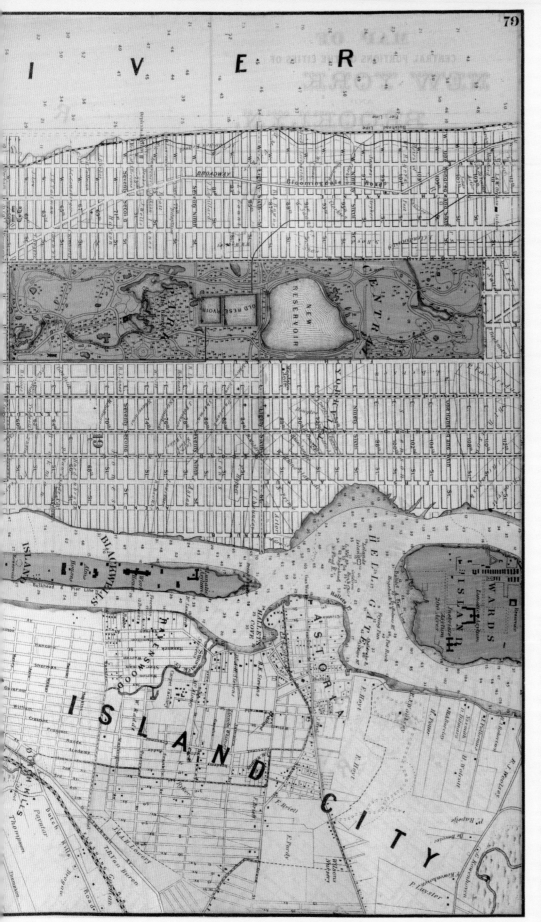

MAP OF CENTRAL PORTIONS OF THE CITIES OF NEW YORK AND BROOKLYN

FROM STATE ATLAS OF NEW JERSEY BASED ON STATE GEOLOGICAL SURVEY AND FROM ADDITIONAL SURVEYS

F.W. BEERS, 1872

Frederick Beers' study refers to both the cities of New York and Brooklyn, due to the fact that it would be another nine years before the Brooklyn Bridge was completed and the process of consolidating the area to become a New York city district began.

Beers' work contains a number of details not often seen on maps of this era, those pertaining to a maritime theme being of particular note. As well as highlighting Brooklyn Navy Yard, a major and active military shipyard which was decommissioned in 1996, this example also rigorously notes depth soundings throughout the waterways of the two cities. Most of the maps of the time which deemed to include river details of this kind utilized contour-style lines, and seemingly decorative ones at that given their consistent nature in comparison to the fluctuating depths shown on this map.

David Rumsey Map Collection www.davidrumsey.com

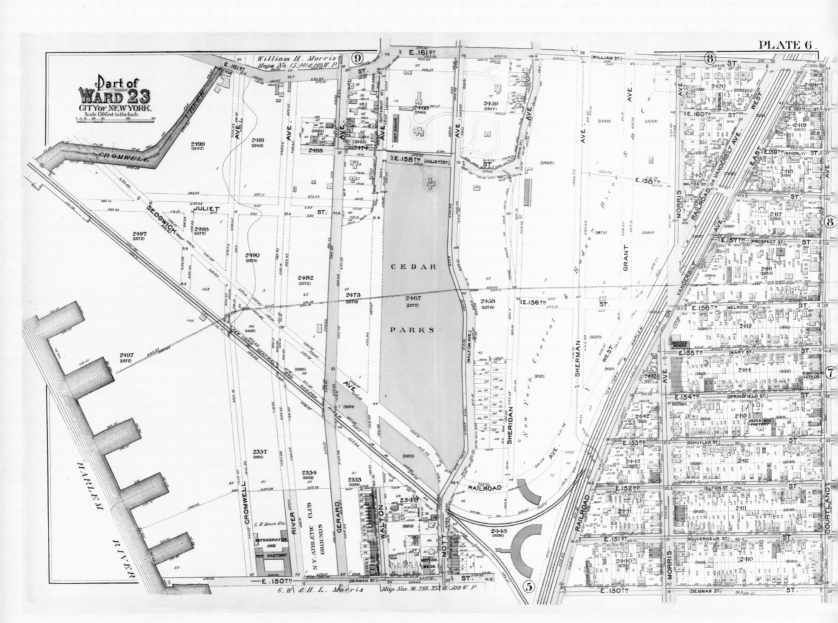

PLATE 6.

Part of
WARD 23
CITY OF NEW YORK.
Scale 150 feet to the Inch.

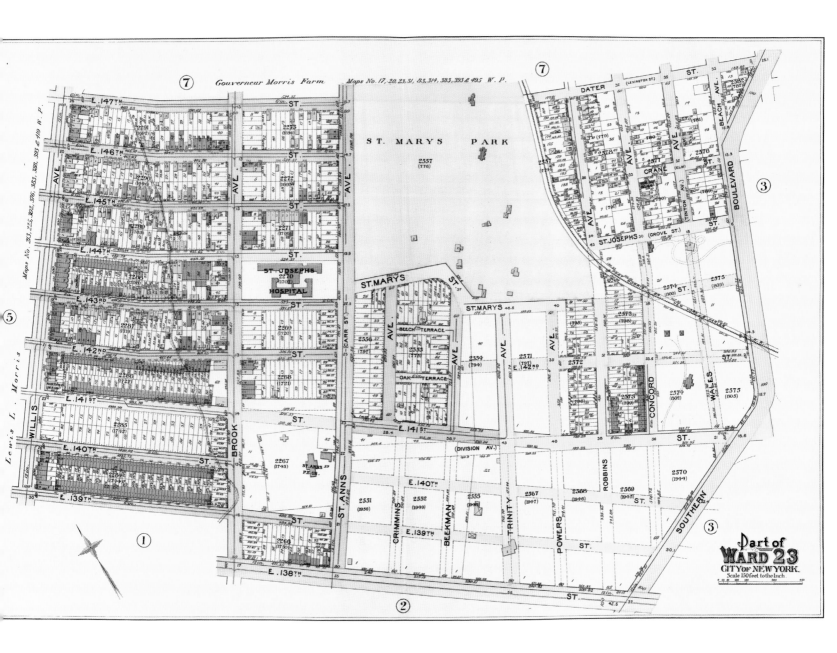

PART OF WARD 23

GEORGE WASHINGTON BROMLEY

AND WALTER SCOTT BROMLEY, 1893

Bromley and Bromley's relatively large-scale
section maps of Ward 23 are derived from
the author's *Atlas of the City of New York*,
1893. Showing a majority of the Ward 23 area,
referential building numbers and street names
are supplied. Particular detail is afforded on
the larger image to the area around St. Mary's
Park, with notable municipal buildings such as
St. Joseph's Hospital picked out and named.

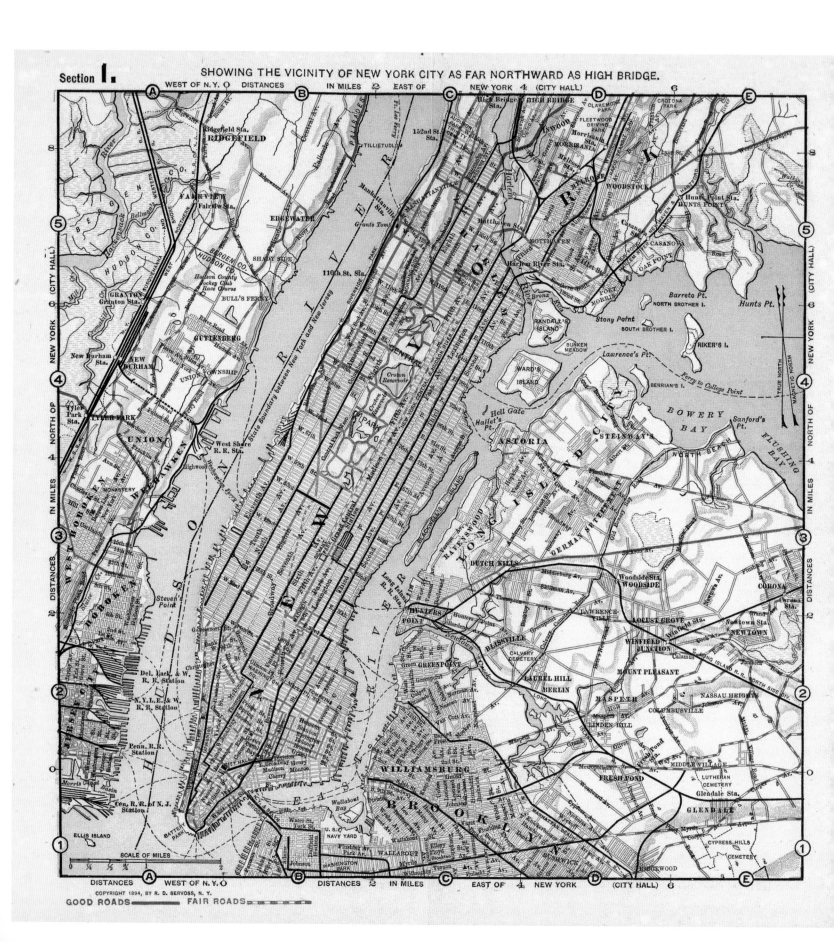

Section **I.**

SHOWING THE VICINITY OF NEW YORK CITY AS FAR NORTHWARD AS HIGH BRIDGE.

WEST OF N.Y. 0   DISTANCES   IN MILES 2   EAST OF   NEW YORK 4 (CITY HALL)

DISTANCES   WEST OF N.Y. 0   DISTANCES 2   IN MILES   EAST OF 4   NEW YORK 6 (CITY HALL)

COPYRIGHT 1894, BY R. D. SERVOSS, N. Y.

SCALE OF MILES

GOOD ROADS ———   FAIR ROADS ■ ■ ■ ■

–OPPOSITE–

SECTION I. SHOWING THE VICINITY OF NEW YORK CITY AS FAR NORTHWARD AS HIGH BRIDGE

R.D. SERVOSS, 1894

R.D. Servoss' Manhattan is a red and white web of 'Good Roads' and 'Fair Roads' intertwined with the streets, ferry lines and railroads of New York City and its surrounding area. The map is part of Servoss' *Sectional Road Map of Westchester County, New York and Part of Fairfield County*—its purpose being to aid the easiest navigation around the city and surrounding counties. Alongside the best roads to travel, the reader is made aware of their position in relation to New York's City Hall— as their distance in miles is mapped in each direction around the edge of the map.

David Rumsey Map Collection www.davidrumsey.com

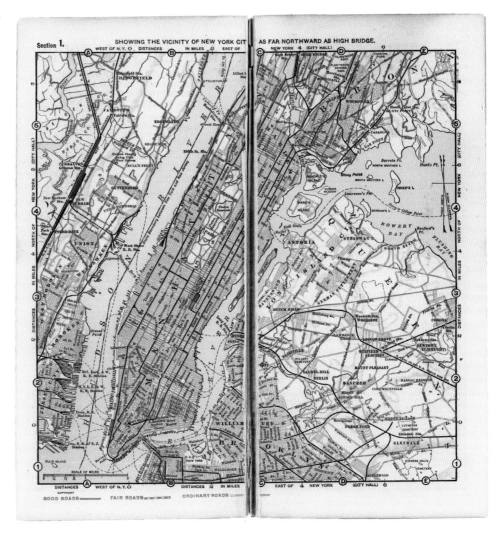

–RIGHT–

SECTION I. SHOWING THE VICINITY OF NEW YORK CITY AS FAR NORTHWARD AS HIGH BRIDGE

R.D. SERVOSS, 1902

Much like its predecessor, this map by R.D. Servoss *Showing the Vicinity of New York City as Far Northward as High Bridge*, shows the 'Good Roads' and 'Fair Roads' of Manhattan and the surrounding area, running alongside the new addition of 'Ordinary Roads'. The rate of development of the city over the turn of the century is made apparent in the 1902 edition, as reflected in the increase in the number of 'Good Roads' on the map—particularly within Harlem and the Bronx.

David Rumsey Map Collection www.davidrumsey.com

–OVERLEAF–

CITY OF NEW YORK. CITY OF BROOKLYN

JOSEPH RUDOLF BIEN, 1895

This striking 1895 map of New York and Brooklyn by Joseph Rudolf Bien shows two colored lithographed maps of Brooklyn and Manhattan, drawn three years before Brooklyn's consolidation with New York City. The Brooklyn map delineates the New York borough as "Kings", in reference to the County of Kings, with which the independent city at the time shared its borders. The map —measuring 24 by 35 inches—shows the extension of Manhattan's ward system into Brooklyn after it officially became a city in 1837, when there were just nine wards. Bien's map shows a growth of up to 32 wards in 1895.

David Rumsey Map Collection www.davidrumsey.com

CITY OF NEW YORK

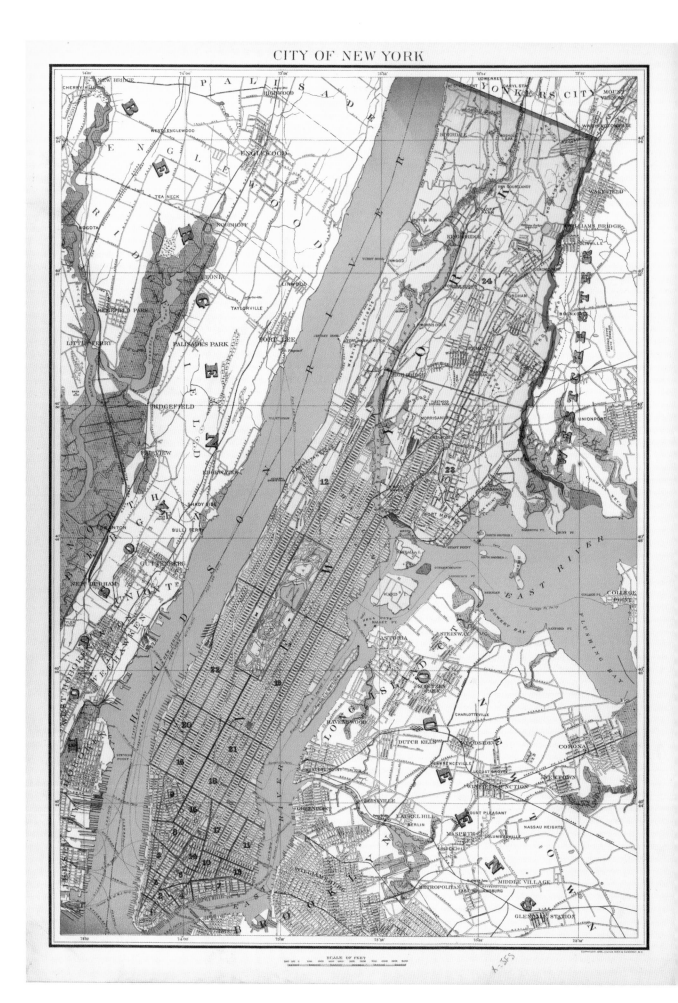

SCALE OF FEET

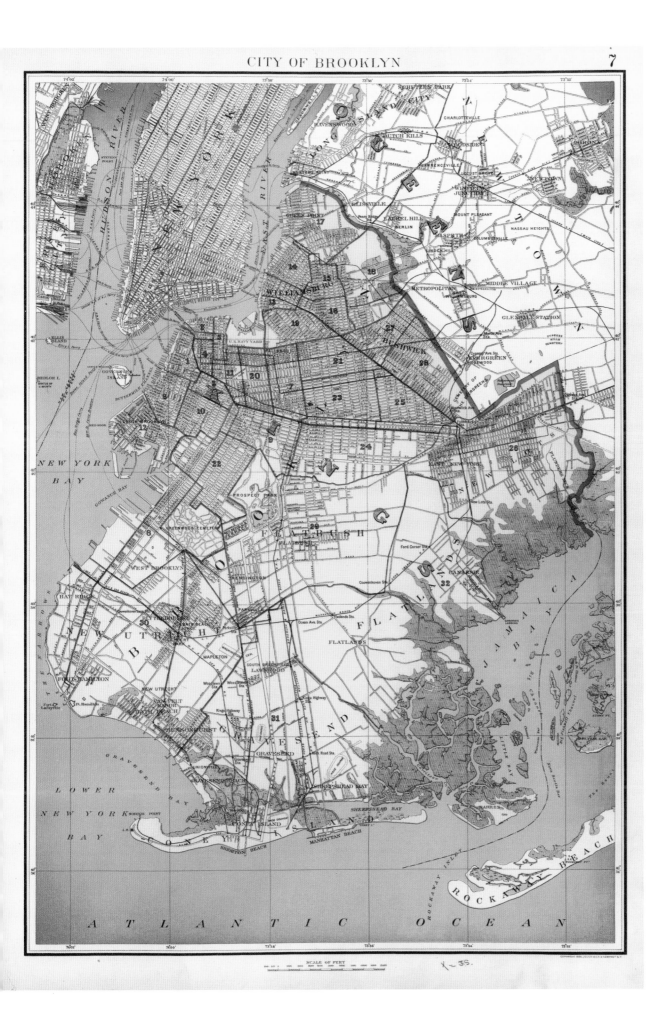

CITY OF BROOKLYN

7

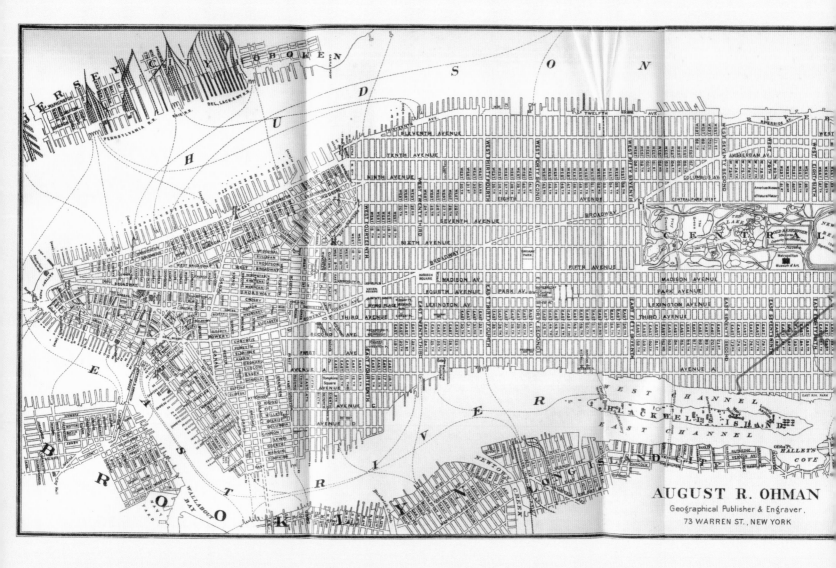

AUGUST R. OHMAN

Geographical Publisher & Engraver,

73 WARREN ST., NEW YORK

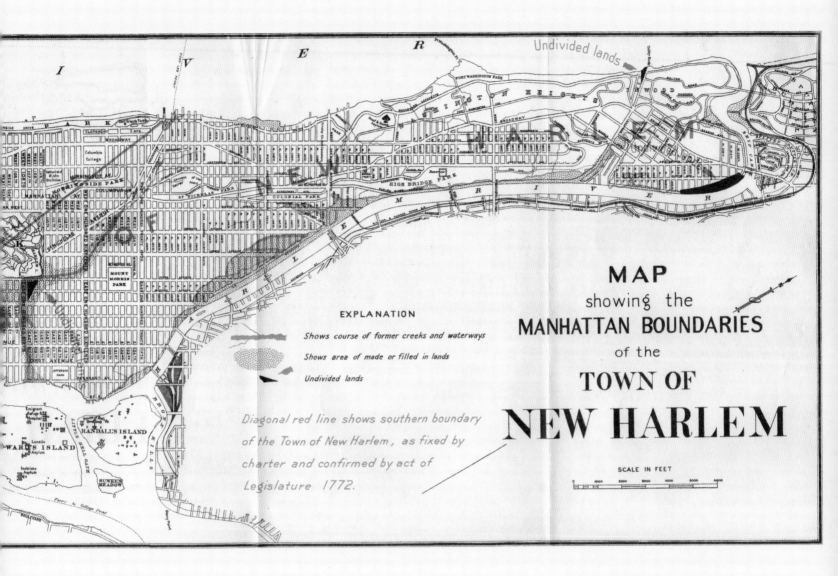

MAP
showing the
MANHATTAN BOUNDARIES
of the
TOWN OF
NEW HARLEM

SCALE IN FEET

EXPLANATION

Shows course of former creeks and waterways

Shows area of made or filled in lands

Undivided lands

Diagonal red line shows southern boundary
of the Town of New Harlem, as fixed by
charter and confirmed by act of
Legislature 1772.

MAP SHOWING THE BOUNDARIES OF THE TOWN OF NEW HARLEM

AUGUST R. OHMAN, 1903

Showing the boundaries of the north Manhattan Town of New Harlem—as set out by legislature officiated in 1772—Ohman's planning map highlights geographical details on top of a functional city plan of the island in an interesting contrast with the dense urban system. The illustrator includes former creek paths, "made or filled in" land, and so-called "undivided" areas.

Map image courtesy of Stuart Brorson

PLAN AND PROFILE OF RAPID TRANSIT SUBWAY
1904

A fascinating contrast to the more recognizable
aerial view of transit railway and subway
maps, this map gives a ground-based,
standing perspective to the routes and lay
of contemporary lines. Clearly a planning
map—no commuter could find their way
accurately with such an illustration—the
author notes the skewed scales used, the
vertical being "27 times greater than the
horizontal", which give the image its almost
mountainous appearance. Street names
and avenues are comprehensively listed
corresponding to relevant distances in miles
between them. An index diagram reveals the
differing pictorial definitions of track
types, as well as showing natural land and
structural materials.

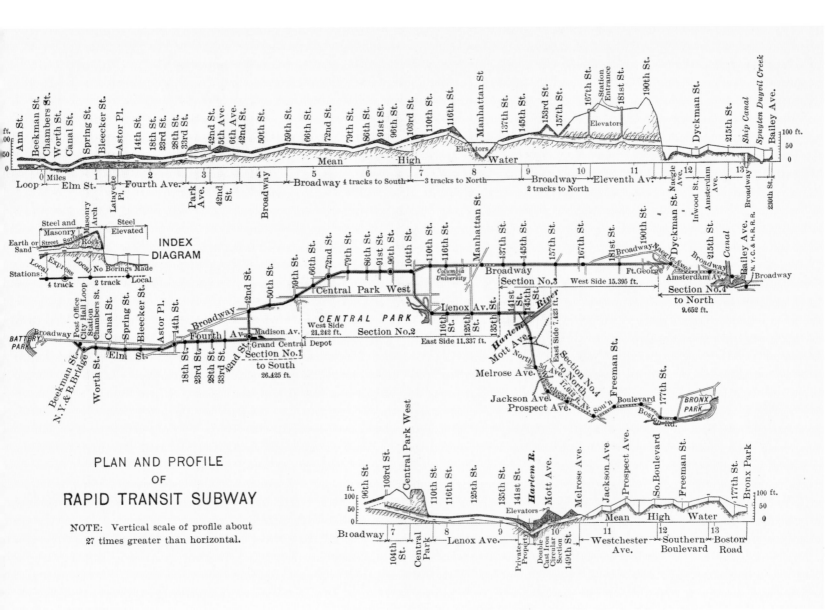

PLAN AND PROFILE
OF
RAPID TRANSIT SUBWAY

NOTE: Vertical scale of profile about
27 times greater than horizontal.

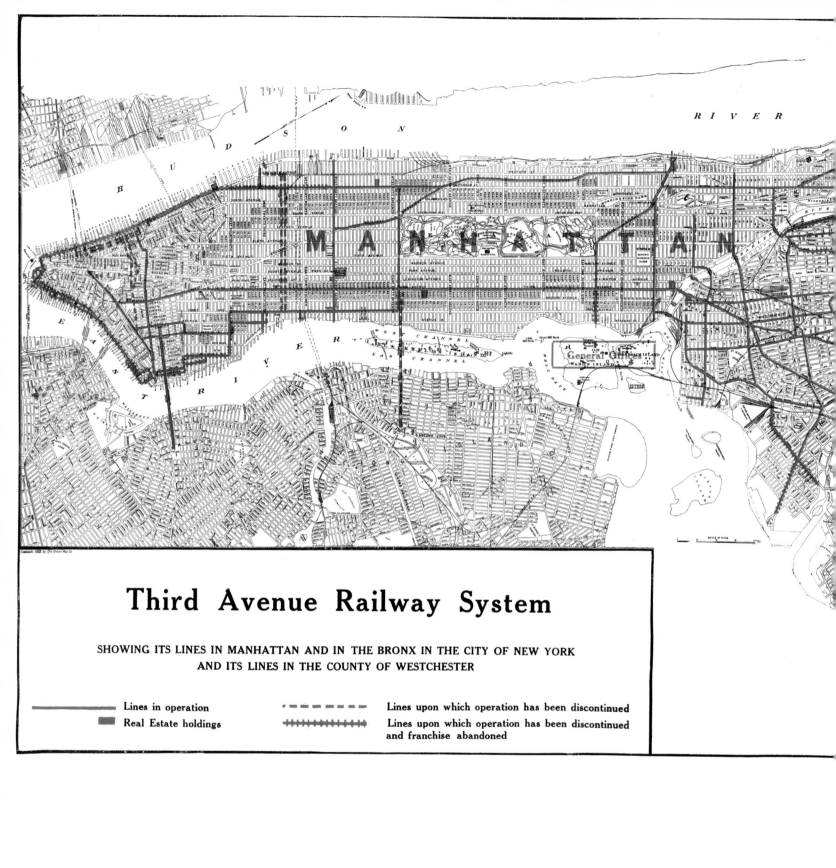

Third Avenue Railway System

SHOWING ITS LINES IN MANHATTAN AND IN THE BRONX IN THE CITY OF NEW YORK
AND ITS LINES IN THE COUNTY OF WESTCHESTER

——————— Lines in operation

▨ Real Estate holdings

– – – – – Lines upon which operation has been discontinued

+++++++++ Lines upon which operation has been discontinued
and franchise abandoned

THIRD AVENUE RAILWAY SYSTEM

1922

The Third Avenue Railroad Company, so-named as it's principle line ran along the eponymous street, was based in New York in the nineteenth and early twentieth centuries, receiving its first franchise on December 18 1852.

This expansive 1922 overview of the Third Avenue railway lines of Manhattan, the Bronx, and Westchester County, stretching as far

north as Hastings and Rochelle, is highly intricate and comprehensive in its key details. The map highlights not only working contemporary tracks, but also discontinued lines and those which had had their franchises fully abandoned at the time of illustration.

Map image courtesy of Jim Poulos

-RIGHT-

BRT RAPID TRANSIT SYSTEM MAP

BROOKLYN RAPID TRANSIT COMPANY, 1912

This railway service map, showing the
Brooklyn Rapid Transit System prior to its
extension under the Dual Subway Contracts
of 1913, highlights the various branches of
suburban lines operated by the company,
just about branching onto Manhattan Island
at this point. The subsequent extension was a
result of the BRT and the Interborough Rapid
Transit Company, operators of the city's first
subway, both signing agreements—hence
the 'dual' contracts—in which the companies
would lease newly constructed lines from the
City of New York. The extensive development
which followed can be observed in the 1937
map opposite.

Map image courtesy of Jim Poulos

-OPPOSITE-

BMT RAPID TRANSIT DIVISION MAP

BROOKLYN-MANHATTAN TRANSIT CORPORATION, 1937

Formed in 1923 as a result of the reorganization
of the Brooklyn Rapid Transit Company, the
Brooklyn-Manhattan Transit Corporation
held an extensive system of railways through
the various districts of New York before it was
officially sold to the City in 1940.

This illustration, clearly showing both subway
and elevated lines, is—as was the case with
maps prior to the design-watershed era of the
1960s—noticeably convoluted and confusing
to read, but effectively shows the wealth of
operating lines in place at this time.

Map image courtesy of Jim Poulos

BRT
RAPID TRANSIT SYSTEM
PRIOR TO ITS EXTENSION
UNDER
DUAL SUBWAY CONTRACTS OF 1913

-OVERLEAF-

INTERBOROUGH RAPID TRANSIT COMPANY MAP

INTERBOROUGH RAPID TRANSIT COMPANY, 1937

This map shows the established and extensive
cross-borough lines of the Interborough
Rapid Transit Company (IRT) circa 1937.
The illustration is dated three years prior to
the City's takeover and consolidation of both
the IRT and Brooklyn Manhattan Transit
Corporation (BMT) to form the unified
system that was to be the basis of the today's
city network.

Map image courtesy of Jim Poulos

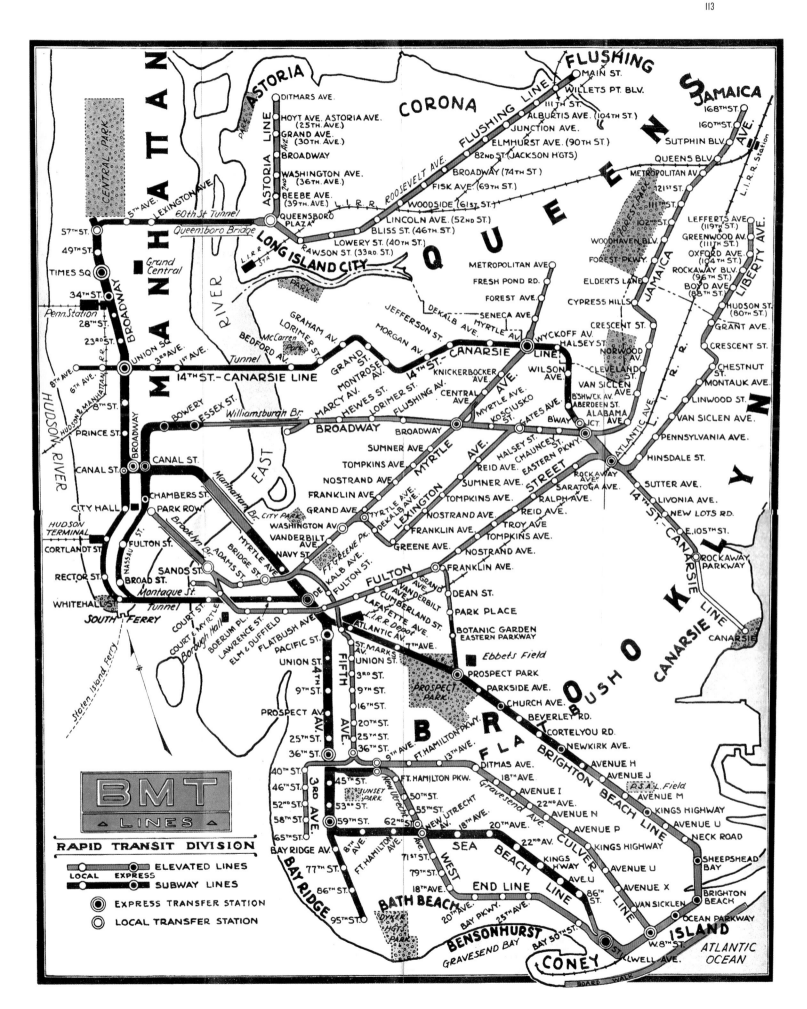

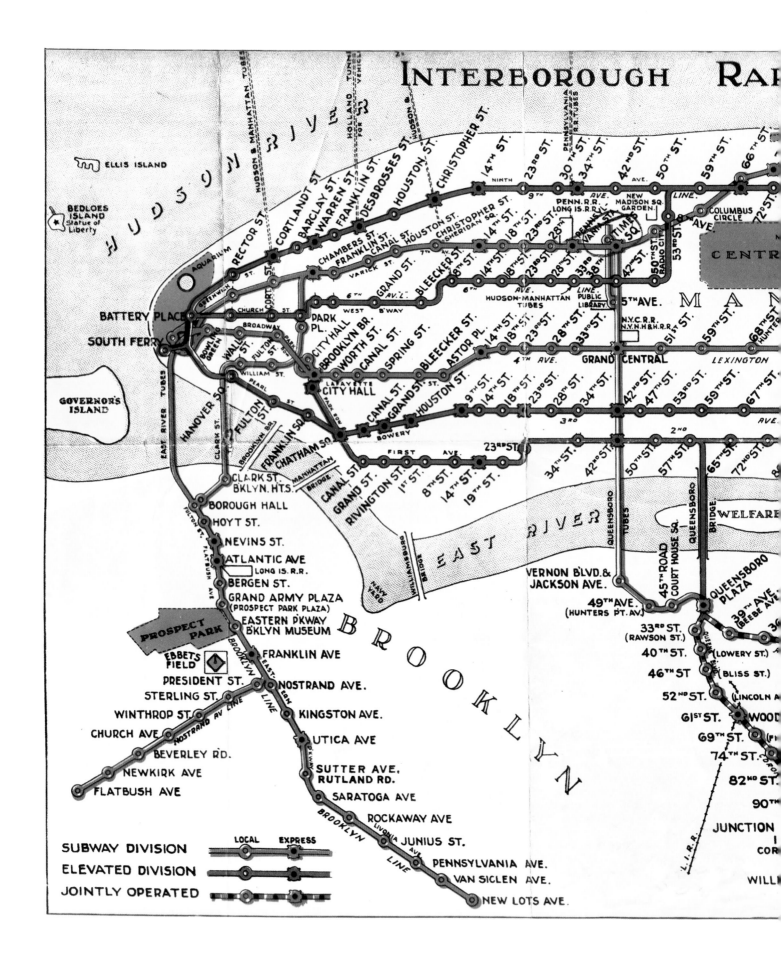

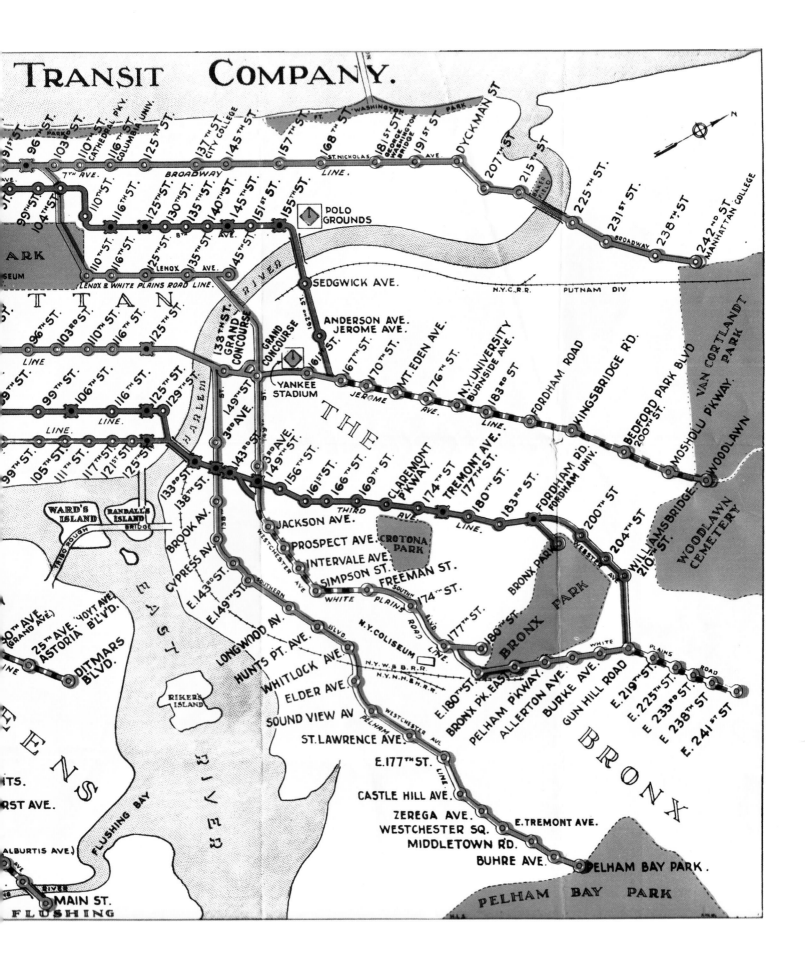

2000 CENSUS TRACTS NEW YORK CITY

THE NEW YORK CITY DEPARTMENT OF CITY PLANNING,
NEW YORK, 2000

This monochrome image, derived from The
New York City Department of City Planning,
rigorously designates each separate census area
around the Five Boroughs. Note the inevitable
concentration of numerous observable areas
around the more densely populated areas of
the city; Brooklyn and Manhattan thus have
a huge number of separate census-specific
areas, whereas Staten Island, far more sparsely
populated, has relatively few.

2000 Census Tracts, used with permission of the The New York
City Department of City Planning. All rights reserved

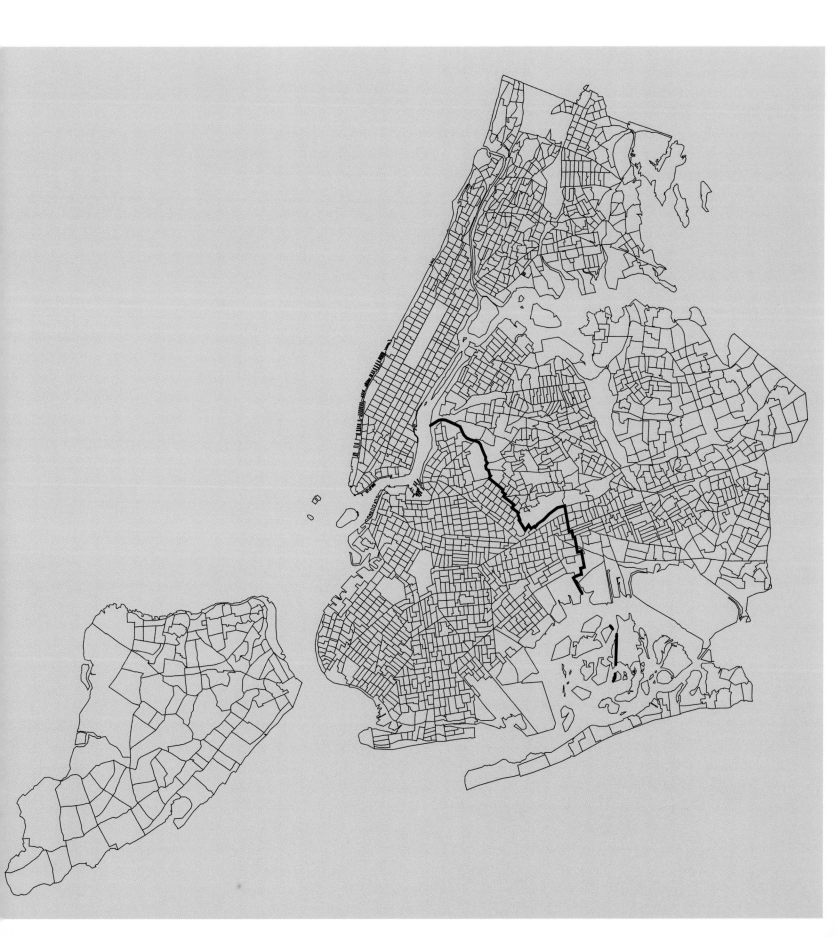

COMMUNITY DISTRICTS, NEW YORK CITY
THE NEW YORK CITY DEPARTMENT OF CITY PLANNING

Drawn up by the Department of City
Planning, this plain illustration shows the
59 defined community districts around New
York City. Officially established in 1975, they
represent a massive diversity of geographical
size and population numbers. District numbers
are specific to the relevant borough; thus the
collections of '1's in Lower Manhattan represent
the collective of district of Civic Center, Wall
Street, Governors Island, Liberty Island, Ellis
Island, and Tribeca, whereas those across
the river in Brooklyn stand for Greenpoint
and Williamsburg.

Community Districts New York City, used with permission
of the New York City Department of City Planning.

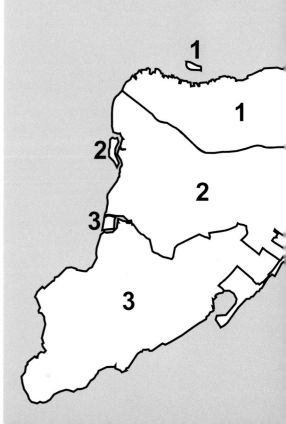

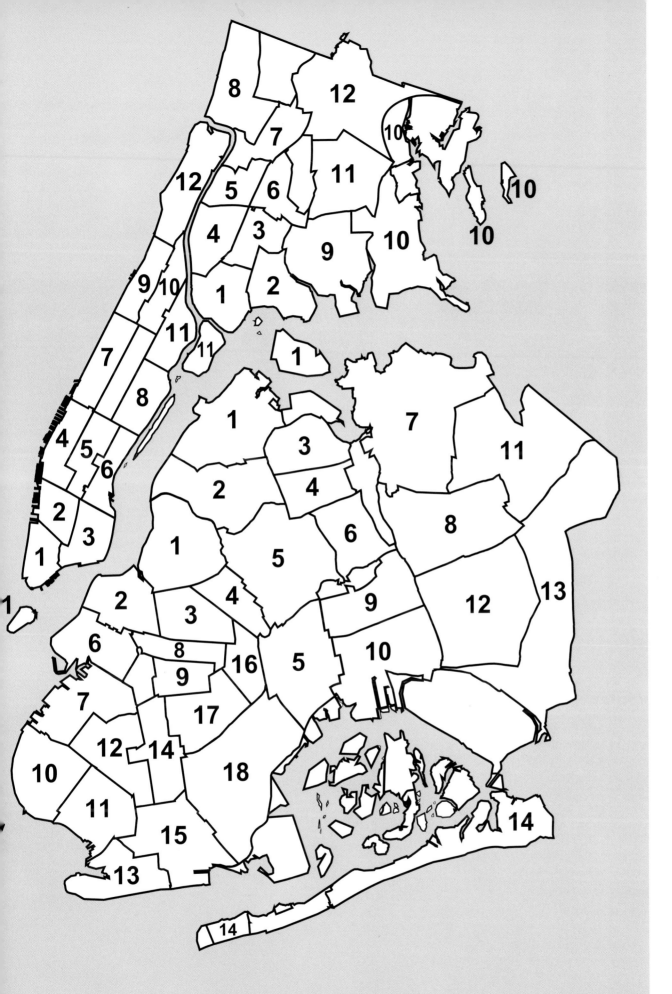

RUDOLPH W. GIULIANI
Mayor, City of New York

JOSEPH B. ROSE
Director, Department of City Planning

Land Use Categories

New York City's land area covers 321 square miles, over 205,000 acres. Excluding streets and major bodies of water, almost 6.9 billion square feet of land (over 150,000 acres) is available for use. Altogether, the city's major land use categories contain:

▪ More than three-quarters of a million (773,000) buildings;
▪ Almost five billion (4,858,560,000) square feet of building floor space;
▪ Almost three million (2,992,000) housing units;
▪ Almost three million (2,904,000) private sector jobs, about 600,000 city, state and federal jobs and about 400,000 people who are self-employed.

One or Two Family Residence

Low-density residences, the largest use of city land, are found mostly in Staten Island, Queens, southern Brooklyn, and the eastern and northwestern parts of The Bronx. They occupy:

▪ 30 percent of the total land area or 47,000 acres;
▪ More than half a million (535,000) buildings with 816,000 housing units;
▪ About 20 percent (992 million square feet) of total floor space.

Multi-Family Residence or Mixed Residence and Commercial

More than two-thirds of the city's residences are in multi-family buildings (three or more dwelling units) or in mixed residential and commercial buildings. Concentrations are in Manhattan's mid- to high-rise buildings and in three to six story buildings in Queens, Brooklyn, The Bronx and Staten Island's north shore. These residences occupy:

▪ 13 percent of the total land area or 20,000 acres;
▪ More than 175,000 buildings containing 2,176,000 housing units;
▪ More than 45 percent (2.3 billion square feet) of total floor space.

Commercial

Commercial uses occupy only a small portion of the city's land, but they use space intensively. From the office towers in midtown and lower Manhattan, downtown Brooklyn and Long Island City, to the regional and local shopping areas and parking garages throughout the city, these areas provide 1,758,000 private sector jobs and occupy:

▪ Almost five percent of the total land area or 7,000 acres;
▪ About 31,000 buildings containing almost 15 percent (704 million square feet) of total floor space.

Industrial

Among U. S. municipalities, New York City's industrial areas have the largest number of industrial jobs. These areas are mostly in western Queens, northern Brooklyn, and midtown and lower Manhattan. They occupy:

▪ About 10 percent of total land area, over 14,000 acres, and provide about 726,000 private sector jobs;
▪ More than 22,000 buildings containing almost ten percent (428 million square feet) of total floor space.

Public Facility or Institution

Institutions and public facilities, including schools, hospitals and nursing homes, museums and performance centers, houses of worship, police stations and firehouses, courts and detention centers are essential services and major sources of employment (420,000 jobs are in the private sector) and occupy:

▪ Almost ten percent of the total land area or 12,000 acres;
▪ Nearly 11,000 buildings containing almost ten percent (466 million square feet) of total floor space.

Open Space or Outdoor Recreation

More than 20 percent, over 33,000 acres, of the city's land is occupied by public and private parks, playgrounds, nature preserves, cemeteries, amusement areas, beaches, stadiums and golf courses.

▪ City parkland and recreational facilities under the jurisdiction of the New York City Department of Parks and Recreation occupy 27,000 acres;
▪ State facilities under the jurisdiction of the New York State Office of Parks, Recreation and Historic Preservation occupy 343 acres;
▪ The Gateway National Recreation Area, under the jurisdiction of the National Park Service, occupies 9,000 acres (much of which is under water).

Vacant Land

More than 12 percent of the total land area, 20,000 acres, is vacant.

Source of Data: Department of Finance RPAD Master File, July 1995, modified by DCP to display condominiums in the correct land use category; DCP research; County Business Patterns, 1992; 1990 Census of Population
Source of Base Map: Department of City Planning COGIS Tax Lot Files Release 95-B
Scale of Map: 1 inch = 1 mile

© 1995 Copyright Department of City Planning, City of New York

NEW YORK: THE CITY'S LAND USES

THE NEW YORK CITY DEPARTMENT OF CITY PLANNING, 1995

This late twentieth century map comprehensively shows land usage throughout the entirety of New York City. An incredibly detailed study of the city street system is color-coded to describe family residences of different sizes, commercial, industrial, municipal, and institutional use, and areas designated for parks and recreation. Inevitably, land designated as vacant is, with the exception of the western shoreline of Staten Island, sparse and often small in size.

New York: The City's Land Uses, used with permission of the New York City Department of City Planning.

NEW YORK:
THE CITY'S LAND USES

DEPARTMENT OF CITY PLANNING
NEW YORK CITY

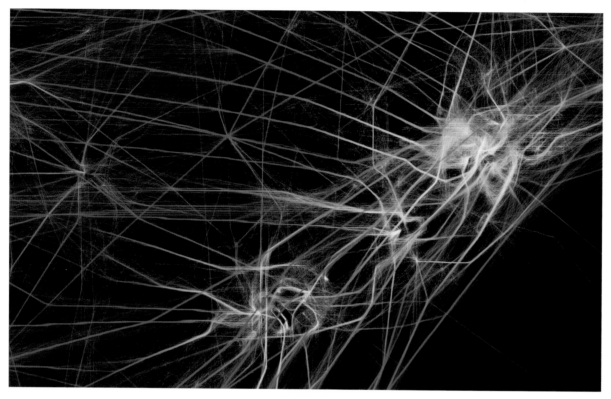

FLIGHT PATTERNS

AARON KOBLIN, 2005

Aaron Koblin's image is an ethereal rendition
of the United States, mapped by the flight paths
of national airlines. This detail of the North
East area sees New York City highlighted as the
northernmost spidery mass of white hairlines
converging on the three state airports—JFK,
LaGuardia, and Newark—from all angles.
Koblin's image was originally developed as
part of a collaborative project at UCLA, and
has since featured at many art festivals and
won numerous awards—including a National
Science Foundation first place prize for
Scientific Visualization.

Courtesy of Aaron Koblin

LIVING IN THE CITY

Over eight million people live in New York's Five Boroughs, with many more commuting to the city daily. Navigating the city's streets has subsequently become a complex task, one that challenges modern day cartographers to continually map and re-map the city's social and geographical landscape. Travel maps remain the most widely produced cartographic sector.

The idea of a pocket companion to aid easy navigation around unfamiliar streets is a theme which runs throughout map-making history—from the early representations of New York, and its humble beginnings on the banks of the Hudson River in William Hooker's elegant *New Pocket Plans*; to today's precise *Block by Block* city guides by master map-maker John Tauranac.

Of course, navigating New York would not be possible today without the city's vast public transportation system; a 24 hour network of trains, buses and ferries, of which maps are available covering every borough, route and time of day. These transportation systems have become such an integral part of New York's history, that retired routes—such as New York's High Line—have been celebrated with their development into public spaces.

The city's subway system—which remains the longest underground train system in the world—continues to fascinate and promote debate between cartographers and graphic designers alike. On the one hand there are the current Metropolitan Transit Authority (MTA) maps that provide a precise geographic guide to riding the New York Subway, whilst on the other, are the likes of Seoul-based design firm Zero Per Zero who favor a simplified map—framing the city's subway lines within a vibrant red heart. This debate is nowhere more apparent than in the graphically celebrated but geographically criticized 1972 *Official Subway Map* by Massimo Vignelli.

Alongside travel "Living in the City" provides a concise cartographic overview of the most densely populated city in the United States. Aided by various maps from the U.S. Census Bureau and New York's Department of City Planning, detailed data on population and immigration has been documented, illustrating the complex social geography of the Five Boroughs area.

In recent years mapping has evolved in order to meet the needs of the technological age. Now not only do we require our landscape to be mapped out by geographical and topographical data but also by virtual space. NYTE's *World Within New York* examines the New York landscape through the AT&T telephone network and its contact with other cities around the world. Whilst, Columbia University's Spatial Information Design Lab has dedicated itself to the unique mapping of our urban environment through data of this kind in *Understanding the Complainers: NYC 311* and *Million Dollar Blocks*.

And finally, as global warming and environmental issues become increasingly prevalent in today's society, maps such as Green Map's™ *Compost Green Map* aim to help us interact with our geography in an environmentally sustainable way.

LIST OF WORKS

———————

———————

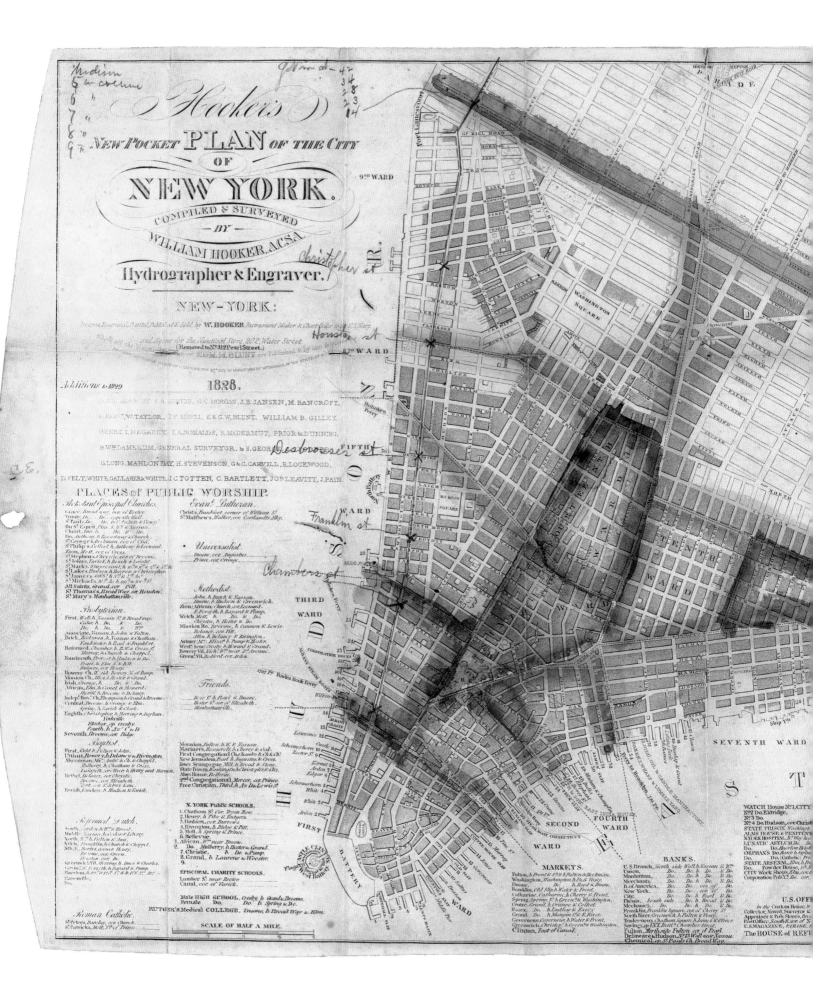

HOOKER'S NEW POCKET PLANS OF NEW YORK

WILLIAM HOOKER, 1829 (LEFT)
AND 1833 (ABOVE)

William Hooker's *New Pocket Plans* are highly descriptive depictions of Lower Manhattan in the early nineteenth century. Producing maps throughout the 1820s and 1830s, Hooker's thorough knowledge of New York City came to life in his *Pocket Plans*. Measuring just 12 by 15 inches, the maps were intended to be read as an everyday guide to the city—much like city guide books in use today, such as John Tauranac's *Manhattan Block by Block*. The *Pocket Plans* provide a comprehensive guide to the city, including references to churches, banks and theaters. When read in conjunction, they reflect the pace of development of New York City, as an increase in streets, buildings and parks are referenced travelling further north on the map—including Union Square and Gramercy Park.

David Rumsey Map Collection www.davidrumsey.com

CITY OF NEW-YORK

HENRY S. TANNER, 1836

A NEW UNIVERSAL ATLAS CONTAINING MAPS OF THE VARIOUS EMPIRES, KINGDOMS, STATES AND REPUBLICS OF THE WORLD

The following three maps were all featured in *A New Universal Atlas Containing Maps of the Various Empires, Kingdoms, States and Republics of the World*. Using the same cartographic template for lower Manhattan and part of Brooklyn, the following maps— each measuring 17 by 13 inches—featured within two different editions of the atlas. Over a 30 year period the same atlas was published under six different authors.

Henry S. Tanner's first edition of *A New Universal Atlas Containing Maps of the Various Empires, Kingdoms, States and Republics of the World* was originally published in parts in 1834, in an attempt by the author to reach a broader market by producing a more affordable atlas. He achieved this by using smaller pages, whilst also documenting a wider geographical area. Tanner's *City of New York* map was released two years later in a complete collection of the atlas in 1836. This map includes an exhaustive list of reference points from churches to hotels. It also clearly indicates the division of the city into electoral districts known as wards— numbered on the map from one to 12 in Manhattan and one to five in Brooklyn.

David Rumsey Map Collection www.davidrumsey.com

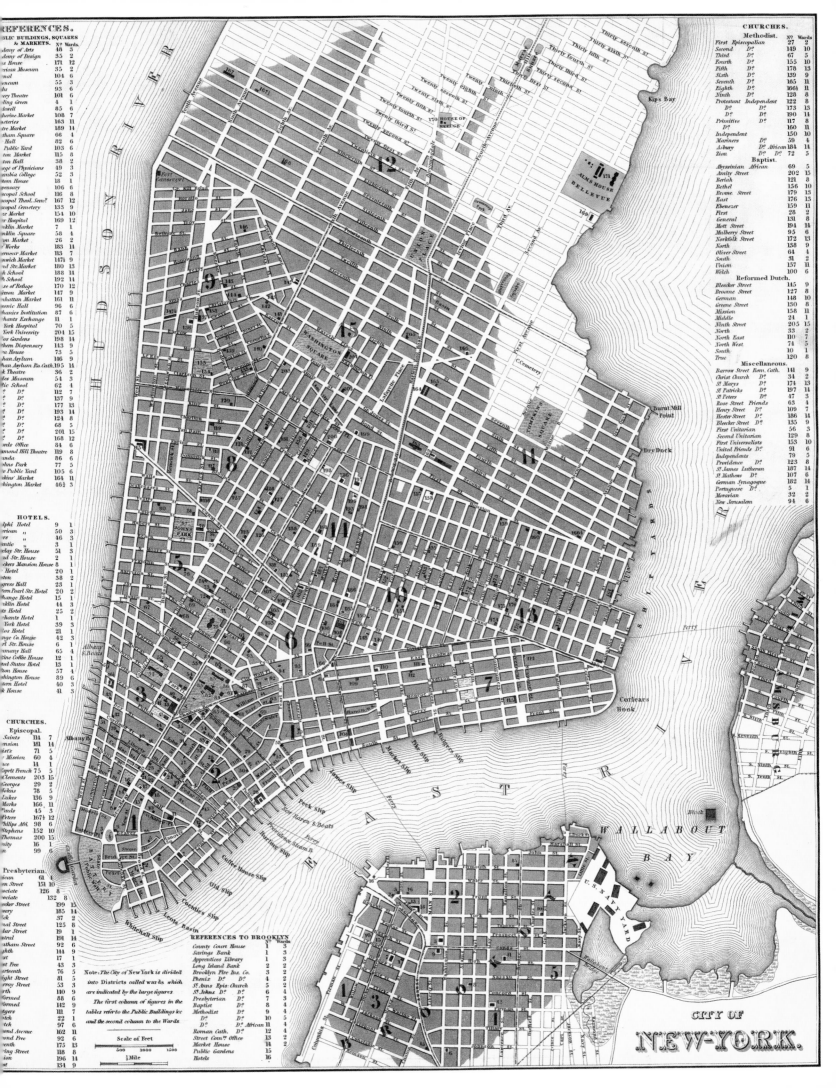

CITY OF NEW-YORK.

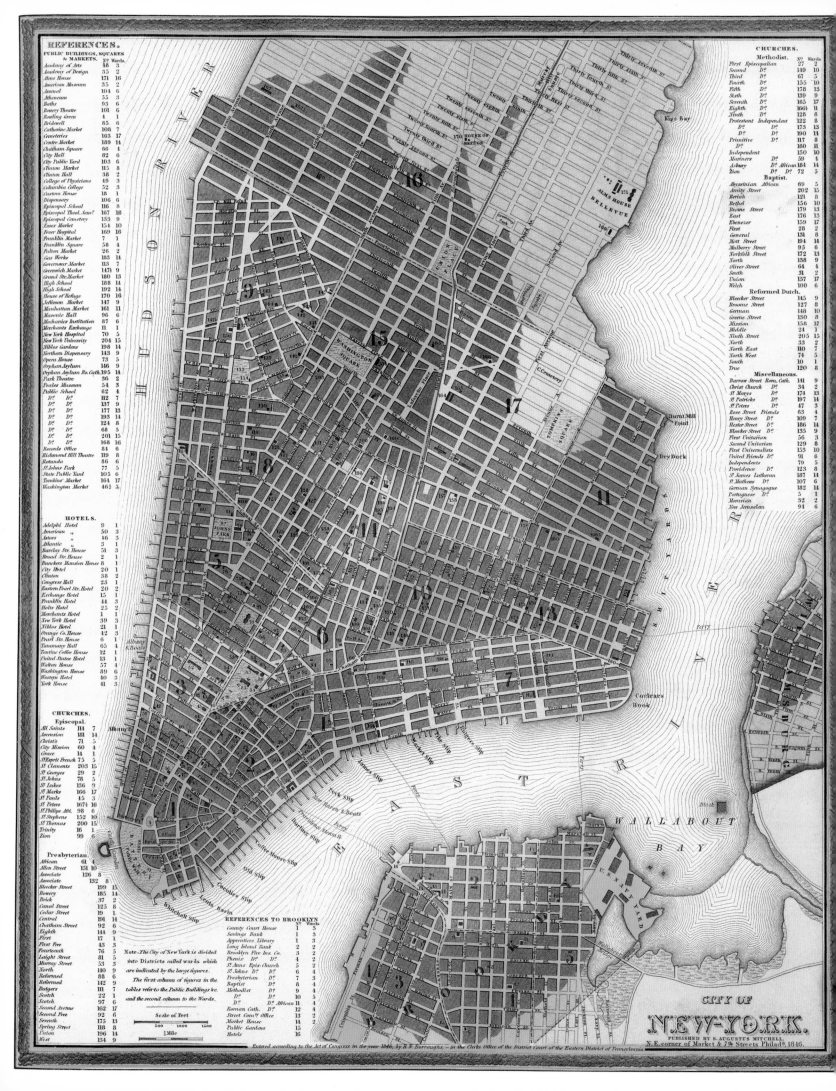

CITY OF NEW-YORK

SAMUEL AUGUSTUS MITCHELL, 1846

Samuel Augustus Mitchell's cartographic interpretation of New York City is considered highly important in the history of American map-making. It was the first American atlas to be converted from engraved map plates to lithographic map plates, in turn reducing the atlas' production cost. Mitchell's full color map shows the addition of four wards to the Manhattan landscape, each depicted in varying colors. The reference points are organized around the edge of the map by its wards, with the majority of landmarks situated in the south of the island.

CITY OF NEW-YORK

SAMUEL AUGUSTUS MITCHELL, 1846

Following the same base template covering
lower Manhattan and part of Brooklyn, this
map featured in Samuel Augustus Mitchell's
1846 *Atlas*. Whilst covering the same reference
points, this map is considered as unusual
in that its wards are divided using a color
combination of red and blue ink. Maps of
this period typically used a "hand-color"
technique, whereby different colors were
layered over a black and white base—as seen
in Mitchell's previous map.

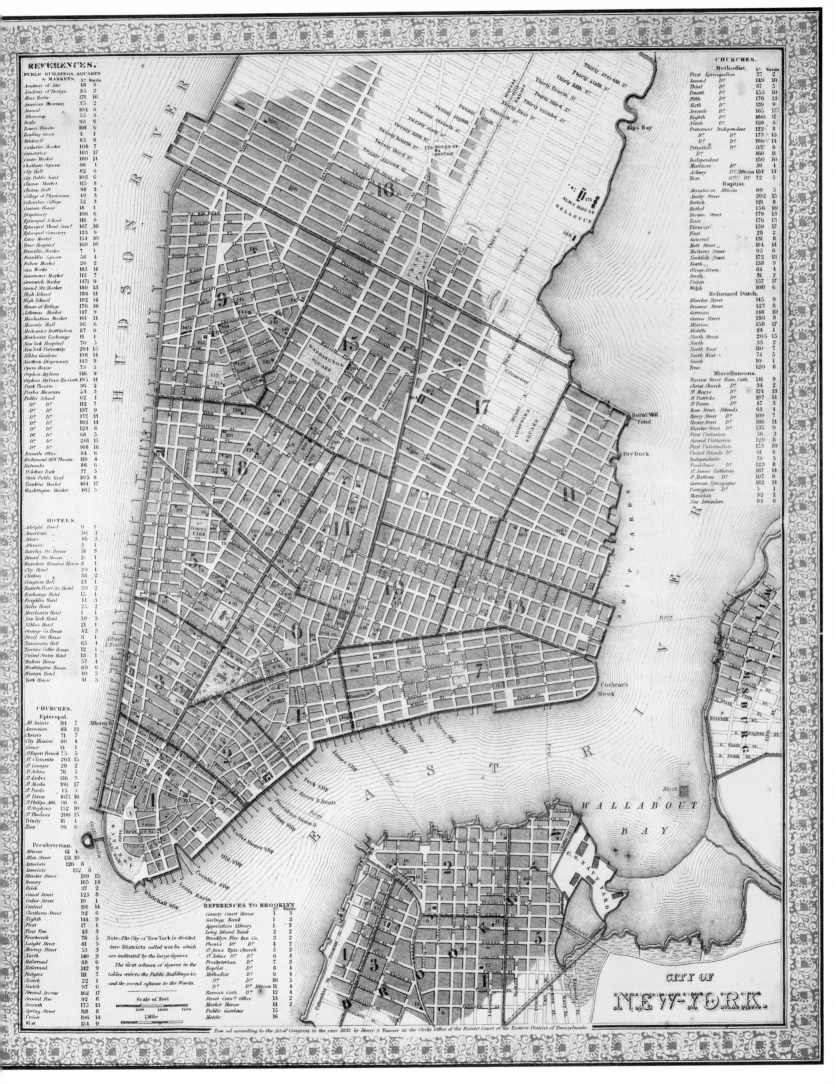

CITY OF NEW YORK
SAMUEL BREESE & SIDNEY E. MORSE, 1845

Published in 1845 by Harper & Brothers as part of *Morse's North American Atlas*, this wax-engraved map documents various period details; wards, park information, a wealth of city parks, major street, and disparate docks and buildings are included, as well as some faintly dotted paths, presumably train lines. Manhattan's shoreline and major streets are picked out in red, whereas the north coast of Brooklyn, seen at the bottom of the map, remains relatively unembellished.

David Rumsey Map Collection www.davidrumsey.com

CITY OF
NEW YORK

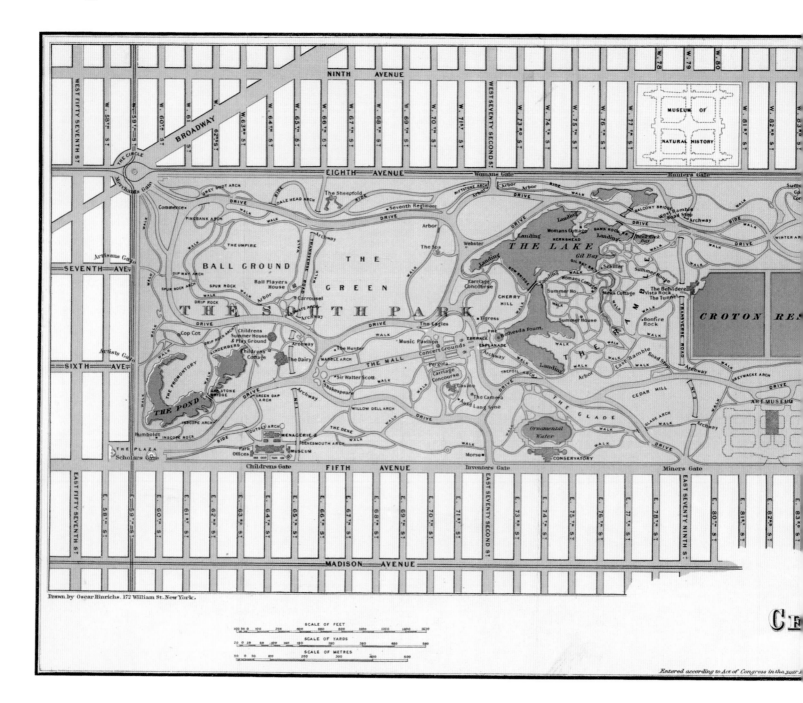

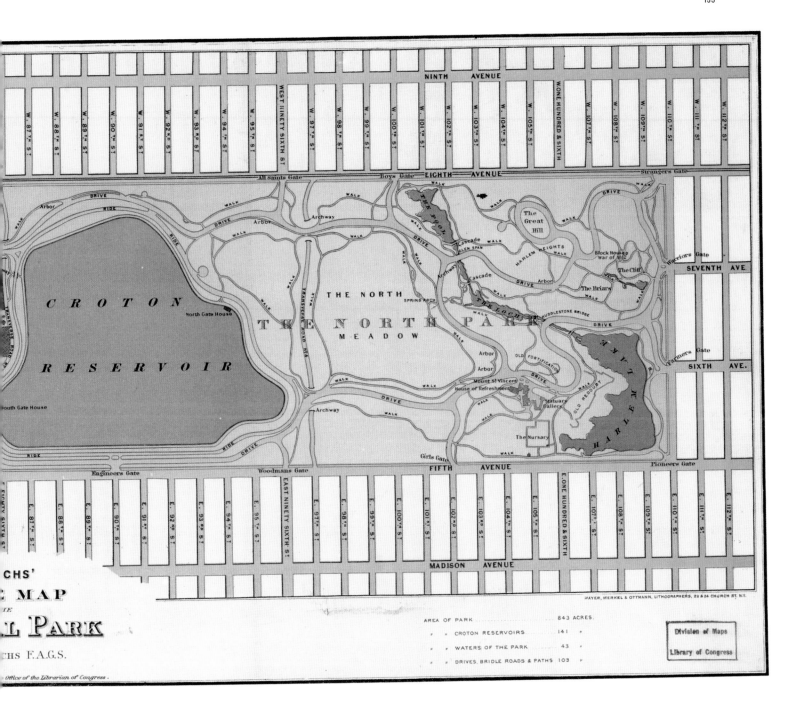

HINRICH'S GUIDE MAP OF CENTRAL PARK
OSCAR HINRICH, 1875

This image of the entirety of Central Park, drawn 16 years after the areas opening, is notable partly for the intricate level of detail afforded to the internal park walkways and roads, but also for the contemporary historical detail hinted at by the original recorded lake names. The Croton Reservoir, now the Jacqueline Kennedy Onassis Reservoir—or the more common eponymous Central Park Reservoir—held drinking water derived from the Croton River in Westchester County, and transported south through the Croton Aqueduct. The smaller, identically named reservoir to the south was an above-ground water distribution container, replete with Egyptian-style facade, and was in active use throughout the nineteenth century.

Library of Congress, Geography and Map Division

HUDSON RIVER

BLOOMINGDALE

Lunatic
Asylum

MORNINGS

Natural History Museum

Womans Gate

Hunters Ga.

Mariners Gate

Merchants Gate

C E N T R A L   P A R K

The Green

The Lake

Strangers Gate

Artisans Gate

Reservoirs

CROTON
RESERVOIR

Warriors Gate

Artists Ga.

The Mall

The Ramble

Obelisk

Harlem Lake

Scholars Gate

Museum

Miners Ga.

Art Museum

Woodmans Gate

Girls Ga.

FIFTH   AVENUE

E A S T

Penitentiary

Hospital

Table or G.ᵗ Mill Rock

Emigrant
Refuge & Hosp.ᵗ

Alms Houses

Work House

B L A C K W E L L S   I S L A N D

Mad Ho.

Lunatic Asylum

W A R D ' S

I S L A N D

LITTLE HELL GA

R I V E R

Halletts Point

Negro Point

Inebriate Asylum

HALLETTS
COVE

HELL GATE

POT
COVE

RAVENSWOOD
PARK

Parade
Ground

Astoria
Park

L O N G   I S L A N D   C I T Y

Hopkins

SCALE OF FEET

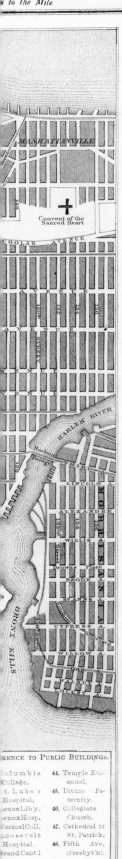

to the Mile

MANHATTANVILLE

Convent of the
Sacred Heart

CHOLAS AVENUE

HARLEM RIVER

LINCOLN A

ALEXANDER

WILLIS

BROOK

ST.ANN'S

CYPRESS A

WILLOW A

OAK

BRONX KILLS

RENCE TO PUBLIC BUILDINGS.

olumbia	44. Temple Em-
College.	anuel.
t. Luke's	45. Divine Pa-
Hospital.	ternity.
enoxLib'y.	46. Collegiate
enoxHosp.	Church.
ormalColl.	47. Cathedral of
oosevelt	St. Patrick.
Hospital	48. Fifth Ave.
rand Cent'l	(Presbyt'n).
Depot.	

Coloured in Wards

NEW YORK (NORTH)
LETTS, SON & CO., 1883

Letts's Popular Atlas was a series of maps: "covering the whole surface of the globe", that included an extensive reference list of over 23,000 place names by Letts, Son & Co., London. This particular colored map, is a curious view of New York (North) from 32nd Street to 138th Street, referencing the lesser known of Manhattan's public buildings. The sparse reference list also includes two Lunatic Asylum's, an Idiot Asylum and an Emigrant Refuge and Hospital, as found on the often unlabeled Ward's and Randalls Islands.

NEW YORK CITY

Rand, McNally & Co's
INDEXED
ATLAS OF THE WORLD
MAP OF

BUSINESS PORTION OF
NEW YORK CITY
ON ENLARGED SCALE.

MAP OF NEW YORK CITY

RAND MCNALLY & CO., 1897

This map, produced by seminal US map-maker Rand McNally, is taken from the company's 1897 *Atlas of the World*, a touchstone in global mapping in the late nineteenth century and notable for its comprehensive indexing. As well as clearly documenting the city's gridded street system in detail, the map highlights shipping and ferry routes through the Hudson, East River, and New York Bay. The 'business portion' of lower Manhattan, Brooklyn and Jersey City is notably enlarged, and supplies further information on the dockland area, numerically labelling every pier, as well as detailing trade depots and business offices.

David Rumsey Map Collection www.davidrumsey.com

BUSINESS PORTION OF
NEW YORK CITY
ON ENLARGED SCALE.

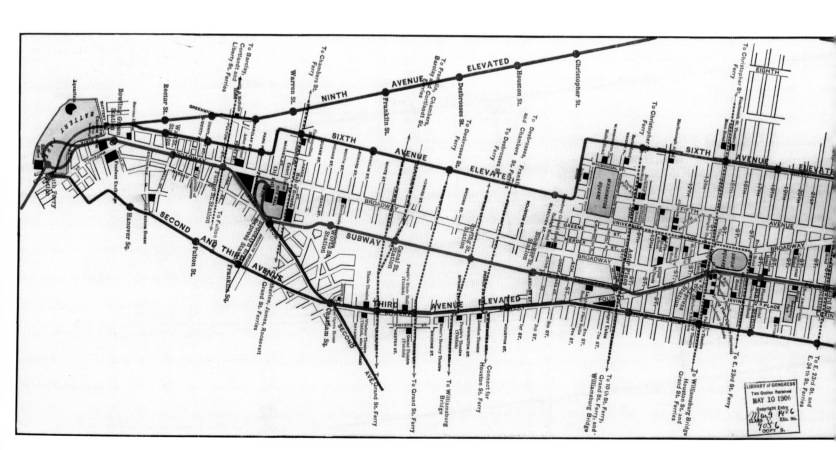

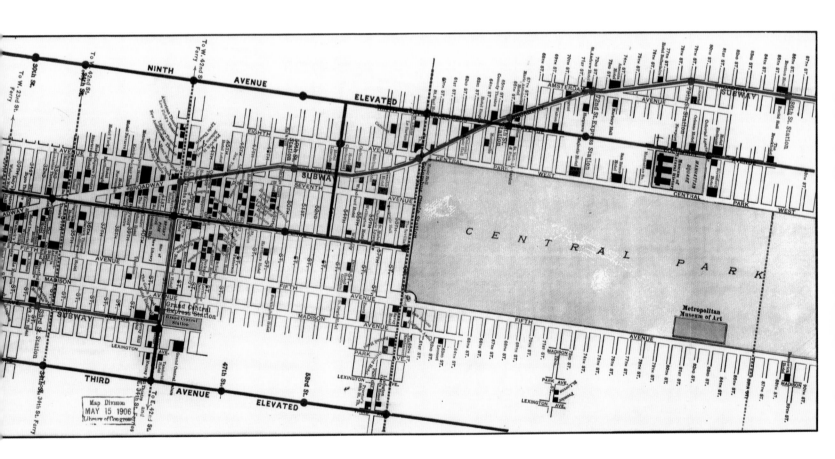

THE MERCHANT'S ASSOCIATION HOTEL AND THEATER MAP

MERCHANT'S ASSOCIATION OF NEW YORK, 1906

This early twentieth century image shows contemporary theaters, hotels, and railways—both elevated, and underground, in black and red respectively—through a long expanse of south and central Manhattan, from the Battery to Central Park. Non-corresponding streets have been removed, giving the image an unusual aesthetic in comparison to the wealth of highly comprehensive maps of this era.

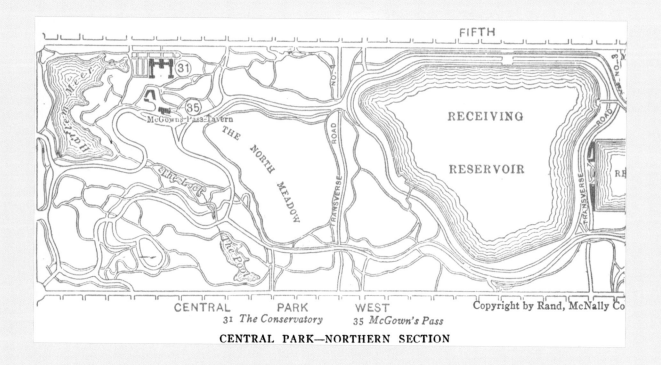

31 *The Conservatory*   35 *McGown's Pass*

CENTRAL PARK—NORTHERN SECTION

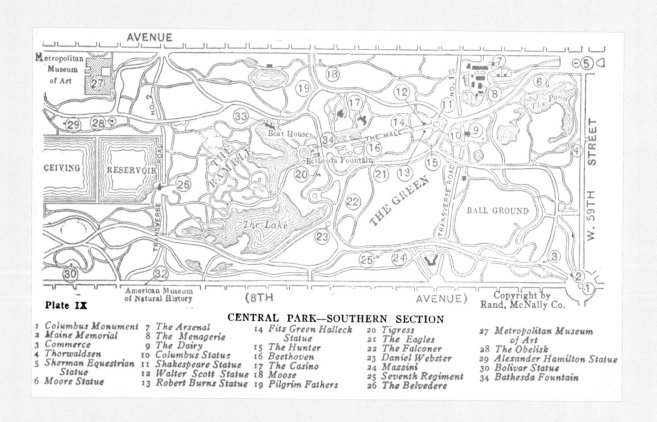

Plate IX

CENTRAL PARK—SOUTHERN SECTION

1 *Columbus Monument*	7 *The Arsenal*	14 *Fitz Green Halleck*	20 *Tigress*	27 *Metropolitan Museum*
2 *Maine Memorial*	8 *The Menagerie*	*Statue*	21 *The Eagles*	*of Art*
3 *Commerce*	9 *The Dairy*	15 *The Hunter*	22 *The Falconer*	28 *The Obelisk*
4 *Thorwaldsen*	10 *Columbus Statue*	16 *Beethoven*	23 *Daniel Webster*	29 *Alexander Hamilton Statue*
5 *Sherman Equestrian*	11 *Shakespeare Statue*	17 *The Casino*	24 *Mazzini*	30 *Bolivar Statue*
Statue	12 *Walter Scott Statue*	18 *Moose*	25 *Seventh Regiment*	34 *Bathesda Fountain*
6 *Moore Statue*	13 *Robert Burns Statue*	19 *Pilgrim Fathers*	26 *The Belvedere*	

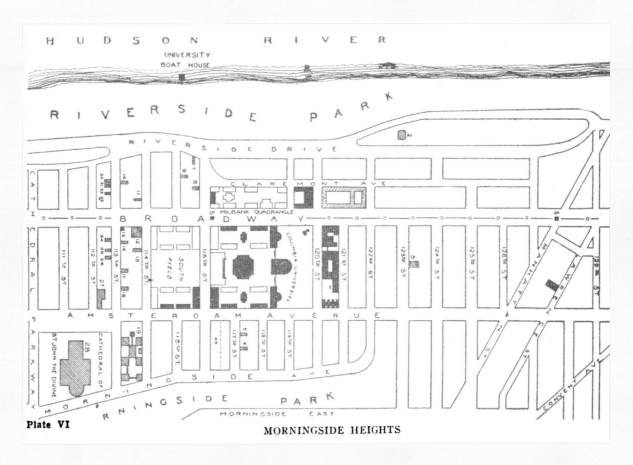

Plate VI

MORNINGSIDE HEIGHTS

MORNINGSIDE HEIGHTS
FROM RIDER'S NEW YORK CITY, 1916

CENTRAL PARK—NORTHERN SECTION AND CENTRAL PARK—SOUTHERN SECTION
FROM RIDER'S NEW YORK CITY, 1916

This overview of Central Park provides an outline of park grounds, paths, and lakes, as well as a clear numerated key of monuments, museums, and with the posthumous inclusion of the McGowns Pass Tavern, a roadhouse. Sold-out of its possessions, including a then-famous parrot named Old Gabe who departed for a mere $45, and closed in 1915 in order to accommodate space for park administration, the tavern marks the spot of a significant lookout post of the War of 1812, which is still commemorated with a plaque to signify the importance of New York City in the fight for American independence.

Morningside Heights, the so-called "Academic Acropolis" of Manhattan due to its density of revered educational institutions, is here documented in notably little detail in comparison to similar examples from the same Rider's publication. Though relatively large-scale, topographic information is limited to some labelling of institutions such as the Cathedral of St. John the Divine and Columbia University—as well as the university boat house on the banks of the Hudson—and street names and numbers. The artist neglects to highlight other significant organizations and buildings such as Barnhard College, the Jewish Seminary of America, and the Union Theological Seminary, all of which would have been well established by this time.

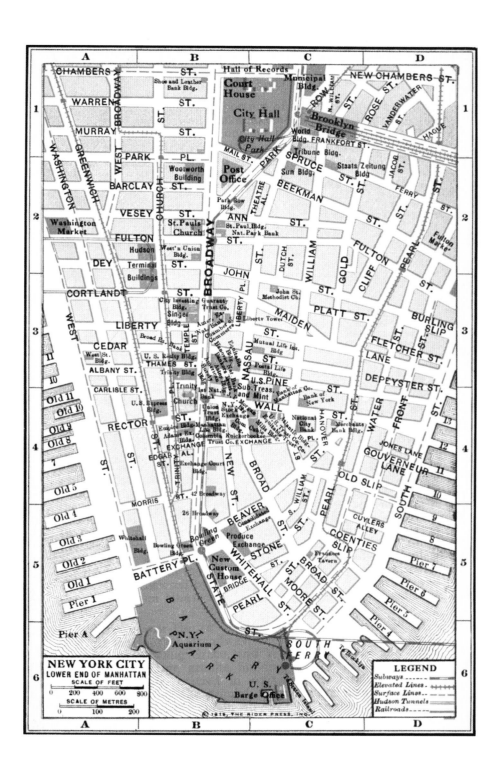

NEW YORK CITY
LOWER END MANHATTAN
FROM RIDER'S NEW YORK CITY, 1916

This eye-catching example of the Manhattan area, south of City Hall, is replete with vivid parks and aquatic contour lines, and serve to reference district rail and subway transport lines, providing particularly detailed legend information in the form of both elevated and surface tracks. Major buildings and religious institutions are labelled, particularly those pertaining to business and finance such as the New York Stock Exchange, the Bank of New York, The Woolworth Building, and the Mutual Life Insurance Building.

Courtesy of University of Texas Libraries

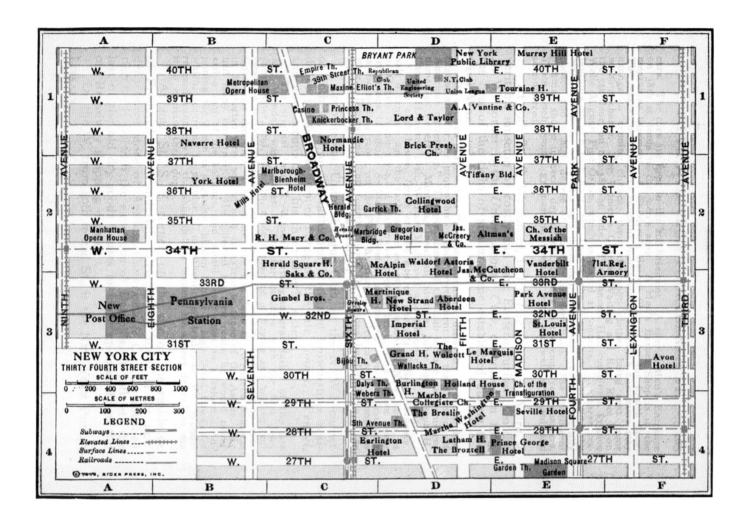

THIRTY FOURTH STREET SECTION

FROM RIDER'S NEW YORK CITY, 1916

Displaying a similar predilection for public railway and subway lines as the image of lower Manhattan from the same publication, this Rider's map details the rectangular Thirty Fourth Street Section between Ninth and Third Avenues, and 26th and 41st Streets. As well as highlighting subways, elevated lines, surface lines, and railroads, the map highlights the great concentration of contemporary hotels east of Hell's Kitchen, around Broadway and Fourth Avenue. One can note the number of clubs situated along East and West 40th Street; the conception and construction of these began around the turn of the twentieth century, though they finally disappeared in 1979 with the selling of the 'Engineers Club'—otherwise known as The United Engineers Society—an iconic association created in memory of the American engineers responsible for the industrial transformation of the country.

Courtesy of University of Texas Libraries

CHIEF POINTS OF INTEREST IN
UPPER MANHATTAN
FROM AUTOMOBILE BLUE BOOK, 1920

This study of upper Manhattan is taken from the *Automobile Blue Book* of 1920, an 11 volume road encyclopaedia of the United States. Surprisingly, given this context, the number of road numbers and names supplied is relatively low. The chief points of interest given by the illustrator are a wealth of municipal buildings, churches, and hotels. The map does contain two inclusions of particular interest, though; as well as noting ethnically significant areas—'Little Africa' and 'Little Italy'—the author has also included a number of personal residences of industrialists, philanthropists, and businessmen of the era, an element which is particularly conspicuous on the eastern side of Central Park, along Fifth Avenue.

Courtesy of University of Texas Libraries

WHERE to STOP in NEW YORK

CHIEF POINTS OF INTEREST
IN
UPPER MANHATTAN

Abbreviations.

Ave.	Avenue	H.	Hotel.
Bld.	Building	Ho.	House.
Ch.	Church	Hosp.	Hospital.
Cem.	Cemetery	Sq.	Square.
Cl.	Club	St.	Street.
		Th.	Theatre.

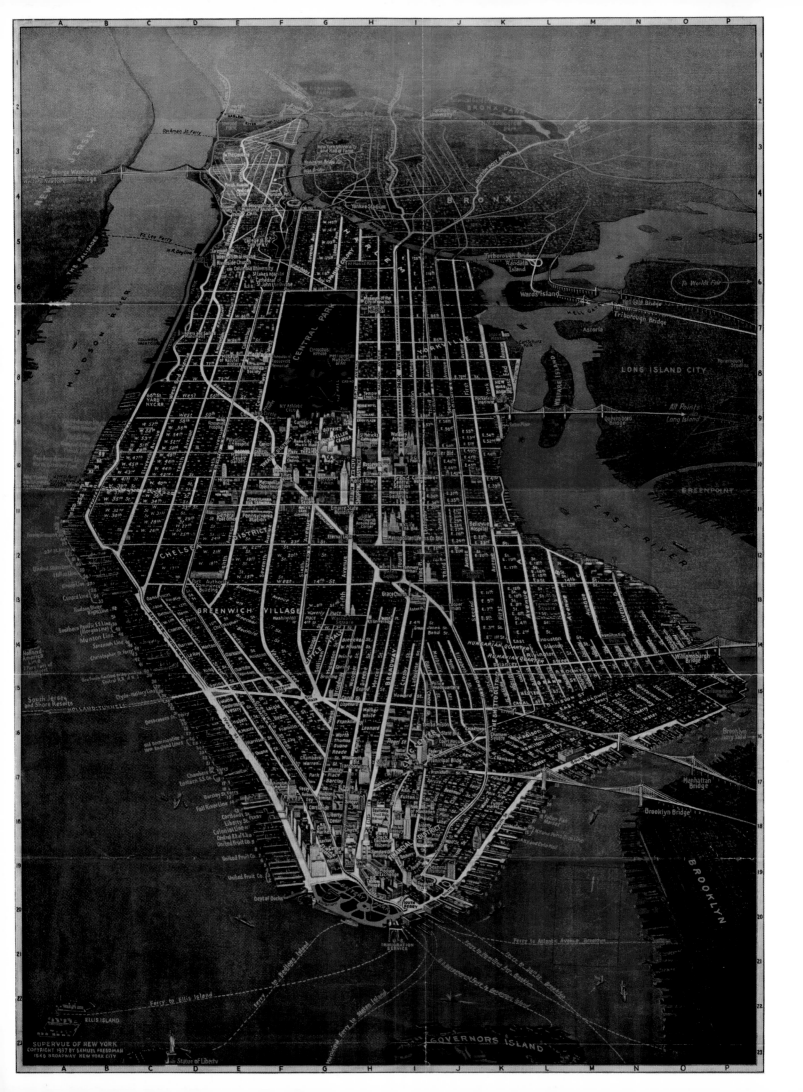

SUPERVUE OF NEW YORK
COPYRIGHT 1937 BY SAMUEL FREEDMAN
1845 BROADWAY NEW YORK CITY

SUPERVUE OF NEW YORK

SAMUEL FREEDMAN, 1937

Freedman's pictorial illustration supplies
a detailed and highly stylized overview of
New York, from the northern reaches of Van
Cortlandt Park in the Bronx, stretching down
to Brooklyn and Governor's Island. The detail
in the landmarks and public buildings of
Manhattan is impressive, both aesthetically
and informatively; as well as highlighting
major tourist attractions, the artist notes
ethnic quarters, municipal buildings, and
even shipping line offices along the island's
west docks.

Freedman's was a souvenir 'map'. The golden
glow which the island borough seems to
emanate is a hint as to its grand status and
allure; disparate bridges act as beacons shooting
into the shadowy districts across the bays,
and the Statue of Liberty, ever a symbol of the
promise of America greeting those arriving
from Ellis Island, matches the brightness of the
city's most attractive mainland monuments.
Also interesting is Freedman's decision to
keep the city's many parks in a shade of dark
green, giving them a suitably rugged appeal
in juxtaposition to the urban glitz of the rest
of Manhattan.

Collection of the University of Toronto Libraries

OFFICIAL NEW YORK CITY SUBWAY MAP
AND STATION GUIDE

NEW YORK CITY TRANSIT AUTHORITY, 1958

The New York City Transit Authority, at
this time, was a public benefit corporation
operating over three-dozen transit lines
and supplying services to around four and a
half million passengers per day. This, their
1958 subway map, shows the extent of the
then contemporary underground services
around New York's boroughs. At this time,
the city subway alone was carrying around
1,355,000,000 passengers per year, more than
three times the total amount recorded on the
entire county's overground railroads.

Collection of the New York Transit Museum

NEW YORK CITY RAPID TRANSIT MAP
AND STATION GUIDE
NEW YORK CITY TRANSIT AUTHORITY, 1967

This 1967 MTA map was the first design to truly form the basis of today's city underground guides. Each route is color coded—a common element of contemporary maps which first concurrently appeared with the 1967 launch of the major Manhattan Bridge connection—and referred to in a detailed legend, whilst regular and part-time services are indicated by solid and broken lines, respectively. Aside from its antiquated appearance, the map's historical context can be seen by the fact that the Third Avenue (8), Myrtle Avenue (MJ), and Culver Shuttle (SS) lines are all still active.

Collection of the New York Transit Museum

New York City Rapid Transit Map and Station Guide

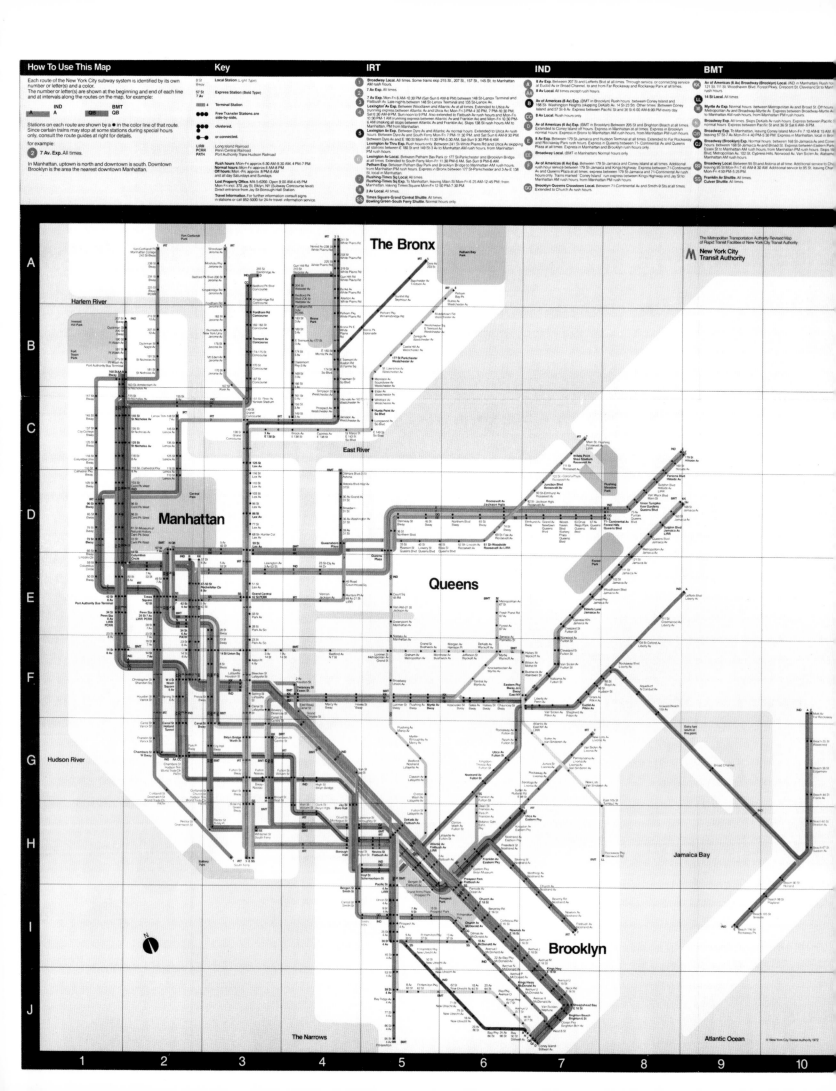

NEW YORK SUBWAY MAP

MASSIMO VIGNELLI, 1972

In common public use for seven years until it was superseded by Michael Hertz's design in 1979, Massimo Vignelli's 1972 *New York Subway Map* is an iconic touchstone of city artwork. Simple in its concept, and aesthetically effective in its execution, each station is reduced to a dot and each route a different colored line, intertwining with its neighboring tracks.

Despite acclaim for its appearance, Vignelli's map also attracted critical disdain for its lack of geographic accuracy; being based on the London Underground map, the tracks are set to a grid and bear no relation to actual street distances and district formations. Further, the feature of Central Park is represented as a square, whereas in reality it is of course a long rectangle.

New York City Subway Map © Metropolitan Transportation Authority. Used with Permission

TAURANAC MAPS

JOHN TAURANAC

John Tauranac's impeccable knowledge of New York geography has been catalogued within his vast portfolio of New York maps. Charting the modern city's development, Tauranac's maps compete alongside the Transit Authority's official publications as the most widely referenced cartographic representations of the New York cityscape. Former chair of the Metropolitan Transit Authority Subway Map Committee (he was the Design Chief for the 1979 subway map) Tauranac left to create what he sees as a fully comprehensive guide to the iconic New York subway system. Alongside his *New York City Subway*, Tauranac's collection boasts *Manhattan Block By Block*, *Manhattan 3 Maps in 1* and *Manhattan Line by Line: A Subway and Bus Map*.

Courtesy of John Tauranac

MANHATTAN LINE BY LINE: A SUBWAY AND BUS MAP

JOHN TAURANAC, 2005

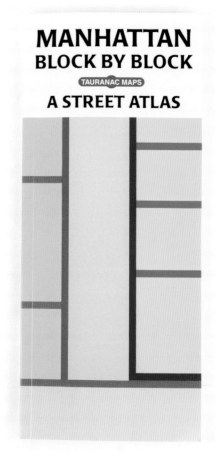

Manhattan Line by Line: A Subway and Bus Map boasts an impressive collection of non-geographic strip maps of each individual subway line operating in Manhattan. Along the way users navigate past parks, cultural institutions and railroads for both day and night transit. The collection also gives room to geographic maps to suit everyone's needs when navigating the city.

Courtesy of John Tauranac

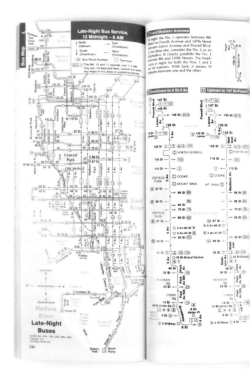

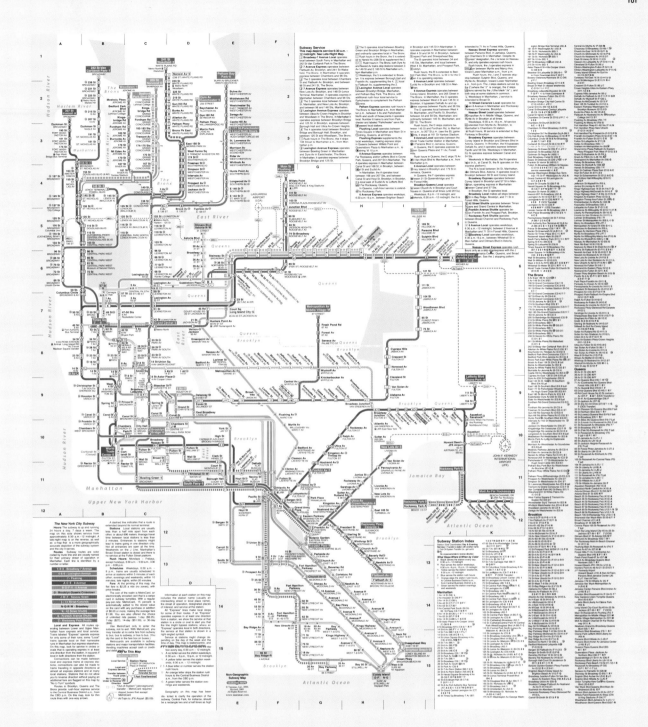

NEW YORK CITY SUBWAY

JOHN TAURANAC, 2007

John Tauranac's *New York City Subway* map provides both a schematic and geographic guide to those travelling the city's iconic subway system. The schematic map provides information on the different services running the length and breadth of the Five Boroughs with a detailed guide referencing each stop and service. The geographic map, found on the flip side, is for those who prefer to travel the subway in perspective with the city—complete with geographic reference points from universities to parks. The *New York City Subway* map also includes a guide to late night services—a foolproof aid to those in transit.

Courtesy of John Tauranac

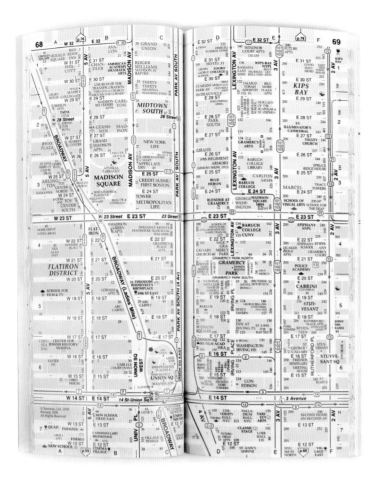

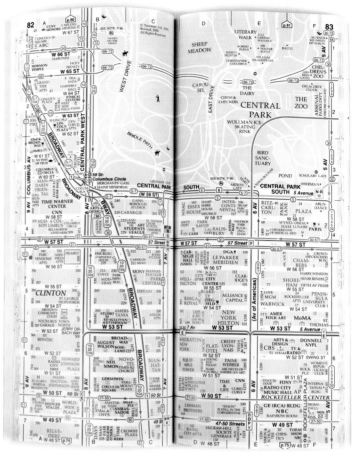

-THIS PAGE-

MANHATTAN BLOCK BY BLOCK

JOHN TAURANAC, 2008

Manhattan Block by Block is a complete guide to all the practical cartographic information a New York explorer might need. Alongside a detailed street map—including formulas for street finding—*Block by Block* includes a subway map, a bus map, and a "places of interest" map.

-OPPOSITE-

MANHATTAN 3 MAPS IN 1

JOHN TAURANAC, 2007

Known as "The Maps that put Manhattan in Perspective" *Manhattan 3 Maps in 1* is an easy to use guide to the streets, places of interest, subways and bus routes of Manhattan.

Courtesy of John Tauranac

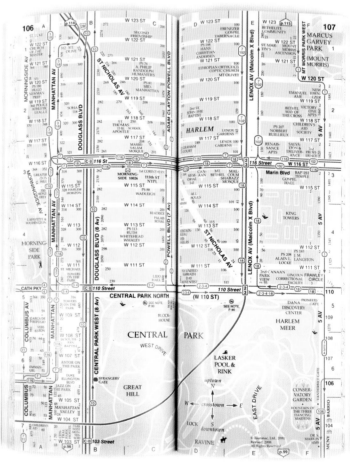

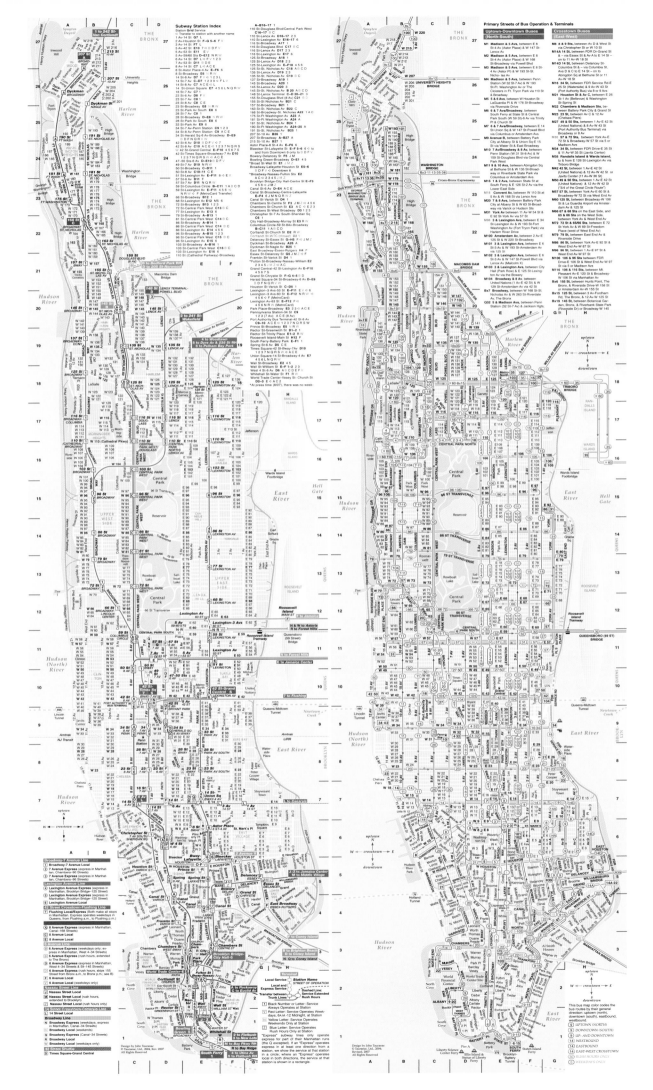

ROUTES OF LEAST SURVEILLANCE

MANHATTAN, USA CIRCA 2001

Based on the iSee project by
the Institute for Applied Autonomy

Camera location data collected by:
- The New York Civil Liberties Union
- The Surveillance Camera Players
- The Institute for Applied Autonomy

Map designed by SITE-R

Key

● = Surveillance Camera
〰 = Path of Least Surveillance

Although born in Brooklyn, Zahid's olive complexion and dark hair makes him unnaturally attractive to surveillance camera operators. He is particularly careful to avoid CCTV on his way to the market from his local mosque after evening prayers.

Ethan is a model Columbia student who maintains a 3.7 average, and is active in student government. However, his unruly hair and military clothing makes him a target for video surveillance – which is especially problematic when he's off to purchase marijuana from the friendly vendors in Tompkins Square Park.

Skye is an anti-globalization activist organizing an April 29th, 2007 anti-war protest march. Knowing that the New York Police Department increasingly relies on surveillance footage to bolster activist prosecutions, she is planning a route that avoids as many cameras possible.

The thought of unsupervised male camera operators ogling her on the way home from the Power Pilates class she teaches at Chelsea Piers gives Wanda the creeps... especially during the warmer months when she isn't wearing her full-length parka!

Eric is a 30-something software engineer who spends his free time reading conspiracy novels and posting to his blog, "Where Was Alex Jones on 9/11?" He only leaves his house once a month (to pick up prescription medication), but when he does, Eric knows that "they" are watching his every move.

ROUTES OF LEAST SURVEILLANCE:
MANHATTAN, USA CIRCA 2001
INSTITUTE FOR APPLIED AUTONOMY WITH SITE-R, 2007

Taken from a collection entitled *An Atlas of Radical Cartography, Routes of Least Surveillance* is an intriguing commentary on the concept of public observation in a major city. The map key contains only two real details: red dots pertaining to the location of CCTV cameras, and the titular "path[s] of least surveillance", routes around the city where one might successfully avoid any unwanted recording or voyeurism. Five presumably apocryphal case studies of individuals keen to avoid observation are drawn out; the dope purchasing student, the harassed Brooklyn-born Muslim, the protest-planning activist, the paranoid conspiracy theorist, and the woman eager not to be spied upon in a state of fitness-derived undress.

Map courtesy of The Institute of Applied Autonomy and SITE-R

SPATIAL INFORMATION DESIGN LAB: MILLION DOLLAR BLOCKS

LAURA KURGAN AND SARAH WILLIAMS, 2005

Columbia University's Spatial Information Design Lab offers a unique cartographic documentation of New York City. 13 separate projects attempt to map urban locations across the United States using carefully selected social data that together form a unique interpretation of the urban landscape.

Million Dollar Blocks is an exploration into 'Justice Mapping'—in which the Spatial Information Design Lab and the Justice Mapping Center have visualized the concentration of residents from New York's neighborhoods currently in prison. This series of maps attempts to explore the 'city–prison–city–prison' migration flow; highlighting, in particular, communities in Harlem, The Bronx and northern Brooklyn. *Million Dollar Blocks* aims to prove the hypothesis that the criminal justice system is so prevalent in the everyday lives of people living in these parts of the city, that public investment in civic infrastructure such as education and health has subsequently been neglected.

Spatial Information Design Lab. Columbia University Graduate School of Architecture Planning and Preservation: Laura Kurgan, Eric Cadora, David Reinfurt, Sarah Williams

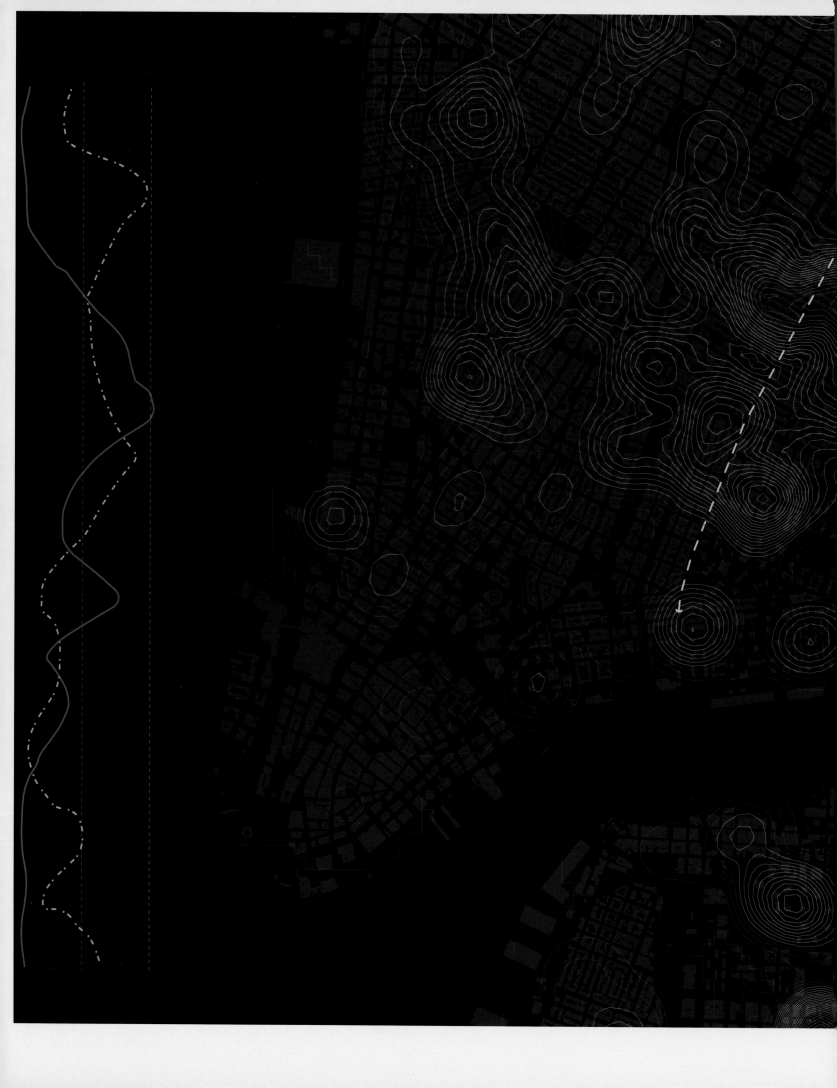

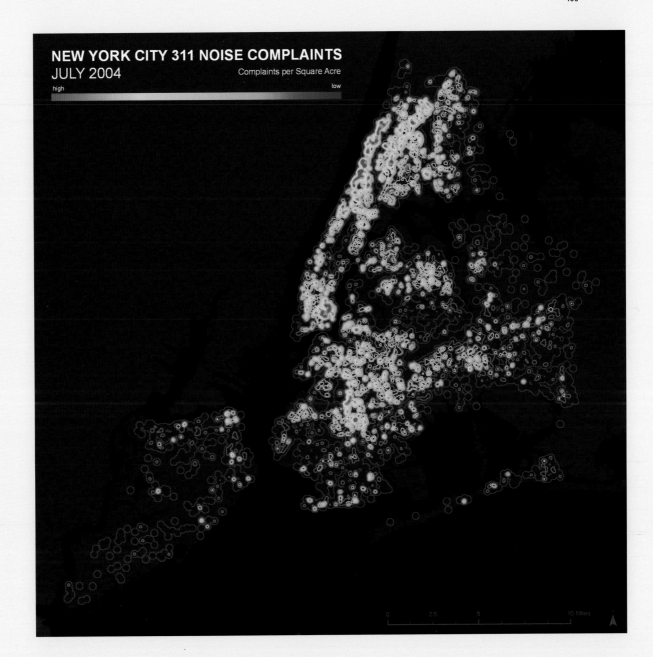

NEW YORK CITY 311 NOISE COMPLAINTS

JULY 2004 · Complaints per Square Acre

high · low

SPATIAL INFORMATION DESIGN LAB:
UNDERSTANDING THE COMPLAINERS NYC 311

SARAH WILLIAMS, 2008

New York's 311 call system for all non-emergency, information and governmental complaint calls—in particular its noise complaint calls—has been mapped by the Spatial information Design Lab in *Understanding the Complainers: NYC 311*. This study has focused on the fashionable area of Alphabet City in Manhattan's Lower East Side, popular for the wealth of bars and restaurants that have appeared in the area over the past decade. A graph is shown corresponding with the contours on the computer generated map that illustrates the number of people living in the area against the number of noise complaints. The corresponding map, above, confirms Manhattan's Lower East Side as one of the city's noise 'hot-spots'.

Spatial Information Design Lab. Columbia University Graduate School of Architecture Planning and Preservation: Study by Sarah Williams

GANGS OF NEW YORK
FROM TIME OUT NEW YORK, 2008

This map of contemporary gang locations within the Five Boroughs is taken from *New York Time Out* magazine. Though highlighting five of the principle organizations around the city, there are in reality many hundreds of active groups. The article from which the image is derived notes that the low statistical representation in the lower Manhattan area is, speculatively, due to the NYPD's secretive attitude towards this issue and a desire to show a control over such groups.

Courtesy of *Time Out New York*

Gangs of New York

Despite strict gun laws and rampant gentrification, gangs continue to thrive throughout the city (even in Chelsea!). Here's a look at the five biggest threats.

Though NYC's crime rate is the lowest it's been in years, gang-motivated incidents have soared 37 percent since 2005—including a recent deadly bout between bangers at high schools in tony Chelsea and Gramercy.

According to the mayor's Preliminary 2008 Fiscal Report, New York is home to some 17,000 gang members. "For a city as large as New York, it has extremely low numbers," says Lou Savelli, retired commander of the NYPD Detective Bureau's Major Case Squad, Gang Division, and editor of Gangs Across America (*gangsacrossamerica.com*).

But don't breathe a sigh of relief just yet. "No area is immune to gang activity—I don't care how wealthy your community is," says Andrew Grascia, president of New York Gang Investigators Association. "When the largest growth of the gang population has been in rural America, to say Brownsville is worse than Manhattan would be inexcusable."

"New York doesn't have clearly demarcated gang territories like Chicago and Los Angeles," adds David Brotherton, chair of the sociology department at the John Jay College of Criminal Justice. Yet in Staten Island, where authorities have identified more than 1,000 members in roughly 55 different organizations, 600 affiliates live within a short distance of the 120th precinct alone. "The exact number is hard to know because they're recruiting new members all the time," says Assistant District Attorney Michael Drews at the Supreme Court Bureau.

Curiously, Manhattan lacks the hardest stats. "The NYPD is extremely secretive and very conscious of its public image," says Brotherton. "It doesn't want to give the impression that anything is outside of its control."

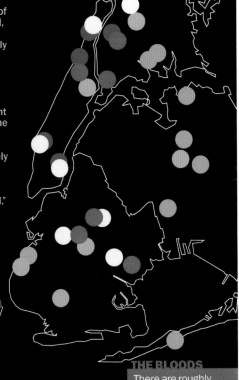

DOMINICANS DON'T PLAY

Battles between DDP and Trinitarios in Gramercy, Chelsea, Harlem, Morris Heights and Washington Heights have garnered lots of media attention, despite its relatively low membership. "It reflects the spike in the Dominican population," says Capital Region Gang Prevention coordinator Ron "Cook" Barrett. "It's a game of 'power by numbers.'"

ALMIGHTY LATIN KING AND QUEEN NATION

ALKQN's 5,000 members operate in Bay Ridge, Sunset Park, Park Slope, East Harlem and the Bronx. "We felt like a family," says former member Brandon Cory, who wrote *Sunset Park Latin Kings*. Grascia calls ALKQN the "the most sophisticated organization out there—the next La Cosa Nostra." ALKQN has filed for nonprofit status in New York.

MARA SALVATRUCHA

MS-13 is a machete-wielding Latin American group that has been assigned its own special task force. "In El Salvador [where it originated], the machete is an acceptable weapon," says Grascia. The gang has members in Corona, Jamaica, Flushing, and the Rockaways in Queens; the Parkchester and Woodhaven sections of the Bronx; and Sunset Park, Brooklyn.

TRINITARIOS

This mostly Dominican gang has chapters in Bushwick, South Williamsburg, Brownsville and Bed-Stuy. Its members recruit heavily at high schools like DeWitt Clinton, often brandish bats and razors, and can be found trash-talking on YouTube.

THE BLOODS

There are roughly 10,000 Bloods in the New York City area. "There is no one leader because there are so many different sets," says Savelli, "but for some reason, they attract the biggest assholes." Sets include Bushwick's Pretty Boy Family and Linden Street Bloods; and the Clay Avenue Bloods in the Bronx. More Bloods can be found in Crown Heights, East New York, Mott Haven and the Stapleton section of Staten Island.

World Within New York

World Within New York shows how different neighborhoods reach out to the rest of the world via the AT&T telephone network. The city is divided into a grid of square pixels where each pixel is colored according to the regions of the world wherein the top connecting cities are located. The heights of the color bars represent the proportion of world regions in contact with each neighborhood. Encoded within each pixel is also a list of the top ranking world cities that account for the communications with that particular area of New York.

NYTE
new york talk exchange

City Ranking
Flushing, Queens

Seoul, KR **11.19%**

Porto, PT **8.19%**

Toronto, CA **5.91%**

Keelung, TW **3.53%**

Shanghai, CN **3.52%**

Santo Domingo, DR **3.00%**

Ho Chi Minh, VN **2.51%**

Quevedo, EC **1.81%**

Fuzhou, CN **1.80%**

Montreal, CA **1.67%**

Guangzhou, CN **1.62%**

Stockholm, SE **1.61%**

Kingston, JM **1.43%**

Moncton, CA **1.31%**

Manila, PH **1.14%**

Cuenca, EC **1.01%**

Geneva, CH **1.00%**

London (Outer City), GB **0.94%**

Halifax, CA **0.92%**

Belize City, BZ **0.84%**

Delhi, IN **0.80%**

Mumbai, IN **0.79%**

Munich, DE **0.74%**

Palermo, IT **0.68%**

Tokyo, JP **0.67%**

Frankfurt Am Main, DE **0.67%**

WORLD WITHIN NEW YORK
NEW YORK TALK EXCHANGE, 2008

Investigating the exchange of information between New York City and the rest of the world, the New York Talk Exchange or NYTE aims to explore the city's real-time relationship with other cities around the world. Exhibited at The Museum of Modern Art in 2008, NYTE mapped the flow of internet and long-distance telephone data in three visualizations. *Globe Encounters* visualized the volumes of internet data flowing between New York and cities around the world, whilst *Pulse of the Planet* looked at the volume of international calls between New York City and 255 cities worldwide.

"2008_NYTE_03" | The world inside New York. *World Within New York* shows how different neighborhoods reach out to the rest of the world via the AT&T telephone network. The city is divided into a grid of two kilometer square pixels where each pixel is colored according to the regions of the world wherein the top connecting cities are located. The widths of the color bars represent the proportion of world regions in contact with each neighborhood. Encoded within each pixel is also a list of the world cities that account for 70 per cent of the communications with that particular area of New York.

Carlo Ratti group director, Kristian Kloeckl project leader, Assaf Biderman, Franscesco Calabrese, Margaret Ellen Haller, Aaron Koblin, Francisca Rojas, Andrea Vaccari research advisors William Mitchell, Saskia Sassen at&t labs research Alexandre Gerber, Chris Rath, Michael Merritt, Jim Rowland

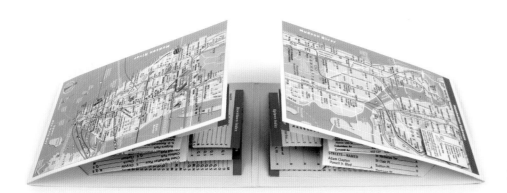

NYC MANHATTAN POP-UP MAP
STEPHAN VAN DAM, 2008

Ostensibly a visitors map, given its compact format and standard list of major city attractions, Van Dam's attractive, clear illustration of Manhattan Island is nevertheless startlingly comprehensive and informative given its small size. Complete street names and a street index, ferry routes, subway lines, and a detailed key are supplied, as well as a separate map and guide to Central Park. A number of skyscrapers and other major buildings are illustrated in lower Manhattan, adding to the casual, informal aesthetic charm of the image.

Courtesy of Stephan Van Dam

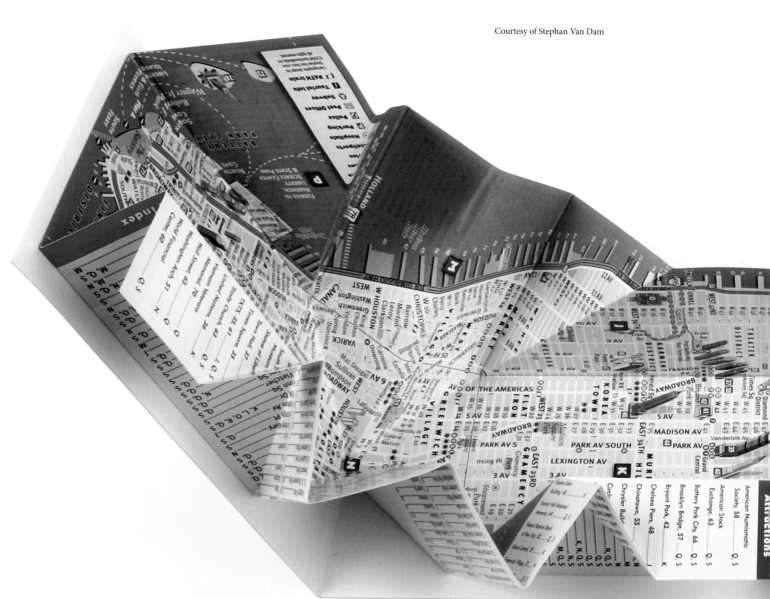

CENTRAL PARK AND SURROUNDING
GOOGLE MAPS, 2009

Google's innovative, adaptable, portable Google
Maps program has made easily accessible
cartographic information available to almost
anyone with a computer or a mobile phone.
Comprehensively mapping all of North
America, most of Europe, and large swathes
of South America and Asia—though coverage
will inevitable increase in time—the software
is an invaluable tool for city guidance, with
zoom and detailed location searches providing
an interactive orienteering tool useful for both
residents or visitors.

Copyright 2009 Google-map data copyright 2009

Tele Atlas-terms of use

NEW YORK

SMALL EVENTS (60 - 100 IMAGES)
MINOR EVENTS (< 50 IMAGES)

MAJOR EVENTS (650 - 1,000 IMAGES)
AVERAGE EVENTS (100 - 200 IMAGES)
BIG EVENTS (200 - 600 IMAGES)

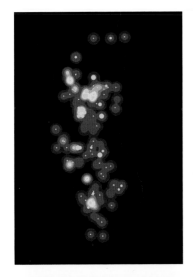
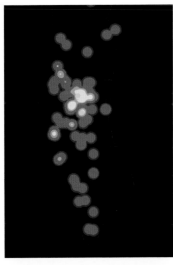
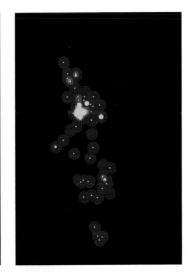
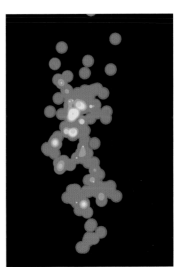

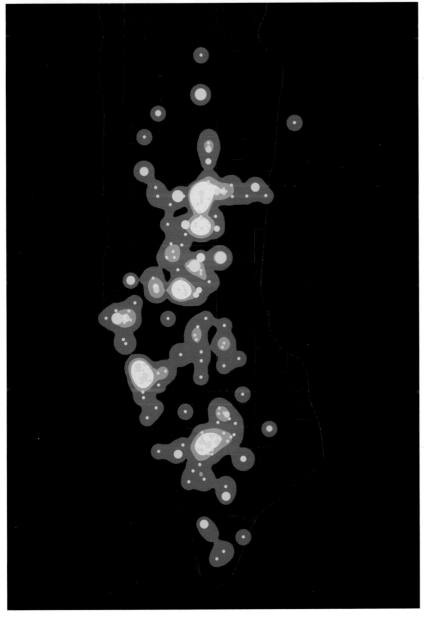

SPATIAL INFORMATION DESIGN LAB: GEOGRAPHY OF BUZZ

SARAH WILLIAMS AND ELIZABETH CURRID, 2008

New York's arts and entertainment industries are a multi-million dollar business. Beginning in 2006, Sarah Williams and Elizabeth Currid, began to map the frequency of film, fashion, theater, music and television industry events onto the New York landscape, by examining over 300,000 photographs from the Getty Image Library. Williams and Currid found that geographical clusters of the different industries began to form in not too distant locales; proving that "event geographies appear to be closely linked to iconic symbols" and that areas such as midtown Manhattan and Chelsea were still more 'buzzy' than the trendy Lower East Side or Brooklyn.

Spatial Information Design Lab, Columbia University Graduate School of Architecture Planning and Preservation: Study by Sarah Williams (Columbia University) and Elizabeth Currid (University of Southern California). Maps created by Sarah Williams and Minna Ninova

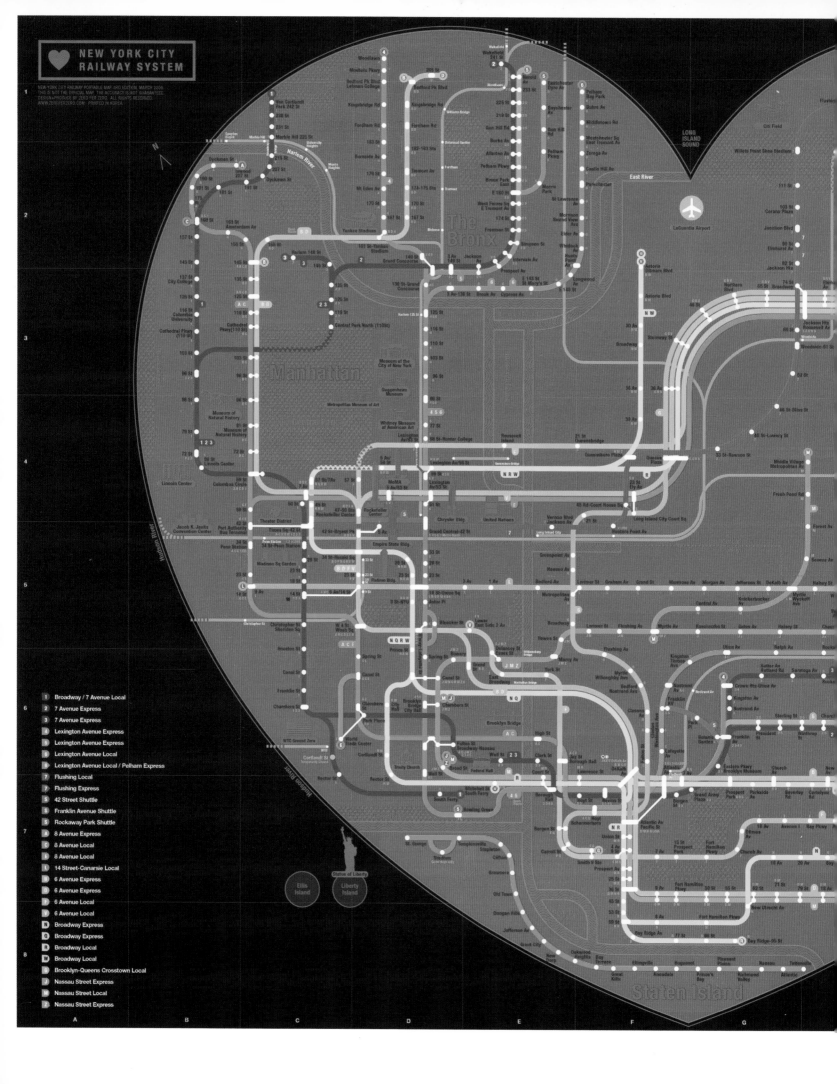

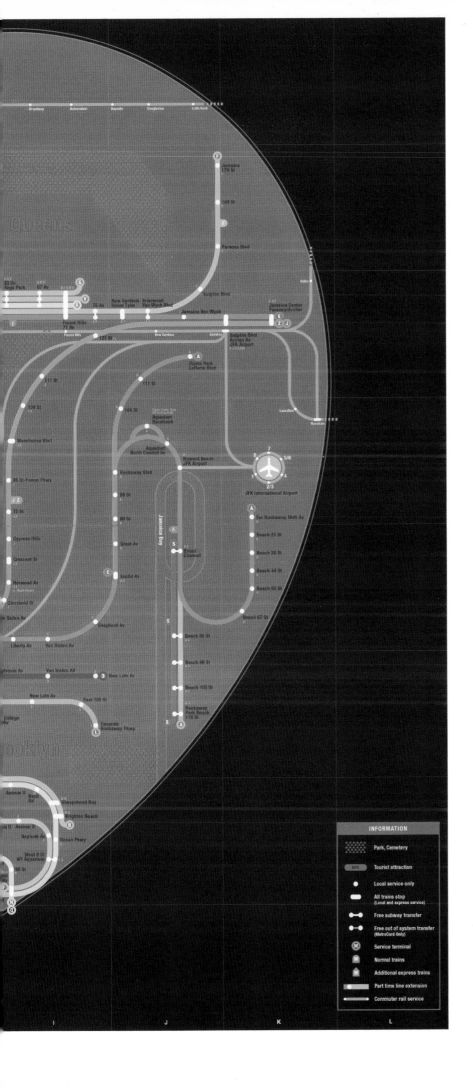

NYC RAILWAY MAP
ZERO PER ZERO, 2008

Paying homage to one of the more iconic, and certainly most imitated, of city images —Milton Glaser's 'I ♥ NY' t-shirt design— Korean design team Zero Per Zero's re-imagining of the New York subway map is a practical urban-orienteering tool as well as an aesthetically charming piece of contemporary graphic design. In addition to standard rail information, the map also shows meticulously illustrated monuments, sights and above ground locations around the city.

Courtesy of Zero Per Zero, www.zeroperzero.com

COMPOSTING GREEN MAP
OF MANHATTAN
GREEN MAP™, 2008

Highlighting the need for efficient waste
management in New York city, Green Maps'
Compost Green Map of Manhattan shows a
plethora of local resources for composting
around the Manhattan area. A stylized key
reveals the high number of schools with
composting facilities and community gardens
around the borough, as well as referencing
in greater detail the functions of its many
noted locations. Further online resources
and information on citywide composting
are also provided.

Composting Green Map of Manhattan 3rd edition, 2008,
Green Map® Green Map System. Lower East Side Ecology
Center, Anya Farquhar, Jane Barber, Risa Ishikawa, Andrew
Sass, Carlos A. Rubio Martinez and Wendy E. Brawer
www.greenapplemap.org/page/compost

Compost Green Map of Manhattan
Worms in the Green Apple

GREEN MAP LEGEND

- 🍂 Public Composting Site
- 🏠 School with Composting
- ↑ Environmental Center
- 🧺 Greenmarket
- 👁 Great Views
- 👫 Parklands/Recreation Area
- ♥ Community Garden
- 🏠 Rooftop Garden
- 🌿 Native Plants
- ☼ Solar Energy
- 🏠 Special Household Waste Station
- 🌐 Info Resources Online

0   1   2
Scale: 1 1/8 inch = 1 mile

GREEN MAP ™

Icons © Green Map System, Inc. 2008 All rights reserved.

1 ↑ 👫
Inwood Hill Park Nature Center
218th & Indian Rd.
Large-scale worm bin for community & Center's food waste. Educational portable worm bin, too.

2 🍂 ☼
Riverside-Inwood Neighborhood Garden (RING)
Dyckman, Riverside & Broadway triangle
3 compost bins, 2 wire holding pens & worm bin. Schools program, butterflies and more.

3 🏠 🏠
Our Lady Queen of Martyrs School
71 Arden St.
Composting cafeteria waste in rooftop garden.

4 ♥ 👁
Riley-Levin Children's Garden Swindler Cove Park
Harlem River Drive & Dyckman St.
Compost bin in children's garden.

5 🍂 ♥
West 181st Street Beautification Project
880 W. 181st St.
Public drop off. Compost in beautiful community garden with youth leadership program.

6 🍂 ♥
West 124th Street Community Garden
Between Lenox & Fifth Aves.
Small but growing bin system and workshops in Spanish & English!

7 🏠
PS 76 A.P. Randolph School
220 W. 121st St.
Fun Roly Pig compost bin and yard waste system.

8 ♥ ☼
Rodale Pleasant Park Garden
437 E. 114th St.
Three bin composters for yard and tumbler for members' food waste built by NY Restoration Project, with rainwater recycling and straw-bale shed!

9 👫 🌿
Central Park Conservancy
Compost Drive, near E. 105th St. behind Conservatory Garden
CPC composts all the Park's yard waste in windrows. Everything from fallen leaves to algae from the ponds!

10 🏠 🌿
High School for Environmental Studies
444 W. 56th St.
Worm bins in classrooms, garden waste composting on the green roof & even a composting club.

11 ♥ 🌿
Clinton Community Garden
West 48th St. btw 9th and 10th Aves.
A "green sanctuary" since 1978 with composting, bee hives and flower, native plant and vegetable gardens.

12 🏠 🏠
NYC Department of Sanitation Special Household Waste Drop Off Station
605 W. 30th St. btw 11 & 12 Aves
Check for info and open hours at 🌐 NYC.gov/wasteless

13 🏠 🏠
The School of the Future
127 E. 22nd St.
Vermicomposting of local business waste and green roof!

14 ↑ ☼
Solar One
E. 23rd St. & FDR Drive
Educational worm bin for food waste. Green building and arts, too!

15 👫 🌿
Stuyvesant Cove Park
E. 18th – 23rd St. & FDR Drive
3-bin compost system for yard waste, mid-park. Riverside refreshment!

16 🍂 ♥
Union Square Greenmarket
17th St. & Park Ave. South
Public drop off & compost outreach at LESEC's stand, every MWF & Sat. 8am to 5pm. Get this map here!

17 🍂 ♥
Lower East Side Garden
E. 11th St. east of 1st Ave.
Composting in Open Road's student-designed garden.

18 🍂 👁
La Plaza Cultural Armando Perez
9th Street & Avenue C
3 bin system with tumbler for members only. Great art & amphitheater!

19 🍂 ♥
Lower East Side Ecology Center Garden
E. 7th St. btw Aves. B & C (north side)
Public drop off, any time through gate opening. Community garden open year-round: Sundays 8am to 5pm.

20 🏠
Franklin Roosevelt PS 34
730 E. 12th St.
Educational composting in historical garden setting.

21 ♥ 🌿
6B Garden & 6BC Garden
E. 6th St. & Ave. B, corner & mid-block
Composting their own yard waste and garden members' food waste.

22 🏠
Earth School
600 E. 6th St.
Outdoor bins in school's garden for yard waste & students' food waste.

23 👫 👁
East River Park
Delancey St. & FDR Drive
LESEC's custom-built in-vessel food waste system composts waste collected from their public drop off sites.

24 ↑ 👫
Grand St. Fireboat House
Grand St. & FDR Drive
LESEC's East River Park Environmental Learning Center. Compost & ecology workshops & events, year-round!

25 🏠
PS 134
293 East Broadway
Classroom worm bins & garden compost site in development.

26 🏠
New York University
Locations in Lower Manhatan
NYU's 13 dining halls began composting in 2008. Averaging 15 tons per day, find out more about their campus-wide greening program at 🌐 NYU.edu/sustainability.

27 🏠
PS 2
122 Henry St.
Classroom worm bins.

28 🏠
City As School
16 Clarkson St.
Project Grow composting entrepreneurship program.

29 👫 🌿
Battery Park City Parks Conservancy
Battery Park Pl. & Thames St.
Advanced compost systems for office & supermarket food waste. Eco-smart "Leave it on the Lawn" policy & windrows for yard waste.

ABOUT THIS MAP:

Every day, more New Yorkers are composting. Almost 200 🍂 community gardens offer Manhattanites a great place to start composting. Most compost their yard waste and members' food waste to improve the soil and help plants thrive. Only 🍂 Sites welcome public drop offs! This map features 🍂 with compost and education programs. 🍂 are a wonderful way to create community and clean air, too. Citywide, find the closest 🍂 at OasisNYC.net.

To grow or know more,
🌐 GreenThumbNYC.org   🌐 NYRP.org
🌐 GreenGuerillas.org   🌐 TPL.org
🌐 MoreGardens.org   🌐 cenyc.org

Indoors, compost can be made in a worm bin (details on reverse). Offices, schools, cafés and food shops are composting, why not you?
🌐 NYCcompost.org provides great workshops & givebacks citywide. In Manhattan, check 🌐 LESecologycenter.org

open
GREEN MAP

OpenGreenMap.org/compostnyc

An interactive Composting Green Map is starting to take shape. Right now, you can explore and add your own videos, images, insights and impacts to Manhattan's compost sites. Starting in Spring 2009, the map goes citywide! Find more and participate online.

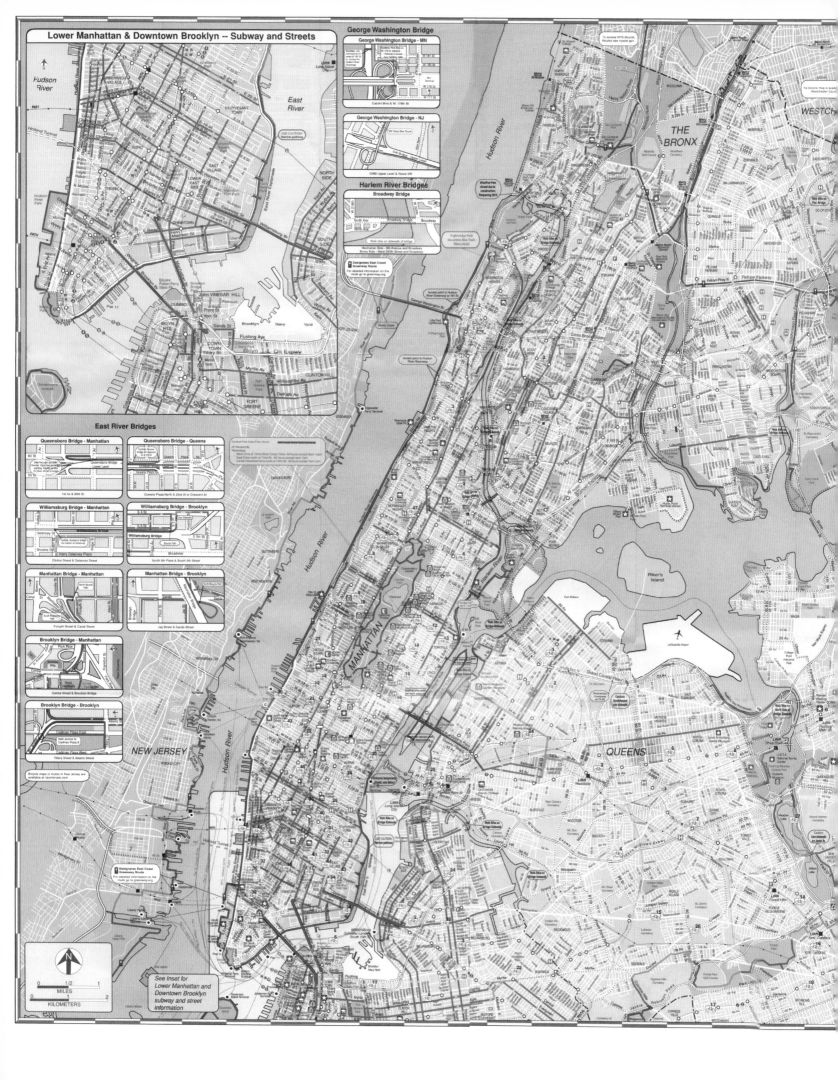

Lower Manhattan & Downtown Brooklyn -- Subway and Streets

George Washington Bridge

George Washington Bridge - MN

George Washington Bridge - NJ

Harlem River Bridges

Broadway Bridge

Designates East Coast Greenway Route
For detailed information on the route go to greenway.org

East River Bridges

Queensboro Bridge - Manhattan

1st Av & 60th St

Queensboro Bridge - Queens

Queens Plaza North & 23rd St or Crescent St

Williamsburg Bridge - Manhattan

Clinton Street & Delancey Street

Williamsburg Bridge - Brooklyn

South 6th Place & South 5th Street

Manhattan Bridge - Manhattan

Forsyth Street & Canal Street

Manhattan Bridge - Brooklyn

Jay Street & Sands Street

Brooklyn Bridge - Manhattan

Centre Street & Brooklyn Bridge

Brooklyn Bridge - Brooklyn

Tillary Street & Adams Street

Bicycle maps or routes in New Jersey are available at njcommuter.com

Designates East Coast Greenway Route
For detailed information on the route go to greenway.org

See Inset for Lower Manhattan and Downtown Brooklyn subway and street information

MILES

KILOMETERS

Hudson River

East River

NEW JERSEY

MANHATTAN

THE BRONX

WESTCH

QUEENS

LaGuardia Airport

Riker's Island

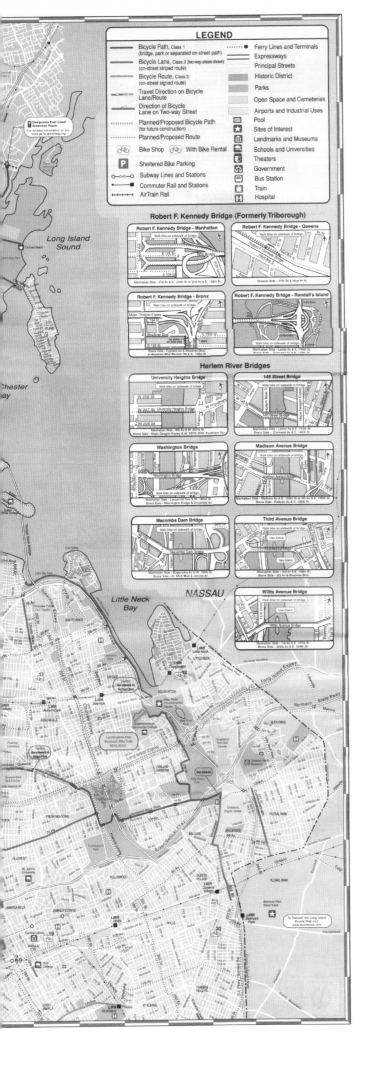

NEW YORK CITY CYCLING MAP

THE DEPARTMENT OF CITY PLANNING, NEW YORK, 2009

Given its popularity in most major cities, the fact that cycling is still largely associated with fringe and courier culture in New York has long been seen as unusual. Traffic dense streets, gung-ho pedestrians, and passive-aggressive motorists, as well as a lack of facilities and commuter awareness, have all played their part in stalling a city-wide embrace of cycling commonplace in places such as Paris or Copenhagen. Despite this, popularity has been growing in recent years, as shown in the annually increasing circulation of the Department of City Planning's NYC *Cycling Maps*. This current edition, incorporating 90 miles of new bike routes and 16 new parking shelters, is dizzying in the amount of information conveyed; full city maps, bridge cycle paths, park auto-access times, cycle traffic markings, subway access, ferry and railway use, and safety guides.

2009 NYC Cycling Map, used with permission of the New York City Department of City Planning. All rights reserved

KICK SUBWAY MAP
KICK DESIGN, 2009

Conceptualized as a hybrid of existing diagrammatic and topographic styles—exemplified in the current MTA and 1972 Vignelli maps respectively—Kick's re-design aims to utilise the strengths of both and provide an easily readable, geographically accurate and up-to-date rendition of the New York subway guide. The color-coding remains the same as the MTA image, though its line kinks are straightened out, moving in line with the standardized angles of the 1972 example, but attempting a greater degree of geographic accuracy than Vignelli.

Station stops, disabled access, commuter line connections, and previously absent information on which stations one can cross directions and lines on without paying twice, are all listed.

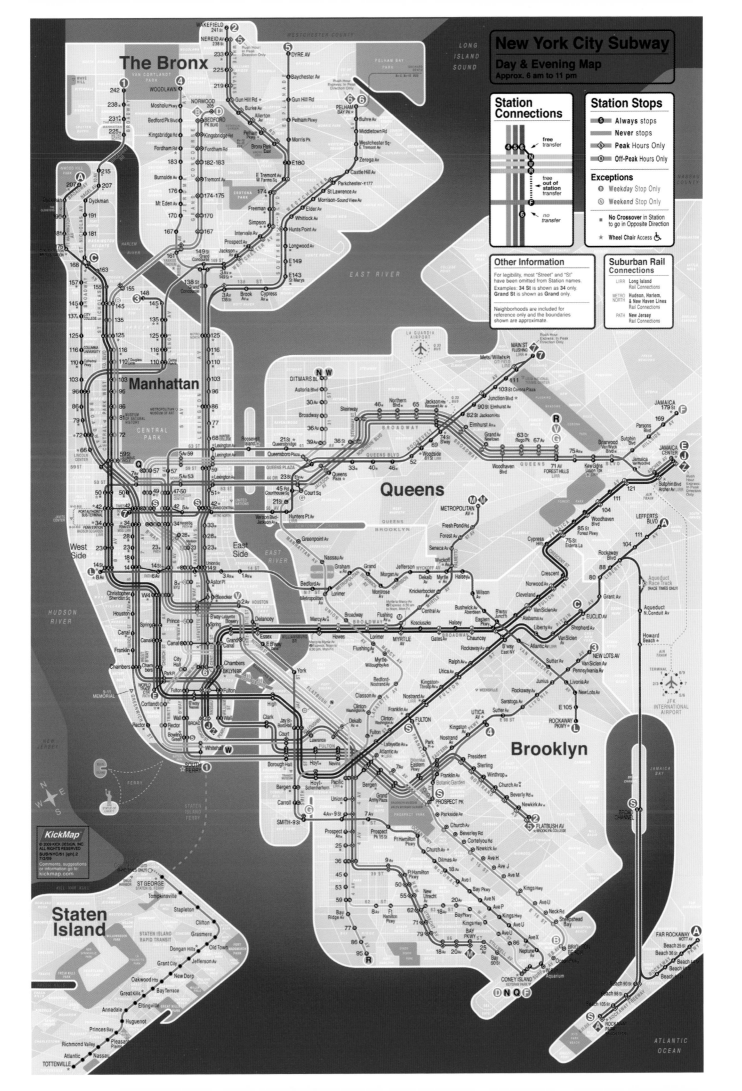

IMAGINING THE CITY

With its often staid and practical purpose, one may forget that cartography is in fact a long established art form with myriad personal uses and interpretative potential. Though largely employed to show practical topographic and municipal detail, the medium is also effective at revealing emotional geography; the desires, memories, instructions, and visions of the particular artist. New York, perhaps the world's single most culturally and socially significant and referenced urban center, is especially open to interpretation.

With the solidifying of New York's physical infrastructure, many artists have begun to re-imagine the city on their own terms. Get Lost, exhibited at The New Museum in

2007 and from which a number of images in this chapter are derived, exemplifies this perfectly. Gathering various personal views of the city, the show highlighted the significance of maps as an expressive art form. Terence Koh's poetic *After Dark* regales promiscuous hotspots visited by the artist, whilst filmmaker Jonas Mekas' *My Downtown* pastes remembered dwellings of friends, musicians, artists, and cinema locations of the era over a standard, functional map of the lower Manhattan area. Practical for the common reader these illustrations are not; but in giving us such a particular insight into the mind of the artist they are invaluable. The city, in this respect, is a canvas both tangible and spiritual. By applying themselves to the cityscape, the creators can become part of the urban landscape, and *vice-versa*.

Even if the city is not familiar or home to an artist, we can gain the valuable insight of the interpretation of the visitor. Though a cartographic study of New York may be perfectly accurate, no visitor to the city sees it in this rigid, emotionally disconnected way. Aleksandra Mir's hand sketches of parts of New York are derived from real maps of the city, though her images are skewed and elaborated upon. Street grids and roads are inserted with almost no accuracy, and her image of Manhattan is dwarfed by that most recognizable of city icons,

the Statue of Liberty. Her drawings reflect the confusion of the casual visitor to a bustling city; detail is disparate, surrounded by blank space and inaccurate understandings of urban order, the one truly filled-out image being that which is famous around the world.

A re-imagining of the city need not be wholly personal, though. Applying different aesthetics to the accepted rigidity of the map can transform recognizable topography into fascinating, fresh imagery. Peter Sis' *MTA Art Card*, with which the artist grafts Manhattan Island onto the body of a giant whale, is a case in point. Similarly, Paula Scher's *Manhattan at Night* and *NYC Transit*, with their vivid depictions of the city's streets and transported networks re-realized in multicolored text maintain a relative accuracy in geographic shape, though draw location and street names away from their real placements and into the waterways of the Hudson and East River.

The different aesthetic styles and commentaries applied to the mapping of New York in this chapter show just how informative and revealing disparate details, seemingly inaccurate renderings, and abstract interpretations can be. The city, with the inclusion of the personal realm, is given yet another layer of meaning.

LIST OF WORKS

———————

———————

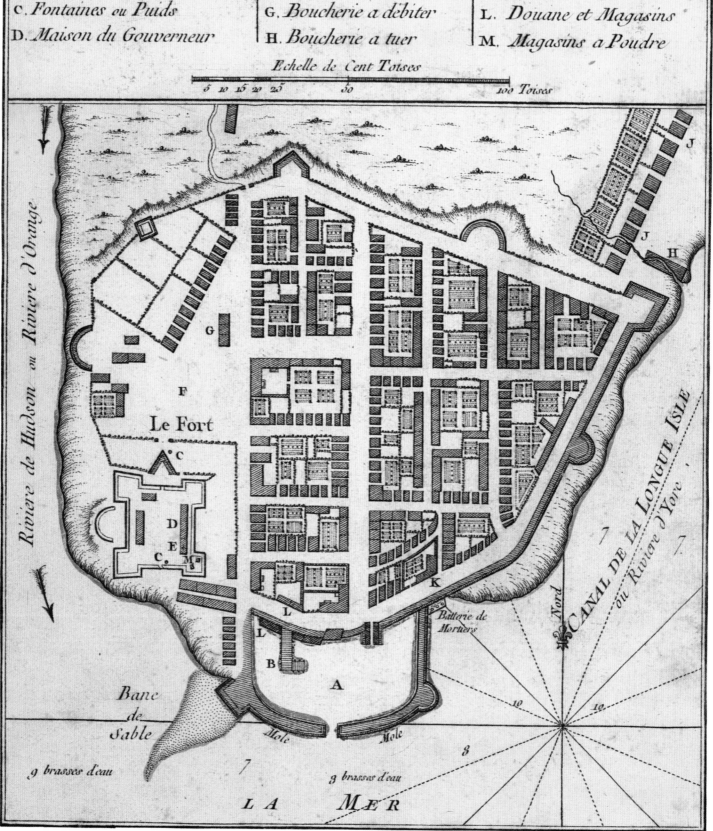

VILLE DE MANATHE ou NOUVELLE-YORC

A. *Le Port des Barques*
B. *Pont pour décharger les Barques*
C. *Fontaines ou Puids*
D. *Maison du Gouverneur*

E. *Le Temple*
F. *Place d'Armes*
G. *Boucherie a débiter*
H. *Boucherie a tuer*

J. *la Basse Ville*
K. *Maison de Ville*
L. *Douane et Magasins*
M. *Magasins a Poudre*

Echelle de Cent Toises

5 10 15 20 25 50 100 *Toises*

Rivière de Hudson = ou = Rivière d'Orange

Le Fort

Bane de Sable

9 brasses d'eau

Batterie de Mortiers

Mole *Mole*

9 brasses d'eau

Nord

CANAL DE LA LONGUE ISLE ou Rivière d'Yorc

LA MER

VILLE DE MANATHE OU NOUVELLE-YORC FROM JACQUES NICOLAS BELLIN'S *LE PETIT ATLAS MARITIME*

JEAN-BAPTISTE-LOUIS FRANQUELIN, 1764

A printed version of a map originally hand drawn by Franquelin in 1693, this image portrays the early-era New York as a fortress of some strength, at a time when an attack by the French seemed inevitable and imminent. With a single wharf at the south and steep inclines approaching the city walls, shown by hachure marks, on the east and west shorelines, Franquelin's image depicts the conurbation as being far more secure than would have been the case in reality; the fort's walls and structure would likely have been in a constant state of relative disrepair and shoreline wharfs were in comparative abundance along the East River at this time.

BROADWAY BOOGIE WOOGIE
PIET MONDRIAN, 1942–1943

Broadway Boogie Woogie is Piet Mondrian's homage to both New York's most famous avenue and the artist's personal love affair with the music from which the painting takes its name. Boogie-Woogie is a fast-paced offshoot of American Jazz, which became popular—particularly in New York—in the 1930s and 40s. The energy of Boogie-Woogie, which fascinated Mondrian on his arrival to New York in 1940, came to represent much more than just music—it was an aural representation of this extraordinary city with which he had fallen in love. The painting's static interspersion of yellow, red, blue and white squares is evocative of the bright lights of Broadway—in particular the stretch that encompasses legendary Times Square. Mondrian's sporadic use of white against yellow creates a striking visual affect; whereby the lights of Broadway appear to be dancing on the canvas. The interlocking horizontal and vertical lines in the painting, reflective of New York's grid system are encompassed by the blinking lights of the passing traffic moving around the billboards of Times Square.

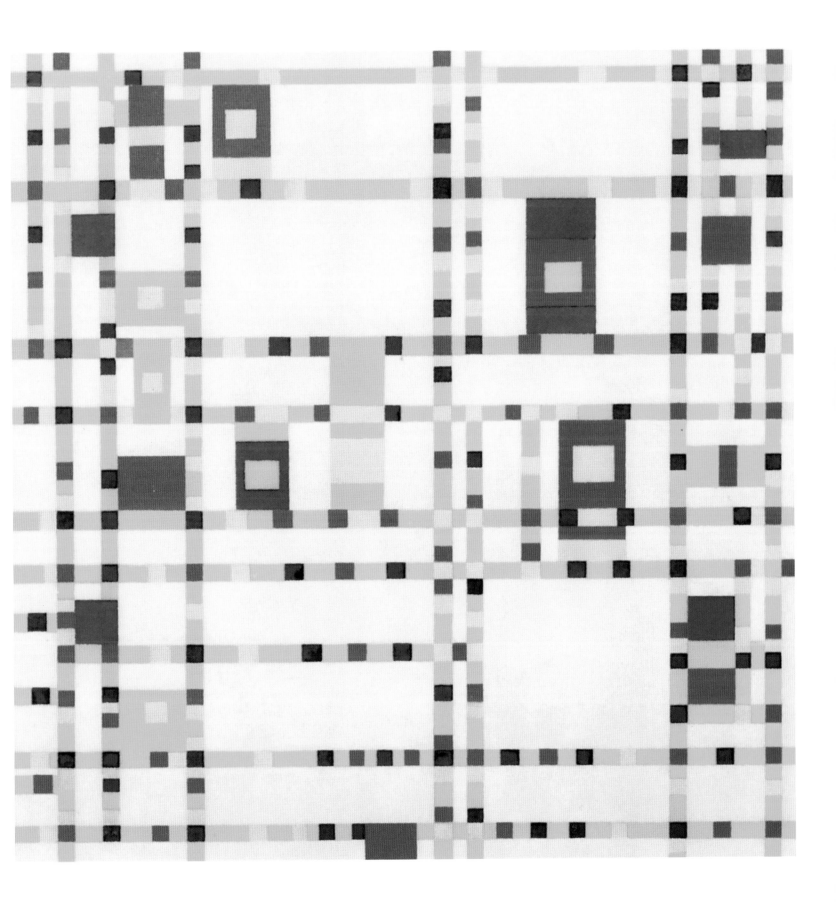

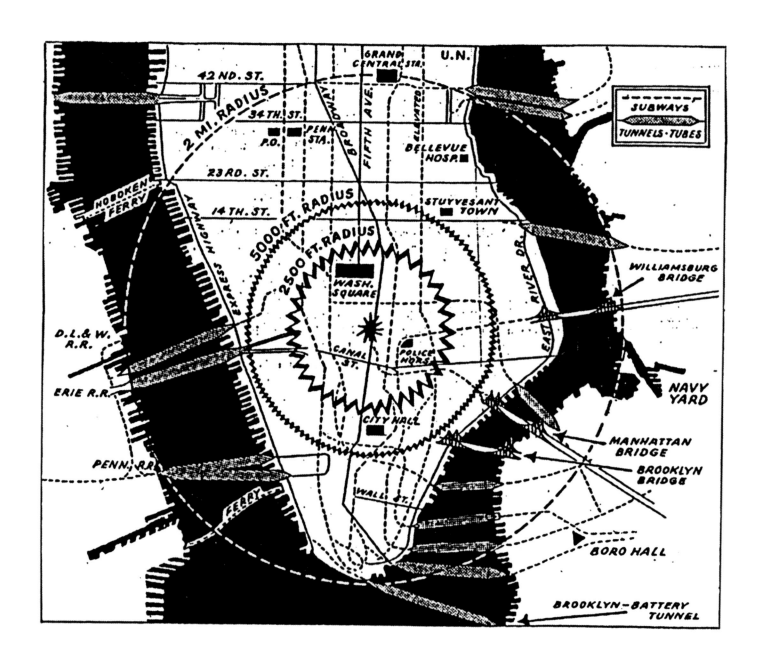

ILLUSTRATION EXTRACTED FROM EDWARD CONWAY 'A-BOMB OVER MANHATTAN'

FROM AMERICA MAGAZINE, JULY 22 1950

This 1950 map was designed to accompany an article published by the Catholic periodical *America Magazine* in alignment with the 'defensive dispersal movements' of the Cold War era. The illustration envisions hypothetical damage zones following an atomic attack on New York City, in this case centered a little south of Washington Square. The map's focus relates specifically to discussions concerning transportation planning in the event of such an attack, and highlights how the majority of the island's escape routes would be theoretically unusable given the projected blast radiuses that the writer, Edward Conway, references in the diagram.

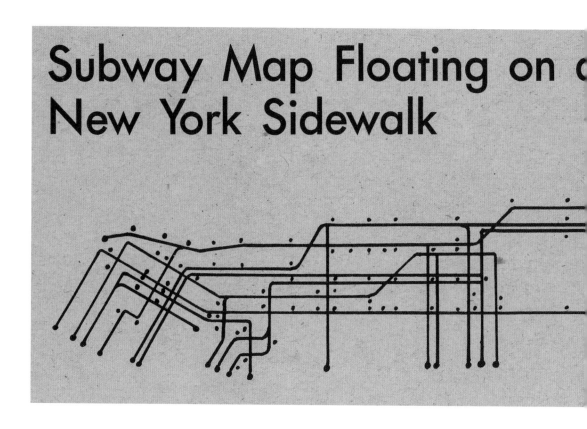

Subway Map Floating on a New York Sidewalk

SUBWAY MAP FLOATING ON
A NEW YORK SIDEWALK

FRANCOISE SCHEIN, 1985

Walking past 110 Greene Street, Manhattan, one comes across a giant steel subway map embedded in the sidewalk. The map, a creation of French artist Francoise Schein, won the 1983 New York City Design Commission's *Award for Excellence in Design*—a government funded project promoting permanent works of art and architecture on city owned property. Schein's long-standing fascination with the New York subway system culminated in this public-funded schematic map. Made from stainless steel, glass rounds (found in the cellars beneath the neighborhood's sidewalks) and L.E.D. lights, the artist created what she sees as "a sort of abstract map of the city".

Courtesy of the artist. Sponsor: Goldman Properties.

For more info about the artist: www.francoiseschein.com

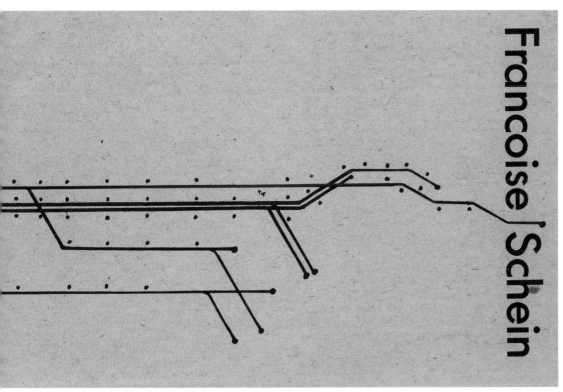

Francoise Schein

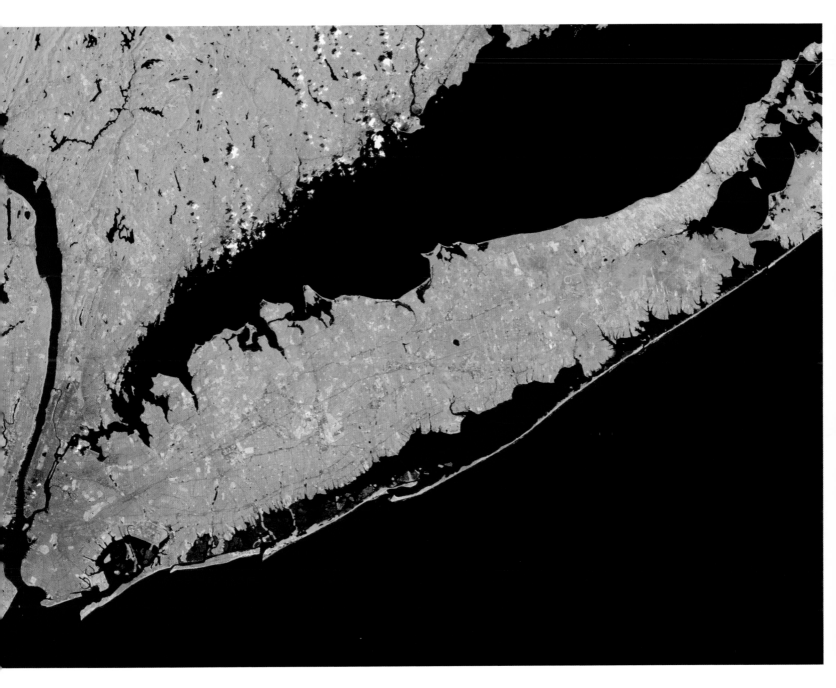

NEW YORK CITY FLYBY

NASA VISIBLE EARTH, 1996

Recorded with the Landsat Thematic Mapper™ instrument, these images—showing Long Island, Long Island Sound, and Manhattan Island—highlight basic geographic data; barren or recently cultivated land is colored red to pink; water is blue; and concrete and asphalt are shown as grey or black.

NASA/Goddard Space Flight Center Scientific visualization studio

NEU-YORK
MELISSA GOULD, 2000

Gould's meticulously detailed image of
a 1939-era New York re-imagined by the
Third Reich is a surreal conceptualization
of a familiar space. The artist describes
her work as a "horrifying counterfactual
proposition", one which adheres to German
cultural ideologies of the time by removing
Jewish synagogues—represented by Jewish
stars—from a contemporary 1939 map
of Manhattan, and, by replicating real
1939 Berlin street names, locations, and
neighborhoods, effectively transposing the
German city across the Atlantic. Thus, the
Statue of Liberty becomes the Siegessäule,
Grand Central Terminal is renamed Anhalter
Bahnhof, and the large lake in Central Park is
replaced by Wannsee.

Gould's system of replacing street and avenue
titles draws in a wealth of German language
and culture: avenues are re-named after kaisers
and kings; those south of West 58th Street—
now Richard Wagner Strasse—are replaced
with German composers associated with
operas, and traditional Teutonic first names;
on the East Side, German rivers, cities and
towns are referenced. Specific nods to the Nazi
era are also included, albeit subtly; both Hitler
and Göring have their minor streets.

"NEU-YORK"© 2000 by Melissa Gould (MeGo). 4-color
lithograph on paper: 27 by 43 inches (68cm by 109cm);
limited edition of 20 prints
www.megaphone.com/neuyork.html

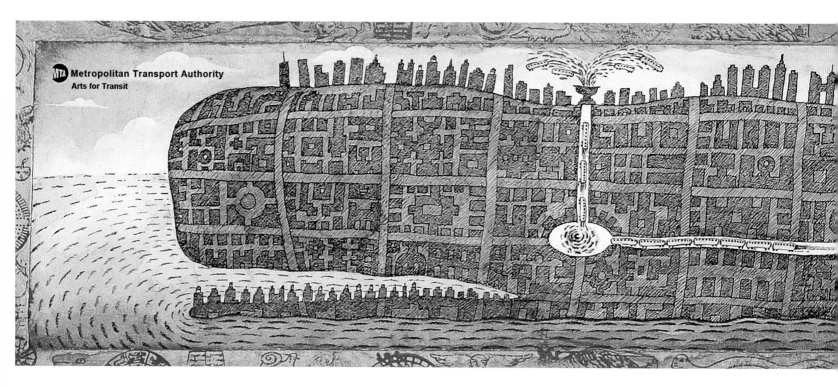

Peter Sis, Artist

MTA ART CARD

PETER SIS, 2001

This poster, designed for the Metropolitan Transit Authority's *Art Card Scheme* by the artist Peter Sis, is an unusual interpretation of the New York cityscape mapped onto the body of a whale. Sis created this amusing illustration using a cross-hatching technique in ink, watercolor and gold acrylic. The *Art Card Scheme* commissions one to two artists a year to create transit related imagery to display in the newest subway cars, in an effort to promote mass transit, whilst also providing amusement for the millions of commuters riding the New York subway each day. Sis' illustration entertained commuters for two years with its maze of subways and streets criss-crossing the whale from tail to mouth.

2001 © Peter Sis. Commissioned and owned by

Metropolitan Transportation Authority Arts for Transit

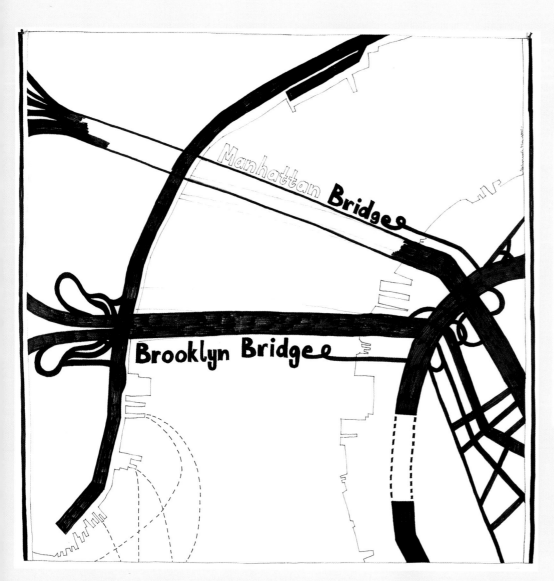

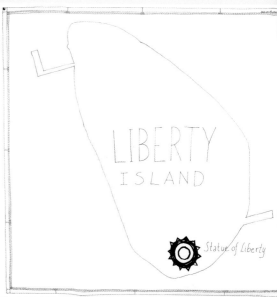

LIBERTY ISLAND AND BROOKLYN BRIDGE, FROM THE WORLD FROM ABOVE (SERIES)
ALEKSANDRA MIR, 2003

Aleksandra Mir's series of 48 by 48 inch black marker drawings, under the collective title *The World From Above*, are derived from mass produced cartography and 'translated' by the artist sketching in freehand. These examples, of the Manhattan and Brooklyn Bridges and Liberty Island respectively, effectively show this simplistic approach: island shorelines are semi-accurate, if rudimentary, and basic feature names appear in place of any actual topographic information. Roads are seemingly shown on the map entitled Brooklyn Bridge, though it is hard to tell where decoration becomes detail as the text loops into the very topography of the map.

The World from Above. Liberty Island; Statue of Liberty, marker on paper, 48 by 48 inches, 2003–04, courtesy of the artist

The World from Above. Manhattan Bridge; Brooklyn Bridge, marker on paper, 48 by 48 inches, 2003–04, courtesy of the artist

MANHATTAN

ALEKSANDRA MIR, 2003

This map, one of several produced by Mir covering the Manhattan area, is derived from Get Lost, a 2007 exhibition of interpretative portraits of downtown New York.

Mir's work, knowingly half-finished and seemingly vague in its intentions, focuses on a grotesquely imagined Statue of Liberty shadowing the western side of Manhattan island. Cartographic detail is limited and sparse; the artist has mapped out some parts of the city's street grid system in a rudimentary fashion, mostly around Central Park, though has seemingly inserted a fictitious Broadway—and a crossed out 'Wrongway'—through the center of the island, as well as a number of invented road systems around the edges of the borough. Bridges through the East River are noted, but those over the Hudson are left out completely. Interestingly, Mir appears to have allowed far more artistic attention to apparently applying a street-grid to the aquatic areas of the image.

Manhattan, marker on paper, 200 by 100 cm, 2006, courtesy of the artist

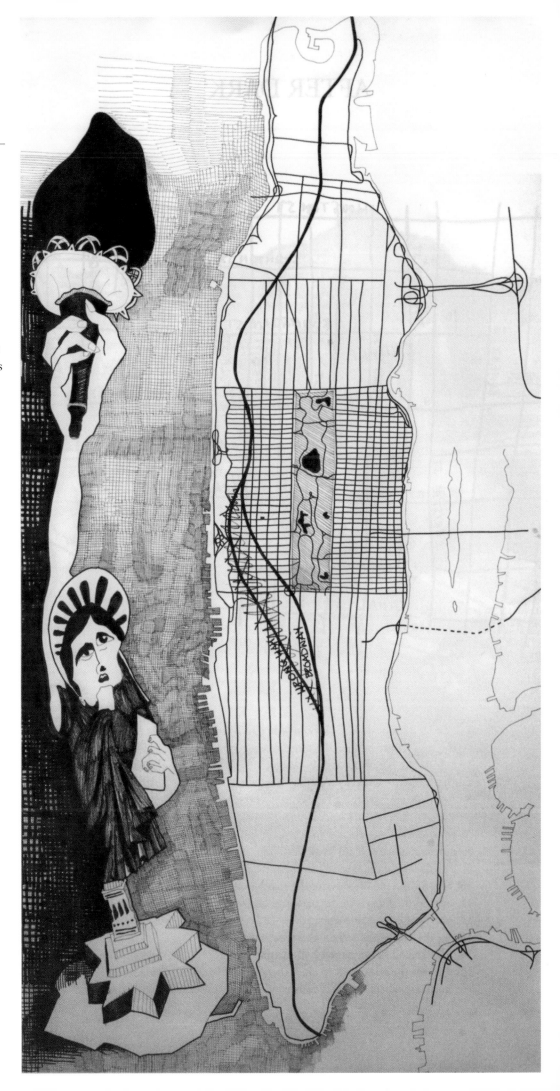

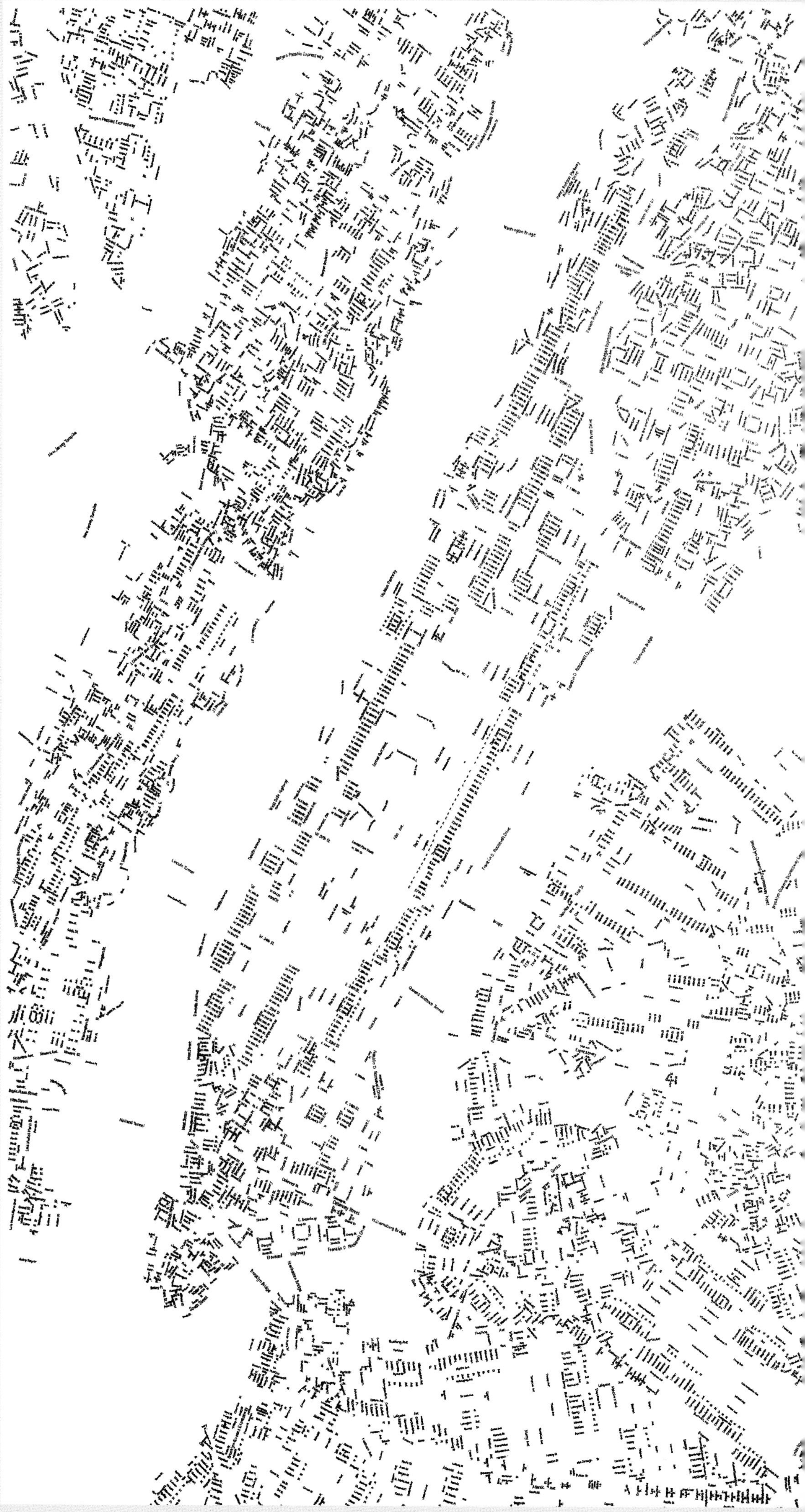

NEW YORK INDEX DRAWING

LAYLA CURTIS, 2003

Striking a balance between the intricate and the sparse, Curtis' 'text' styles New York as a dense mass of hand-written street and bridge names. Despite the distinct lack of topographical boundaries, owing to the map's atypical construction, city details are visible through the lack of cartographic information afforded to the viewer; parks are clearly shown—or rather, not shown—throughout Manhattan, and the disparity of bridges and tunnels over and through the Hudson and East River give clarity to the paths of the city water systems.

Courtesy of Layla Curtis

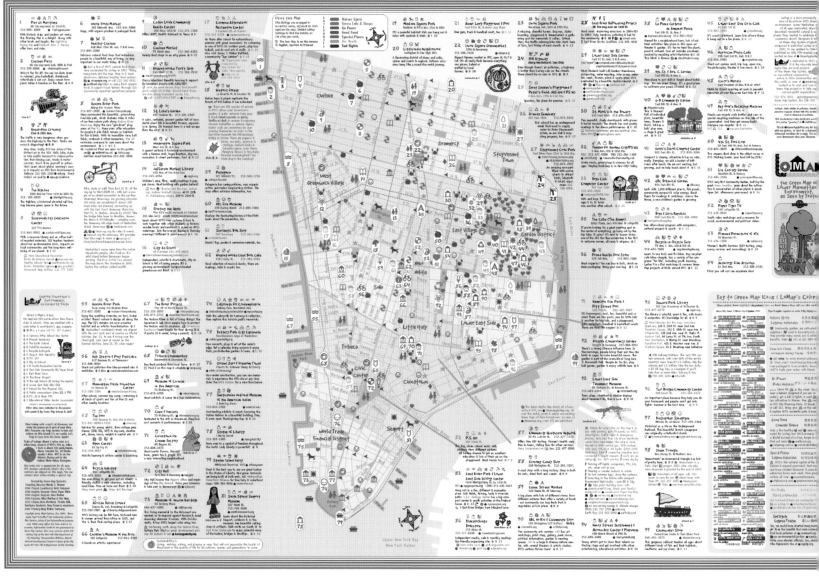

LOMAP: THE YOUTH AUTHORED GREEN MAP
OF LOWER MANHATTAN
GREEN MAP™, 2004

LoMap: The Youth Authored Green Map of Lower Manhattan is a vast project compiled by over 250 ethically informed New York youngsters between the ages of seven and 19. Through color-coded illustrations and descriptions, the map—published by The Green Map System™—describes around 100 natural and cultural sites located around Lower Manhattan. Many more places of interest are identified by a comprehensive list of icons including "Eco-Spiritual Spot" in red and "Sunset Views" in green. Amongst downtown Manhattan's green spots to celebrate are *The Green Triangle: Between Henry St. and Madison Avenue*: "'Greenstreets' environmental triangle has lots of pretty trees" and the *Labyrinth for Contemplation: Battery Park, North West Side*: "Walk the Labyrinth for harmony and reflection".

LoMap, the Youth Authored Green Map of Lower Manhattan,
2nd edition, published 2004, Green Map®

NEW JERSEY IS THE ONLY
THING POSSIBLE

WILLIAM POPE L., 2007

William Pope L.'s Lower Manhattan is a
carefully censored landscape, identifiable only
by its safe houses or secure refuges marked out
in thick, black pen. All recognizable landmarks,
including the Statue of Liberty, have been
disguised beneath layers of correction fluid
and tea stains to reveal a distorted view of the
once recognizable cityscape.

Courtesy of the artist

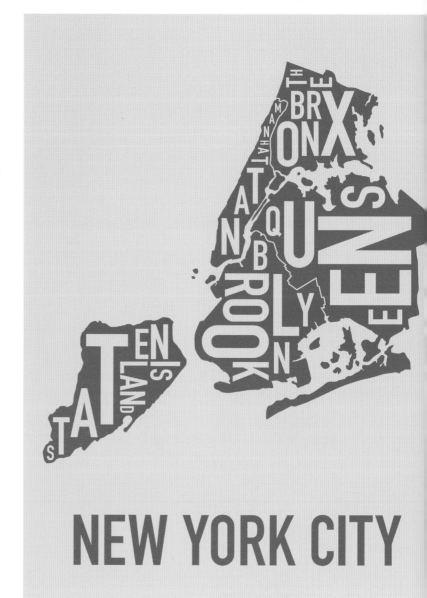

NEW YORK CITY

MANHATTAN

ORK POSTERS

JENNY BEORKREM, 2007

Ork Posters' typographic prints map out the neighborhoods of various cities around the United States, in an attempt by graphic designer Jenny Beorkrem to create a sense of identity through the communities we belong to. Beorkrem created this series of New York City posters and screen prints in a range of colors from "Classic Black and White" to vibrant "Pop-Red", mapping out the Five Boroughs: Manhattan, Staten Island, Brooklyn, Queens and The Bronx. The posters, measuring 18 by 24 inches, are all printed on recycled paper, using local printers whenever possible to reflect their community driven message.

Courtesy of Ork Posters: orkposters.com and Jenny Beorkrem

BROOKLYN

AFTER DARK

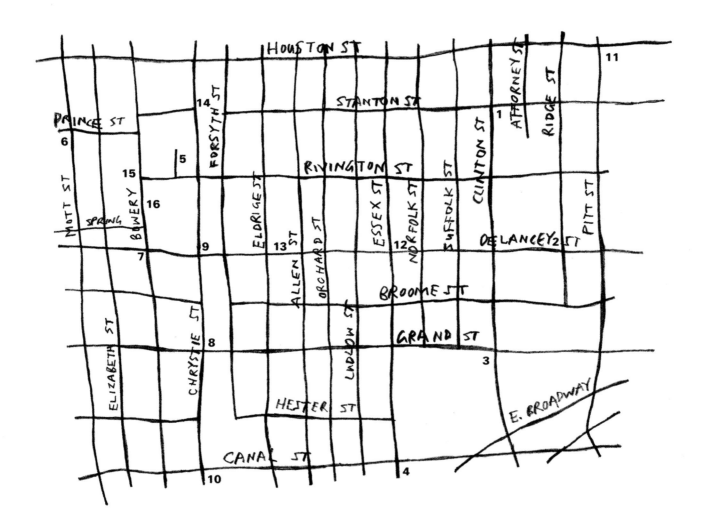

1. a squat surrounded by chicken wire and warning signs
2. the small space behind the fence, keeper of the dark
3. behind the big maple tree in the gardens
4. an old rusty swing. a young boy died there?
5. freemans ally just round the corner of the building
6. steps of the old shoe store where the white secrets lurk
7. walk quietly into the car park, watch out for the attendant!
8. on the steps of the old bank building
9. choose any of the benches in the public gardens, but the best one is the green one
10. keep in the shadows under the manhattan bridge. don't let the river lights catch you
11. behind the bushes in the park and best when the wind is blowing strongest
12. just by the subway entrance
13. see the old public toilets, there we can go
14. a basketball hoop, its net half missing
15. wait for the restaurant to close then use the bench just outside
16. sneak anywhere into this construction site. consecrate it with yourself.

AFTER DARK
TERRENCE KOH, 2007

Claiming to have personally visited every one
of the locations he lists, Terence Koh's sparse
map serves as a guidebook of sexual and
promiscuous hotspots in the area between
downtown Houston and Canal Streets. The
obscure, unexplained notes to his locations
are rich in subtext and mystery; Koh writes of
secrets lurking by old shoe stores, the danger
of being "caught" by river lights, and in noting
that the Houston Street bushes are "best when
the wind is blowing strongest", a kind of
unsalubrious advice to the reader. It is hard
to tell whether the details Koh highlights are
incidental or intrinsic to the map's purpose,
or even exactly what this purpose is: what
acts take place at these locations remain only
hinted at and left to the reader to imagine.

Courtesy of the artist

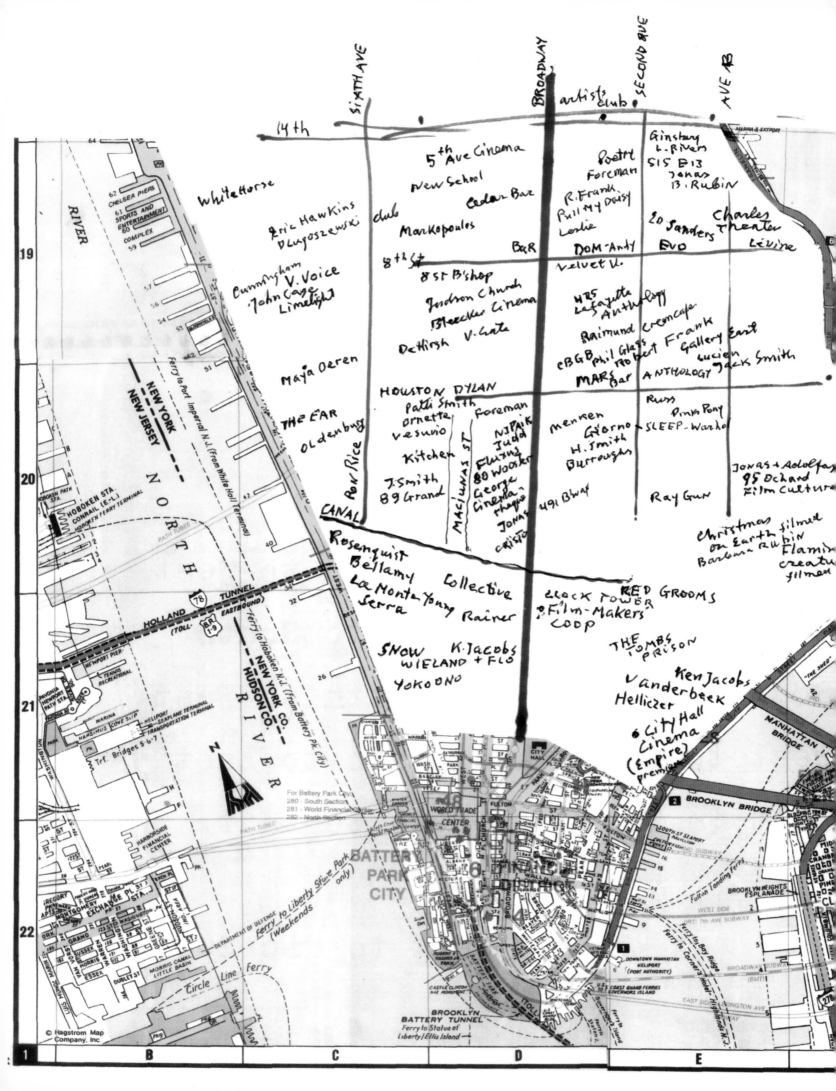

MY DOWNTOWN
JONAS MEKAS, 2007

By erasing the common cartographic representation of downtown Manhattan and replacing it with a personal map of people and locations particular to the artist, Mekas' image provides a fascinating juxtaposition between the personal and public conception of New York City. The noted content is a veritable who's who of musical and artistic dignitaries, filmmakers, and contemporary references; the viewer would never be able to practically find his way around with the map, but we can see where Bob Dylan and Patti Smith resided, where John Cage, Philip Glass and the Velvet Underground were based, and where Mekas may have viewed films essential to his own career. Tellingly, we can see that Wooster Street has been re-named as Maciunas Street, in tribute to the pioneer of the Fluxus movement.

Courtesy of the artist

UNTITLED
LAWRENCE WEINER, 2007

Lawrence Weiner's contribution to the Get
Lost exhibition, discusses mapping and
geographical positioning in terms of human
beings relationships with the objects around
us. Using Lower Manhattan's manhole covers
as his starting point, Weiner presents a unique
cartographic interpretation from Bleeker
Street Playground to St. Marks in the Bowery,
whereby "Material reality itself allows each
manhole cover to offer a certitude." Through
Untitled, Weiner opens up a cyclical discussion
in which both person and place are highlighted
as necessary in the cartographic exploration
of the city "the relationship of human beings
to objects in relation to human beings".

Courtesy of the artist

GIVEN THE LIGHT
URBAN PEOPLE DO NOT IN FACT HAVE ANY MEANS OF DETERMINING
WHERE THEY ARE FROM LOOKING TO THE STARS
THE MATERIAL REALITY OF THE WORK ITSELF ALLOWS EACH
MANHOLE COVER TO OFFER A CERTITUDE
AT THAT MOMENT WIHTIN THE SPHERE WHERE DETERMINING
WHERE YOU ARE IS OF SOME USE IN UNDERSTANDING
THE RELATIONSHIP OF HUMAN BEINGS TO OBJECTS IN RELATION
TO HUMAN BEINGS

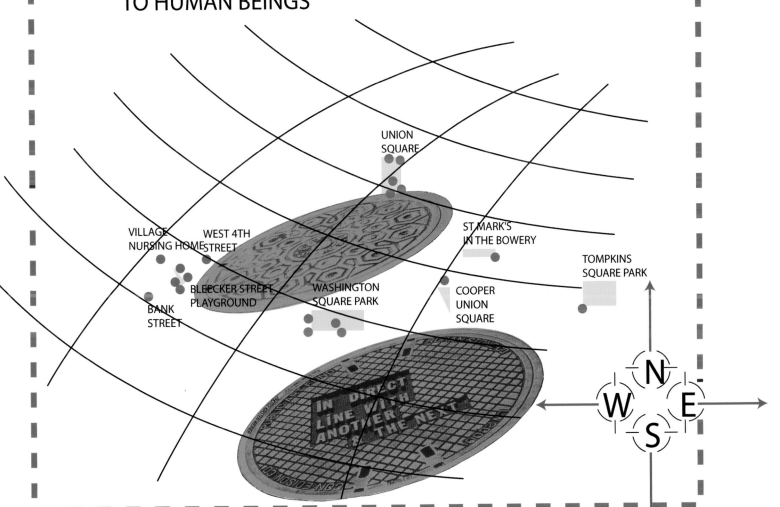

-RIGHT AND OVERLEAF-

MANHATTAN AT NIGHT
AND NYC TRANSIT

PAULA SCHER, 2007

Manhattan at Night's tangible relationship
with reality allows Paula Scher to re-imagine
her landscape through subtle social comment.
Within the hazy glow of the Hudson and
East Rivers, purposefully selected New
York addresses are interspersed with figures
representative of the city's neighborhoods'
average incomes—of which a marked
disparity has been mapped. A difference
of $17,320 in Spanish Harlem and $80,406
on Manhattan's Upper East Side reveals
Scher's glittering landscape as merely a
backdrop to the political message the artist
employs. *NYC Transit* (overleaf) presents a
similar landscape of cluttered street names and
illuminated transportation routes that together
convey the city's sense of urgency.

Paula Scher/Pentagram

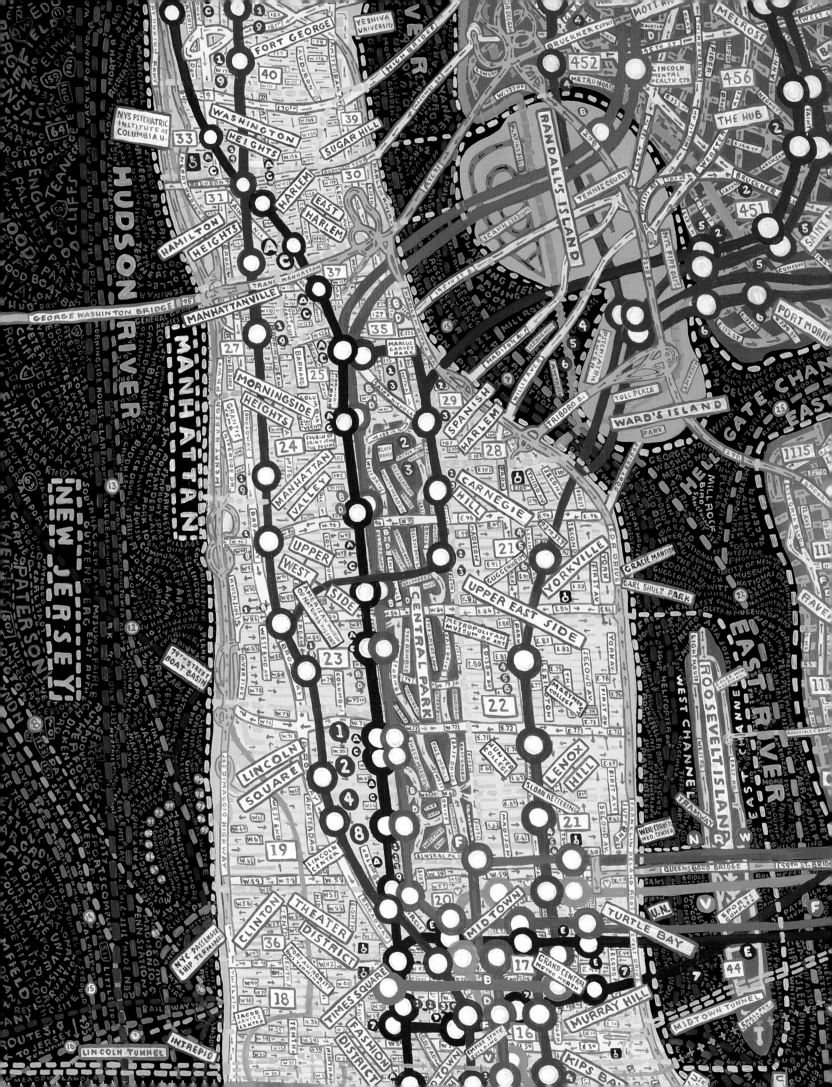

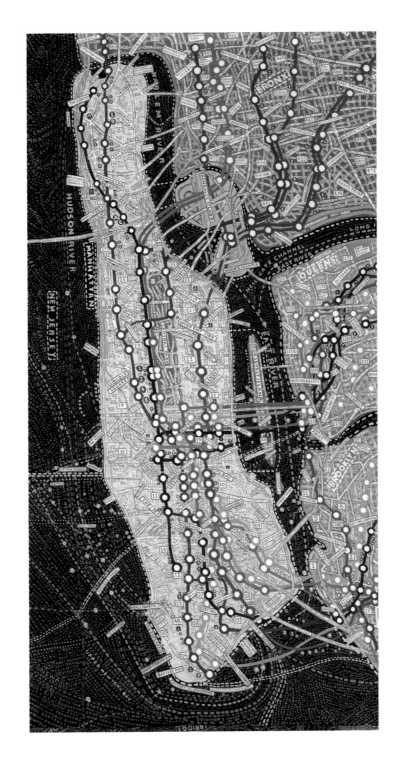

NEW YORK BY WALKMAN
SAATCHI AND SAATCHI SYDNEY, 2008

New York by Walkman is a tangled web of headphones mapping out the New York subway system. The ad, created by Saatchi and Saatchi Sydney, in July 2008, is part of a series of advertisements for SONY Walkman depicting the maps of some of the most highly travelled subways in the world including London, New York and Sydney. Along the way commuters can expect to stop at George Michael where Bedford Avenue normally resides on the L train and the Electric Light Orchestra where 116TH Street Station previously stood on the Lexington Avenue Local.

Courtesy of Sony and Saatchi and Saatchi Sydney

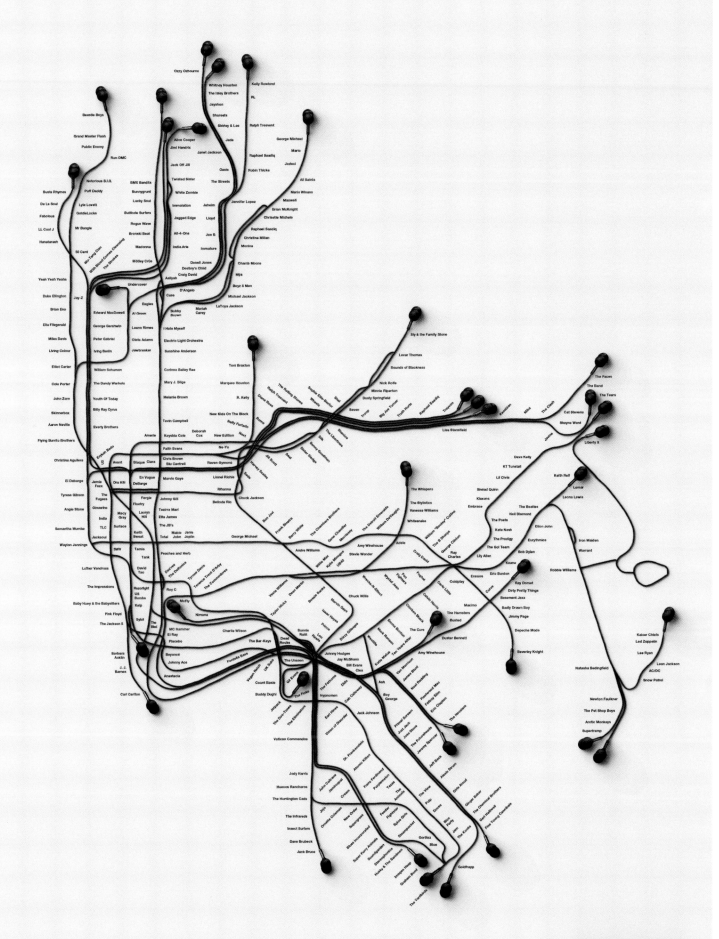

NEW YORK DINNER MAP

SELETTI, 2006

From pretzels to pastrami, to the finest cuisine
reflective of the City's multicultural character—
Italian design firm Seletti celebrates New York
gastronomy in their amusing *New York Dinner
Map*. Part of the *World Dinner Map* Series,
the accurate cartographic depiction of Mid to
Lower Manhattan—complete with places of
interest—is an entertaining accompaniment
to the dinner table.

Courtesy of Seletti, Italy

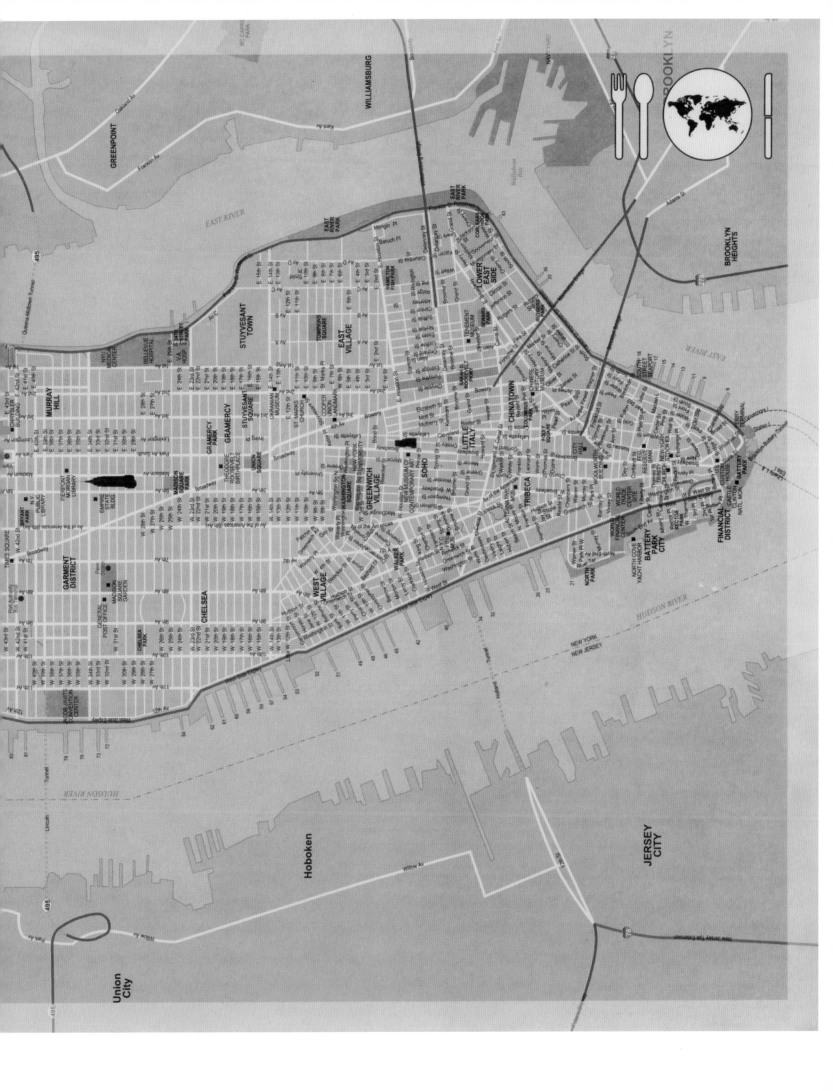

POWERFUL GREEN MAP OF
NEW YORK CITY

ENERGY EDITION, BY GREEN MAP™, 2006

Promoting eco-responsibility and sustainable
practises, this extensively detailed collection
of maps, low-emission travel information,
contemporary climate change science, future-
thinking energy management tactics, and
city-wide green resources is intricate in both its
message and aesthetic. An idiosyncratic legend
provides a dense, but clear, guide to Green
Map's affiliated and promoted associations and
initiatives, whilst still maintaining a degree of
accuracy in borough geography, park locations,
and a number of major streets and avenues.

Powerful Green Map of New York City 2006,

Energy Edition, Green Map®

www.greenapplemap.org/page/power

Every Day Savings

Powerful Green Map Spectrum

- ● Nature
- ● Recycling & Rethinking
- ● Empowerment
- ● Food for Body & Mind
- ● Human Power
- ○ Hot Spots
- ● Predicted Change

Long Island Sound

BRONX

QUEENS

Conserving Embodied Energy

⚡ Conserving Energy is easy: Turn off lights, computers, TVs, A/Cs when not in use. Wear a sweater indoors in winter so you can turn down the heating. Close curtains on hot summer days. Find tips in English, Chinese and Spanish at ⊕ GreenAppleMap.org. See **19** ☀ SolarOne energy education center on *Side 2*.

Check your progress – is your energy bill shrinking? Want a cleaner electricity source? Click "Power Your Way" at ⊕ ConEd.com, compare at ⊕ PowerScoreCard.org. Get advice from ⊕ IdealBite.com, ⊕ greenhomeNYC.org and NY State's ⊕ GetEnergySmart.org ☽ 1-866-GRN-POWR. Ready to re-invest? See *Side 2*!

♻ **Waste Reduction and Reuse** means don't waste energy buying disposables or tossing good stuff. Julia Butterfly Hill of ⊕ CircleofLife.org says, "Bring your own mug, take-out containers, and shopping bags." Make stuff you have last longer – if we bought and tossed less, we'd see, smell and breathe less garbage every day. Too much junk mail? Free list removal ⊕ DMAconsumers.org. Prevent charities from bombarding you – give through ⊕ NetworkforGood.org.

📖 Libraries are a classic energy-saving resource. Each borough's major library is mapped; citywide, there are over 200 branches! Check locations and hours: ⊕ brooklynpubliclibrary.org ☽ 718-230-2100 ext 4 ⊕ queenslibrary.org ☽ 718-990-0700 ext 3 New York Public Library: ⊕ nypl.org, which serves The Bronx ☽ 718-579-4200, Manhattan ☽ 212-661-0626 and Staten Island ☽ 718-442-8562.

♻ Second-hand shops are chic, cheap and prevent waste, too. NYC has far too many to chart but find them through ☽ 1-877-NYC-STUFF, ⊕ nyc.gov/NYCwasteless or ⊕ ReUseAlliance.net. Trade via ⊕ freecycle.org, or set up a free Exchange Shelf in your community center or lunch/laundry room. See **39** ♻ on *Side 2*.

♻ INFORM has WasteFree NYC, a Community Waste Prevention Toolkit, and more online ⊕ informInc.org

♻ Cultural non-profits and art schools can take a wide variety of items donated by companies from Materials for the Arts ⊕ mfta.org ☽ 718-729-3001.

♻ Recycling really does save resources and energy. Really! Get your neighbors to separate metal, glass, paper, plastic for NYC's deluxe weekly pickup. ⊕ nyc.gov/sanitation ☽ 311 has details, free posters and schedules. Radio Shack and Staples stores recycle batteries and cellphones, see ⊕ earth911.org.

♻ Composting means recycling kitchen scraps and yard waste into fertile soil. This "black gold" is the most efficient form of recycling. How-to and drop-off info at ⊕ NYCcompost.org or Lower East Side Ecology Center's stand at **16** ● Union Square Greenmarket every M, W, F and Sat. ♻ LESEC also arranges electronic "eWaste" recycling days for computers, etc. around NYC ⊕ LESecologycenter.org ☽ 212-477-4022. Recycle rain too ⊕ rainbarrelguide.com!

Nature's Way

👫 Ever felt an "urban heat island"? Every summer, our streets and buildings concentrate the heat. Our 👫 Parks, ♥ Community Gardens and other green spaces provide cooler, cleaner air. Chill out by nurturing a small oasis: water a windowbox or a street tree, see

⊕ TreesNY.com. There's about a half-million street trees in NYC – get one planted ☽ 311.

♥ Join a community garden and help cultivate a formerly empty lot with ⊕ GreenGuerillas.org ☽ 212-402-1121 or NY Restoration Project ⊕ nyrp. org. Find ♥ on NYC's open space map ⊕ oasisnyc.

net – South Bronx, north Brooklyn, Harlem and the Lower East Side are major ♥ districts.

👫 Natural refreshment is free every day at NYC parks! With 28,000 acres, we have the nation's largest urban park system. The City is re-planting a diversity of native plants and restoring habitats for butterflies and birds ⊕ NYCparks.org ☽ 311.

≈ Waterfront park views and breezes air-condition our spirit – see Metropolitan Waterfront Alliance's events and maps ⊕ waterwire.net.

✿ Enjoy and learn at lush Botanical Gardens in the Bronx ⊕ nybg.org, Queens (see **41** ⊠ on *Side 2*) ⊕ queensbotanical.org, Staten Island

⊕ sibg.org, Brooklyn ⊕ bbg.org. Find more ✿ like The Bronx's ⊕ FriendsofBrookPark.org on map.

Food Matters

● 27 seasonal and ● 15 year-round Greenmarkets bring the freshest seasonal tastes to your table. Buy local to keep our region green. Open days vary, get the current schedule at any Greenmarket or ⊕ cenyc.org ☽ 212-788-7476. The biggest one, Union Square Greenmarket, is **16** ● on *Side 2*.

🌱 Grow your own food at a ✿ City Farm like East New York Farms ☽ 718-649-7979, or connect with regional organic farmers through a Community Supported Agriculture "subscription" program. 37 CSAs are at ⊕ justfood.org ☽ 212-645-9880.

🍴 Fuel for you: Meat production and imported foods waste lots of energy and vitamins. Alternatively, resource-efficient locally grown and/or pesticide-free organic foods offer vitality – see ⊕ TrueCostofFood.org and ⊕ GraceLinks. org. Fish facts: ⊕ seafood.audubon.org helps you avoid eating endangered fish and ⊕ GotMercury. org helps you avoid endangering yourself.

🍴 With new healthy local and/or organic dining, delivery and shopping options opening all the time, we can't chart them all – find 'em online ⊕ happycow.net or ⊕ vivavegie.org ☽ 212-242-0011. A vegetarian or vegan (totally free of animal products) diet is a great way to save energy.

ℹ Mind Food: public radio like WBAI 99.5 FM or WNYC 820 AM/93.9 FM; magazines like *Plenty*, *Organic Style*, *Metropolis* and *E*; community papers like *The Villager* and books galore. See ⊕ grist.org, too.

HERE & THERE—A HORIZONLESS PROJECTION IN MANHATTAN
BERG, 2009

A project by Jack Schulze and Matt Webb concerning, in the artist's words, "speculative projections" of the dense urban space of Manhattan, *Here & There*'s aesthetic is dizzying. The city seems to curve vertically away from the observer, skewing relative distances as it appears to recede at an ever-increasing pace, the surrounding areas of Queens, New Jersey and Brooklyn appearing almost as a wallpaper backdrop to the island. The 3-D mapping of structures throughout the city seems rudimentary, but fits in perfectly with the basic aesthetic of the rest of the map. Contrast is found in major streets being picked out in yellow, notable buildings in gold, and parks in green. The labelling of streets and particular buildings, seeming to float in front of the viewer when at the forefront of the image, transforms to the format of a standard map as the image flattens out with the gradient.

-LEFT-

NEW YORK CITY

NASA, 2003

This false-color satellite image depicts
Manhattan Island and parts of Staten Island
and Long Island. Produced with the use
of NASA's Advanced Spaceborne Thermal
Emission and Reflection Radiometer
(ASTER), vegetated surfaces appear green,
water is dark blue, and urban areas show
up as a grey-blue color.

Image courtesy NASA/GSFC/MITI/ERSDAC/JAROS,
and U.S./Japan ASTER Science Team

-OPPOSITE-

MANHATTAN 2409

HEIDI NEILSON, 2009

Mannahatta: The "Island of many hills"—so-
called by its native Lenape, who populated
the land until the Dutch and British invasions
in the seventeenth century. This image, taken
from *Mannahatta: A Natural History of New
York City*—a ten year research project into
the ecological history of New York City, by
landscape ecologist Eric Sanderson and The
Wildlife Conservation Society—predicts
how the cityscape will appear in the year
2409. The imagined landscape shows how
sustainable living will have reshaped New York
City, with dense pockets of cities replacing
suburban sprawl—their boundaries revised
by climate change. Farms and woodland are
shown covering much of the land, serving the
cities they surround with an abundance of
renewable crops year round.

Eric Sanderson and Heidi Neilson

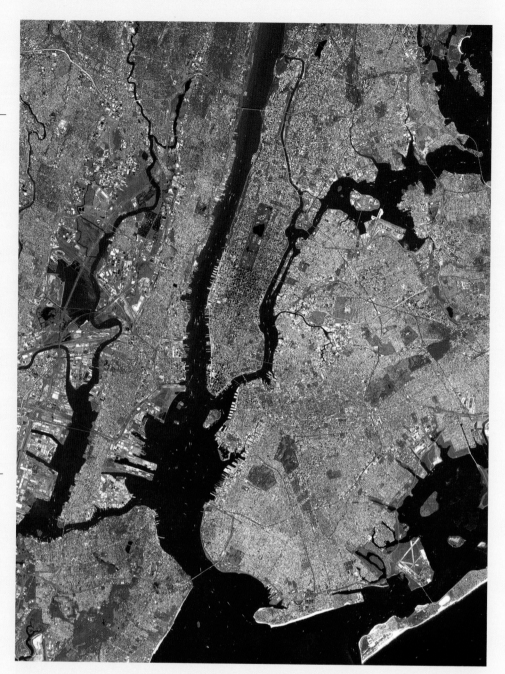

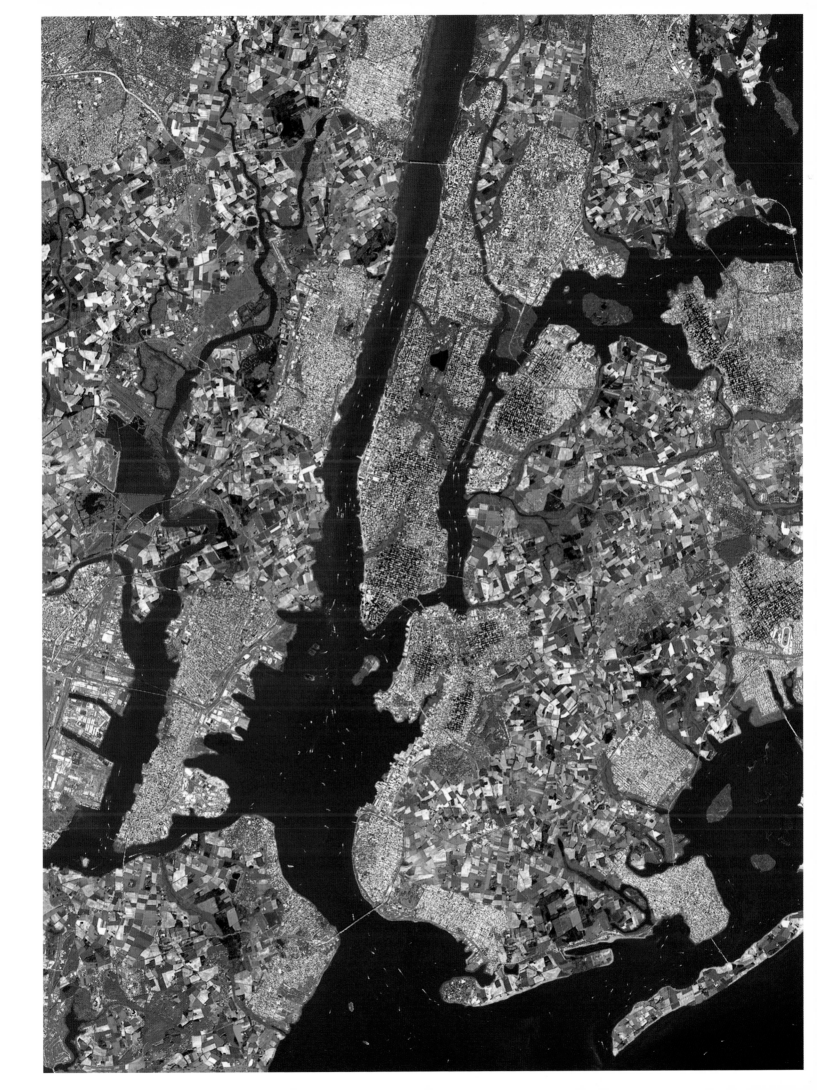

BIOGRAPHIES

Seth Robbins and Robert Neuwirth have written on New York and
its history for a variety of publications, including *Metropolis* and
Time Out New York. Robbins teaches history at New York City's High
School for Environment Studies and was a founding board member
of OpenHouseNewYork. Neuwirth is the author of *Shadow Cities: A
Billion Squatters, A New Urban World*, and of a forthcoming book on
the rise of the global informal economy.

——————

ACKNOWLEDGEMENTS

This book would not have been possible without the dedicated help of the map enthusiasts involved, whose passion for the subject has helped to unearth New York City's diverse history.

Firstly, special thanks must go to Kenneth Cobb at the New York City Department of Records, whose guidance and advice helped to form the foundations for this project.

Gratitude must also be given to David Rumsey, whose vast collection of historical maps proved to be an invaluable resource for the earlier material used in the book, and to John Tauranac for his never-ending knowledge of the geography of New York City.

Certain individuals and institutions must also be mentioned for their support throughout the project. Paul Rascoe at The University of Texas Libraries, Jill Slaight at The New York Historical Society, Wesley O'Brien at The New York Planning Department, Julee Johnson at Historic Urban Plans, Paul Johnson at The National Archives, Kitty Chibnik at Columbia University Libraries, and the librarians at the New York Public Library.

Thanks also to Jenny Beorkrem, Green Map™'s Wendy Brawer, Sarah Williams and Laura Kurgan from the Spatial Information Design Lab and the artists involved in the New Museum's Get Lost Exhibition—all for their unique interpretations of the New York landscape.

And finally, a special thanks to Brooke Sperry for her help with the early research for the book.

——————

Black Dog Publishing Limited
10A Acton Street
London WC1X 9NG
www.blackdogonline.com

info@blackdogonline.com

Edited by Phoebe Adler, Tom Howells and Duncan McCorquodale

Designed by Emily Chicken at Black Dog Publishing with thanks to
Ben Jeffrey and Alex Wright.

British Library Cataloguing-in-Publication Data.
A CIP record for this book is available from the British Library.

ISBN 978 1 906155 82 7

Black Dog Publishing Limited, London, UK, is an environmentally
responsible company. Mapping New York is set in Minion and
Knockout. Printed in The EU on FSC certified paper.

architecture art design
fashion history photography
theory and things

www.blackdogonline.com   london uk